Looking for God in All ~~the Wrong~~ *Right* Places

OTHER BOOKS BY FLORENCE LITTAUER

After Every Wedding Comes a Marriage
Blow Away the Black Clouds
How to Get Along with Difficult People
It Takes So Little to Be Above Average
Lives on the Mend
Out of the Cabbage Patch
Personality Plus
The Pursuit of Happiness
Say It with CLASS
Shades of Beauty (co-authored with Marita Littauer)
Your Personality Tree

Looking for God in All ~~Wrong~~ *Right* the Places

Florence Littauer

WORD BOOKS
PUBLISHER
WACO, TEXAS

A DIVISION OF
WORD, INCORPORATED

Scripture quotations are from the following sources (when consecutive quotations
are from the same source, abbreviated identification is not repeated):

The King James Version of the Bible (KJV).

The Living Bible (TLB), copyright 1971 by Tyndale House Publishers, Wheaton,
IL. Used by permission.

The Holy Bible, New International Version (NIV). Copyright © 1973, 1978, 1984
International Bible Society. Used by permission of Zondervan Bible Publishers.

The *Good News Bible,* Today's English Version (TEV)—Old Testament: Copyright
© American Bible Society 1976; New Testament: Copyright © American Bible
Society 1966, 1971, 1976.

An effort has been made to locate sources and obtain permission where necessary
for the quotations used in this book. In the event of any unintentional omission,
modifications will be gladly incorporated in future editions.

The names and certain identifying details have been changed in some of the
stories used in this book to preserve the privacy of the parties involved. Other
stories are composites of a number of experiences the author has encountered
through the years.

Library of Congress Cataloging-in-Publication Data

Littauer, Florence, 1928–
    Looking for God in all the right places.

    1. God—Knowableness. I. Title.
BT102.L56 1987   248.4   87–21662
ISBN 0–8499–3083–9

7 8 9 8 RRD 9 8 7 6 5 4 3 2 1

Printed in the United States of America

Contents

◇ ─────────────────────── ◇

◇

PART III

Finding God Face to Face in the Right Place

◇

◇

Taking the First Step

◇ ———————————————————————————— ◇

"Whenever times get bad, the desire for God gets stronger." These are words I've heard most of my life, but events in the last few years have brought new meaning to this old statement. As morals have declined, as money has eluded many, and as life in the fast lane has hit a dead end, I have seen a new and intense search for the sacred.

Sometime in the early part of 1987, I read a Roper poll which asked, "What are Americans interested in?" The top choice was religion with an 81 percent rating. A cover article for *U.S. News and World Report* also tells of "Religion's new turn," saying it cuts across denominations and shifts emphasis from church involvement in social issues, so popular in the 60s, to personal spirituality. Rev. Don Browning, professor of religion at the University of Chicago Divinity School, says, "Now there's the feeling that you must first develop spiritual depth before you can be really successful in helping others."[1]

The article goes on to say that there is "a gnawing disillusionment with science and secularism as the driving forces in U.S. society. Sensing this disillusionment, "churches are growing more aggressive in proclaiming the spirituality that is the root of their very existence. Talk of prayer, meditation, worship and Bible study have replaced social crusades in many a church. Pastors are spending more time honing their skills as shepherds of souls."[2]

The same article tells that Catholics are "no longer content to follow meekly behind bishops and priests." The lay people "are so absorbed in their religion" that they have formed spiritual study groups.[3]

Also, "in a society grown increasingly impersonal and

unpredictable, many Jews are seeking solace and sustenance in a more personal brand of religion. . . . As people have more time for leisure and reflection, they have more of a chasm of emptiness that is not filled by the latest digital hi-fi or the newest big screen television."[4]

Whether we are Protestant, Catholic, or Jewish, we are looking for God to fill that "chasm of emptiness" in our souls.

One evening as I was sitting alone in a coffee shop in Palm Springs, I overheard a conversation from the booth behind me. A ten-year-old girl was having her once-a-week night out with her father who obviously didn't live with her mother. He was somewhat bored and tried to think of something to talk about. "What grade are you in now?" he asked mechanically. She replied simply, "The third." After an awkward pause, he thought of another question, "Can you read?"

She was insulted and answered quickly, "Of course I can read. I can even read the Bible."

"The Bible?" He was stunned. "Why would you read the Bible?"

"A lady on our street has a Bible Club, and she gave me a Bible of my own."

"Is it a Catholic Bible? We're Roman Catholics you know."

The child had no idea what kind of a Bible she had, and when she asked him to explain what Roman Catholic was, he could come up with nothing more theological than "It's one of the world's great religions, and you should stick with it."

"Are there Roman Jews?" she asked. He wasn't too sure, but didn't think so.

By this time I was writing down the whole conversation on my place mat, and even I was amazed when this precious child spoke up proudly and said, "I even know what sin is."

"You do?" He hardly dared to ask for a definition. "What would a good little girl like you know about sin?"

"It's when you do something wrong to someone and aren't sorry. Daddy, if you say you're sorry is it still a sin?"

He had no idea, so he suggested, "That's when you go to a priest and confess to him what you've done wrong, and he'll tell you what kind of a sin it is."

The father was happy with his inspired answer until she asked, "Why should I confess to a priest?"

"Because a priest can talk to God. Only priests can talk to God."

Relieved that he had concluded this uncomfortable conversation with a lofty thought on godly communication and feeling he'd had enough doctrinal discussion for one night, the father headed for the door. The child was deep in thought as she pulled her way out of the booth. Just as she walked by me she brightened up and called to her father, "I've just decided what I'm going to be when I grow up. I'm going to be a priest so I can talk to God!"

Everyone's looking for God, but if this child wanted help from her father she was looking in all the wrong places.

Whatever church background we come from, we're in a search for the sacred, a quest for a personal relationship to God. For some the institutional church has held little meaning and for some sitting in a pew on Sunday morning has seemed to solve few difficult situations.

For those of you who are looking for God, or if you are not satisfied with your current relationship to the Father and desire to fill that chasm of emptiness in your life, this book is written for you. It's neither religious nor preachy, yet it's not simplistic. My purpose is not to suggest that you change churches, but to give you a step-by-step plan for finding God no matter what your religious background may be.

In addition to reading this book for your own pleasure, growth, and edification, you can use *Looking for God in All the Right Places* in either a personal or group Bible study or as a teaching tool for those seeking spiritual direction. This book doesn't bring up doctrinal dilemmas or social issues and then shake its little head in despair, but it does present a plan and prepare a path for all those who want to find God.

So let's put on our walking shoes and take the first step as we start looking for God in all the right places.

"It is time to seek the Lord" (Hos. 10:12, NIV).

Preparing for the Journey

◇ ———————————————————————————— ◇

As I was growing up, I had an underlying desire for God. I didn't know what caused that disquieting feeling, but I was drawn to church and involved in all they had to offer. Good works, moral principles, and Bible stories summed up our focus, yet I always knew there had to be something more. When the late R. G. LeTourneau, a wealthy businessman turned evangelist, came to our church I went each evening to hear him. To my remembrance he was the only hint of revival our church ever had, and I listened to every word he had to say. On the last night he must have touched my heart with the word of God for when he asked for those of us who wanted to work for God and someday go into Christian service, my eight-year-old brother Jim and I walked down the aisle hand in hand. When Mr. LeTourneau asked Jim what he wanted to do for God, he replied that he wished to be a minister when he grew up. The large balding, bespectacled man patted him on the head and then asked me the same question. I said something about not knowing what girls could do for God, and he suggested being a missionary. Even though I was only twelve, I knew I didn't have a feel for jungles. Mother had often stated her hope that "they"—her mythical "they"— would never send her to Africa. "They" never did, but she had instilled in me a fear of the mission field. "What else could I do?" I asked as I stared up at him in hopes of an alternative suggestion.

"You get ready, and when you grow up God will show you his plan."

I didn't like waiting in suspense, so I asked my Sunday school teacher if a girl could become a minister. She answered quickly, "Good heavens no. They'd never let us stand up there in a black robe and preach." She knew the same imposing "they" as my mother, and I accepted the fact that "they" would never let me be a minister.

In college at the University of Massachusetts, I went to church faithfully while others slept on Sunday mornings, and I even attended the Protestant student meetings peopled by some of the dullest and least sophisticated coeds on campus. After graduation I returned to my church in Haverhill, got married in it four years later, and then found I was expected to go to Fred's church—one of the major cults.

At that time, I didn't know what a cult was, and the fact that this religion put another book on an equal level with the Bible and another person above Jesus didn't deeply concern me. For ten years, we went every Sunday and smiled back at all the people. We had no idea we were wandering in the wilderness, dying in a spiritual desert.

Within three years, I gave birth to two sons who were both fatally brain damaged. Practitioners from Fred's church tried to heal them, and I was told it was my lack of faith that prevented their cure. If I could embrace their beliefs and look at these babies as perfect, they would be healed. Once again, I started looking for God. I cried out to the Lord, prayed as the church instructed, and went for lessons and counseling, but the boys both died. If there was a God, how could problems like these come to such a good person as me?

Fred and I gave up on church. We intended to give up on God. We both felt let down by religion, ignored by pious pretenders, and depressed by our circumstances. One night Fred came home with an armload of big books on the various religions of the world. He'd been looking for God in the library. "There must be some church that is right for us," he stated as he placed the books on his desk. Every evening he studied and made a comparison chart on cardboard of the doctrines and beliefs of different denominations in the hopes of finding something to replace his religion. How I wish we still had that chart, for while we didn't know it at the time, that was the first step in Fred's search for God. Although we'd turned our back on church, we both knew there was something missing in our lives besides our sons. We had a "chasm of emptiness" that nothing seemed to fill. Even the chart didn't help; it only categorized choices of churches none of which seemed to suit our needs. Fred systematized synods and delineated denominations. He created his own special church on cardboard, returned the texts to the library, and never mentioned the study again. Fred was a deep, thoughtful, and analytical melancholy, and once he had placed a perfect God on paper, he was through with the project.

One feature Fred had found in his search and had added to his composite religion was a practice in pantheism where the Greeks worshiped God amongst the trees and found spiritual truth in nature. On Sunday mornings, Fred would put on his white shorts, take his racquets in hand, and head to the country club saying, "You can be just as close to God on the tennis courts as you can in church." The fact that he made an excuse each week showed that he felt guilty, but the statement somehow eased his conscience.

One day Fred's brother Dick, who had been brought up in the same cult, told us he had been watching a religious program on television and at the end he and his wife Ruth had knelt in front of the TV set and asked Jesus to come into their lives. We had never heard of someone finding God—or even looking for God—on television, but we did see some changes in their lives as we observed them critically over the next year.

When Ruth took me to Christian Women's Club I must have been ready, for I felt the speaker Roy Gustafson was addressing me personally. Using Romans 12:1–2 he expressed that God wanted us to present our bodies as a living sacrifice. I had no idea what the Bible said about bringing a sacrifice to the altar, but when he got to the part of not being conformed to the world, I suddenly realized I had spent my whole life wandering in the wilderness of the world, and for what? The speaker then explained that God would transform our minds if we'd let him; he would come into our lives and show us

what was his good, acceptable, and perfect will for each one
of us.

When he told us we could find God right in that restaurant,
I prayed with him as he instructed and asked the Lord into
my heart, taking my first baby step toward knowing God.
Within a year, Fred, Lauren, and Marita all dedicated their
lives to the Lord. We had been committed Christians for less
than two years when we were invited onto the staff of Campus Crusade for Christ and moved our family from Connecticut to San Bernardino, California. It was there I began to
study God's Word seriously.

Because Bible stories had always been exciting to me, and I
knew the people and places so well that I had won a district
award in my denomination as a pre-teen, I felt I had a firm
grasp of the Scriptures. When I attended my first Bible study
on Genesis, I assumed I would be the star pupil as I could
recite the genealogy from Adam to Joseph and I knew the
order in which God created the world. Imagine my surprise
when in the first verse of the first chapter of Genesis, the
teacher showed us that God was plural and that Christ was
with God the Father in creation. In way of explanation, she
referred us to the first chapter of the Book of John where we
learned that Christ the Word was in the beginning. "The
Word was with God, and the Word was God. He was with
God in the beginning. Through him all things were made;
without him nothing was made that has been made" (John
1:1–3, NIV).

That seemed to clearly point out that Christ and the Father
are one and that Jesus was present and active during the
entire creation of the world. It didn't say that he showed up
now and then but that without him nothing was made. That's
a clear statement. I couldn't refute the evidence. Here in the
opening verse of the Bible, I found I didn't know what I'd
thought I knew. I didn't know Christ was a part of the Old
Testament. I thought he made his first appearance in the
manger. Hadn't I recited the Christmas story from Luke in
church when I was three years old! As I was running this

question through my head, but not wanting to appear igno-
rant, another lady asked, "You mean he was around before he
was born?"

Others nodded and Barbara, our teacher, replied that although it didn't make human sense, God was a tripartite God:
Father, Son, and Holy Spirit. We all agreed we'd heard that
but didn't think it happened before the gospels and Acts. So
Barbara had us read John 1:10, "He was in the world, and
though the world was made through him, the world did not
recognize him" (NIV).

Our little group was proof of that. Barbara showed us that
when he came to earth no one believed he was God in the
flesh, but John 1:14 says, "The Word became flesh and lived
for a while among us. We have seen his glory, the glory of the
one and only Son, who came from the father, full of grace and
truth" (NIV).

We all agreed it did say that, and then Barbara showed us
John 1:12 which told us that if we would believe in Jesus and
receive him into our lives he would make us children of
God—a part of his family.

That day as two others prayed and asked the Word to come
into their lives and dwell in them, my eyes were opened to
my ignorance of the depth and the power of the Scriptures.
We hadn't gone beyond the first verse of Genesis, yet we had
met the Father, the Son, and the Holy Spirit and had two new
believers in the kingdom.

As it turned out, we spent months in that verse-by-verse
study of Genesis, and during that time I became a compulsive
Bible student. Two years later, when Barbara moved to Atlanta, I was able to step in as the teacher.

When she returned to visit the group, she observed me and
said, "The best thing about your Bible teaching is that you are
unencumbered by theological training and therefore not
deep enough to be confusing." I wasn't sure how to take that
at the time, but over the years I've kept my teaching simple
because I don't want to be confusing.

One lady told me her Sunday school teacher was really

deep. When I asked her how she knew, she answered, "I've been attending class for six weeks and haven't understood a word he's said yet." That's deep.

This book is not a theological treatise, but a personal plan for finding God, so join me as we start *Looking for God in All the Right Places.*

"You will call and the Lord will answer; you will cry for help and he will say: Here am I" (Isa. 58:9, NIV).

Part I

◇

Looking for God in All the Wrong Places

Ten False Starts

◇ ─────────────────────────────────── ◇

Everyone wants to find some kind of a god, some prophet to foretell the future, some father to protect them, some mother to kiss life and make it well, some guru to give them mountaintop experiences, some priest to confess to, some superman to come to the rescue. Everyone's looking for God, but so many are looking in all the wrong places. As Pascal is so frequently quoted as saying, "There is a god-shaped vacuum in the heart of every man that cannot be filled by any created thing but only by God the creator."

◇

1. ATTENDING CHURCH
FOR THE WRONG REASONS

Our first thought, in most cases, is to look for God in church, yet some have tried church and found that the one they chose is no more than a social club with a steeple, an auditorium where the minister impresses his congregation with the slides of his recent trip to Russia. I once visited a church where a richly robed reverend intoned, "The one constant in our Christian life is the church coffee hour." On another occasion I visited a church where the only mention of Jesus was, "If he were alive today he would probably be the president of the Rotary Club." Yes, you can go to church and not find God.

Marjorie Holmes in an article for *Christian Herald* tells of her looking for God in different churches. Brought up in a main-line denomination she was dissuaded from her beliefs by an atheistic college professor who told her she was too intelligent to believe the Bible. She went through some rebellious years, but by the time she had three children and a writing career, she realized intellect wasn't enough.

Marjorie began "praying up a storm" for divine help. Her subsequent search for God led her through numerous church doors. While living in Texas she attended both Methodist and Congregationalist churches. When she moved to Pennsylvania, she visited a Unitarian church and a Hindu swami. When she settled in Virginia, she worshiped in an Episcopal church at the invitation of two neighbors.[1]

It was in this church, after many denominational adventures, that Marjorie settled into a personal relationship with the Lord.

Yes, you can find God in church!

Some people change churches in their search for God, thinking that their present sanctuary is too simple. Perhaps a cathedral would do, one with vaulted ceilings where God himself fades into the fuzzy frescoes—one where tall candles flicker, choirboys chant, patriarchs recite, parishioners respond, angels smile, incense wafts, cymbals clang. "Surely," they think, "God must be here." But, are they looking in the right place?

Fred and I formerly chose churches by whether we could picture our daughters getting married there. Was there a long center aisle with red carpeting? A stained-glass rose window like Notre Dame? One structure I liked had a flood of fountains in the foyer, but I didn't find God there.

◇

2. MISGUIDED BIBLE STUDIES

Many have found God in Bible studies, but others have met, instead, a hypocrite who halted their progress, a person who didn't practice what he preached, a legalistic leader who frightened newcomers with more than ten commandments. So these pitiful pilgrims quit their search almost before they got started.

When our daughter Lauren was a teen, we allowed her to date non-believers as long as they would attend the weekly Bible studies we taught in our home. At one point she had four boyfriends coming; they all found the Lord there, and she later married one of them. Yes, you can find God in Bible studies.

◇

3. PASTOR WORSHIP

Some put their faith in the pastor, and while the majority of our leaders are dedicated spiritual men trying prayerfully to shepherd their flock into life everlasting, we shouldn't expect them to be the Lord himself. When I was first looking for God, I worshiped the pastor and hung on his every word as if each thought he uttered had been divinely inspired and was ready to be embroidered onto a sampler. Yet two years later when I announced proudly that Fred and I were going

to leave our little church and go into full-time Christian service, he was so angered that he threw a Bible across the room,
causing him to lose his spiritual balance and fall off the
pedestal on which I had placed him. We shouldn't make idols
of our pastors, but we should let them know that we need
their help in finding God.

4. TELEVISION

Some people who don't go to church look for God on television in the quiet confines of their home, but He seems so
expensive. "Does God really cost that much?" they wonder.
To be religious do you need cassettes of all last year's mes-
sages plus the taped Book of Revelation to study at home? Do
you need a personalized leather Bible with hundreds of concordance pages including colored maps of the entire Tigris-
Euphrates valley? Without your immediate support will the
entire student body of the pastor's personal college have to
sleep on cement floors for the winter? Will God call us home
if we don't raise enough money? Does the God of TV want
you to send for a little pewter bell to tinkle when a sinner
repents or carry your keys on a ring stating, "The lost have
been found" or go to bed next to a plastic night light that
gives off the aura of the Holy Spirit?

Recently I read a satirical article entitled "And the Greedy
Shall Inherit the Airwaves—Praise the Lord and Pass the
Contributions." Author Robert Steed questioned "the growing number of electronic evangelists who are swarming like
heavenly moths to the bright video light."[2]

He feels that "The old-fashioned church in the wildwood is
rapidly giving way to an incredible array of electronic Elmer
Gantrys cavorting all over the cable systems. On virtually

every other notch you'll find a number of show-biz preachers competing for contributions from the sick and shut-in along with an amazing and cunning variety of space-age, plate-passing techniques.

"These folks have always been around, but television has given them a splendid new dimension."[3]

In one week during the early part of 1987, a sudden scandal in Christian leadership was the cover article in three major news magazines. Televangelists were pictured as lusting after the flesh, after money, and after power. Scripture was quoted in derision, splits in the Holy Wall were dramatized, and every Christian was suddenly on the defensive. *Newsweek* (June 8, 1987) proclaimed on its cover "Heaven Can Wait While the Holy War Heats Up."

When Christian leaders stray from the straight and narrow, or try to purge each other in public, or appear to be planning hostile takeovers of rival ministries, the press delights in publicizing the fall. And when these leaders hit the sidewalk below their ivory towers, we all feel the blows and bear the bruises.

Is it still possible to find God on television among the tinsel, the testimonies, and the tears? Will public persecution purge out the pretenders and put Christ back on the throne where he is seated at the right hand of the Father?

With God all things are possible. Fred and I trace our Christian birth back to television, for it was Fred's brother Dick and his wife Ruth who watched a Billy Graham rally and were convicted by the power of God to get off the couch and confess their sins while kneeling in front of the TV set. Their commitment to Christ that night has held true for more than twenty years. They have raised four outstanding Christian children, and it was their prayers and persistence that prepared Fred and me to find God.

While on a speaking tour in Australia I met several men who had received the Lord while watching the "Hour of Power" and listening to Robert Schuller, who is considered an evangelical beacon shining in that spiritually dark continent. One man who had made fun of a certain female evangelist told me he had to eat his words when his mother, whom he had tried to lead to the Lord for years, joyfully told him how she had found God through the TV ministry of the woman he had ridiculed.

God can use television or any other medium to reach the world, but we should be careful not to be "carried away by all kinds of strange teaching" (Heb. 13:9, NIV).

◇

5. CULTS

Some who have given up on church and TV search for God in cults. Many times it seems that young people who have been given everything, and of whom little has been required, flock to these receptive groups where they live a Spartan existence in a secluded commune and renounce all worldly possessions in order to serve a saintly pseudosavior.

Because everyone is looking for God somewhere, a father figure who appears to offer love and discipline can attract young people to his ways, bizarre though they may appear to the rest of us. Surely, the bearded, shaggy guru from India, the Bhagwan Shree Rajneesh, preaching self-denial while owning a fleet of Rolls-Royces, held no appeal for me; yet, he was able to magnetize over three thousand apparently normal human beings into sacrificing their lives for him and moving to Antelope, Oregon, a town of twenty residents.

One day when I arrived at the Portland airport, I was curious as to why so many good-looking young men and women were dressed in odd orange outfits. I thought there must be some kind of costume party, but my hostess explained these were the followers of the Bhagwan awaiting his arrival. I asked myself, "Why do these young people follow this guru? What makes intelligent people pull out of life to do menial tasks on a commune?" The answer, I think, is an inner hunger for God, a void that can't be filled by money or success, a need for loving discipline, a desire to belong to a supportive community, and a passionate hope that there is something out there somewhere that is bigger and better than we know ourselves to be.

Sundeep Waslekar, an Indian journalist, explained, "For kids whose lives were unhappy and frustrated, due to the uncertainty and alienation resulting from excessive materialism, an esoteric Eastern faith seemed to provide answers to all their problems.

"For them the guru provided a highly emotional atmosphere, evidence that there was a god."[4]

Ironically, there is a recent book about the Bhagwan entitled *Bhagwan: The God That Failed*. Gratefully this man has been deported, and his sixty-four thousand acres are on the market for $28.5 million. A former commune resident says, "Being on the commune was like going to camp for two years. Now I've got to worry about paying bills and being practical. Bhagwan never taught us much about that."[5]

The Radio Bible Class has published an excellent booklet entitled, *What About Those Dangerous Religious Groups?* It warns us to be discerning in associating with those who mention Christ but revere a religious leader, who put the word of men over the Word of God, who direct the lives of followers in a dictatorial manner, who isolate their members from family and friends, and who demand the flock work their way to heaven, often by perverse methods or sexual acts. This booklet explains why the young person hungering for acceptance and approval is attracted to these groups:

> Rebounding from the trauma of a broken home, drugs, a sexual relationship, or a poor self-image, he is captured by the idealism, the intelligence, and the brashness of some gifted religious leader. He is taken in by someone who, if he doesn't say he is God, at least claims to speak for the Almighty.
>
> And all too often it is the new Christian who is blinded by the seductive arguments of deceivers. He accepts their claim of an alternative to the hypocritical materialism and spiritless worship they accuse established churches of having.[6]

A new movement that worships the dead Ethiopian Emperor Haile Selassie as the Messiah is catching on as the new cult for young Americans. Can you believe that some of our youth are matting their hair into long "dreadlocks," praying to the black god Jah, and smoking marijuana as a sacred ritual? Can you picture former Christians carrying Bibles to Rastafari gatherings, rejecting worldly possessions and gainful employment, while calling America Babylon and heading for Utopia in the slums of Jamaica?

All of these practices represent the newest cult of youth, an avant-garde theology of liberation connecting the Bible with the ancient civilization in Ethiopia. Jehovah becomes Jah for short and is black because Haile Selassie, who was both black and God, created people in his own image. One faction is named "the twelve tribes of Israel." They all move to the Jamaican music of "reggae" popularized by Bob Marley who, after his death in 1981, was virtually deified by his followers.

Concerning this latest cult, the *Los Angeles Times* says the following:

> Across the country, cliques of white upper-middle-class youths are becoming devoted followers of this back-to-Africa, back-to-nature religious subculture that began in the shanty-towns of Jamaica in the 1930s and then spread to blacks worldwide.
>
> Probably because it's just beginning and still only involves a relative handful of young people in Southern California, the Rastafari trend has not sparked much alarm. Parents and school officials worried about the anti-God and pro-drugs lyrics of the darker elements of rock music seem to look upon reggae's Rasta overtones as almost benign by comparison— despite its recurring theme of revolution or the on-stage campaigning by some of its leading musicians to legalize marijuana.[7]

Using religion as a front the followers of this movement excuse drugs and violence, and one Los Angeles youth explained his murder of a 5 1/2-year-old girl as helping her get into "the spirit world."[8]

George Robinson, administrator at Torrey Pines High School near San Diego, California, explains the appeal of Rastafari to the student follower, "It sets him apart from his peers. So that out of two thousand students, he's not just another face in the crowd. And that's important for adolescents."[9]

Music promoter Makeda Dread says Rastafari fills a void for youth and claims "they are looking for something extra in life."[10]

Everyone's looking for "something extra"—for some kind of a God—but so many are looking in all the wrong places.

◇

6. NEW RELIGIONS

Well-meaning adults, who don't want to retreat to communes yet feel a spiritual void, are being attracted to new religions where apparently euphoric people act rich and well-adjusted. They discuss their underground shelters, well-stocked with gourmet dinners in preparation for nuclear war. And they all sit on soft sofas of self-satisfaction pretending to be happy. One desperate lady cried out to me, "I've tried everything—even transgressional medication!" Little did she realize in her mistaken memory of her transcendental meditation experience that her misnomer was what she needed: a soothing medicine to eliminate her transgressions!

The social gospel of the '60s and '70s, which said that busing and bare feet were signs of spirituality, is now being replaced by a new prosperity gospel which says that God will reward you with wealth if you follow certain principles. I once saw a poster with the words, "I've been rich and I've been poor. Rich is better." Few would disagree with the conclusion, but is a religion of the rich God ordained? Rich may be better, but being poor does not mean you cannot find God. The prosperity gospel sounds good, but we must remember, "The love of money is the root of all evil" (1 Tim. 6:10, KJV).

One Sunday evening I watched four Christian TV programs in a row. The first preacher stated with authority that God wants us all to be rich and healthy, and that we have but to claim our rights. He had the entire congregation standing up holding their Bibles in the air and calling out to God for blessings.

The second pastor spoke clearly against this fairy-tale philosophy and called the prosperity gospel "a bunch of baloney."

The third man cried into the camera and pleaded with us to double our giving because even though he had "done everything right" he was at that moment millions of dollars in debt.

The fourth speaker was remarkably happy and told us to think positive thoughts and all would be well with our souls.

I couldn't help but wonder if a new viewer to Christian TV would have thought God didn't know his own mind.

7. COLLEGE

In a survey responded to by 617 students enrolled in California institutions of higher learning, I was surprised to read that 88 percent of them answered yes to the question, "Do you believe in God, or some other being?" The survey was definitely not spiritual as it asked things such as: "When did you first lose your virginity? first get drunk? get high? How many sex partners have you had this year?" In spite of the general tone of the questions, the favorite book was the Bible and among admired persons Jesus Christ was in third place, after parents and grandparents, four points ahead of Ronald Reagan and ten ahead of Abraham Lincoln.[11]

On many of the responses the survey drew, the editors felt led to bring in the comments of "experts." Stating "sometimes the Tree of Knowledge bears weird fruit," they chose to balance the apparent interest in God by inserting a disclaimer from Brian Lynch, spokesman for American Atheists—hardly an impartial judge![12]

> That so many of them accept blindly such an irrational and useless idea as God indicates a serious failure of our education system. It shows they are not being taught to think critically. Our studies show that if you ask professors, as many as 50 percent of them don't believe in God. And if you probed deeply, you would find the belief of most students in God is very shallow and will fade with time.[13]

What a shame that some student, reading about the 88-percent-affirmative belief in God and thinking *I must find God for myself,* would be told immediately that he was blind, irrational, and a shallow thinker. Let's hope that the 88 percent who said they believed in God never read the survey results and atheistic comments.

One might assume that it would be easy to find God in seminary, but that's not necessarily so. My brother Jim, a minister in Bath, Ohio, recently took his daughter Cindy to evaluate different seminaries where she might do graduate work. At one of the best-known in the country, he was stunned to see announcements on the bulletin board, "for every liberal cause you could think of," plus several which had never crossed his mind. One lounge at the end of a shabby hallway was fittingly called "the Pit," and another was set aside for gay and lesbian theology students. An ad on the wall told of a woman who read tarot cards, and the one student they talked with had what she called a "Kamikaze ministry." Jim explained, "By that she meant that she took on churches that were going down for the third time and guided

them to a peaceful rest, a dubious task at best." As Jim and
Cindy concluded their visit, they learned that unmarried
male and female students can room together in the seminary
dorms. If a young person, eagerly looking for God, came to
this graduate school of religious studies, what in the world
might he or she find?

◇

8. PSYCHIC PHENOMENA

Currently, astrology, psychic phenomena, and reincarnation are of top interest among those who are trying to find
meaning in life. Once while I was in Houston, there was a
Psychic Mini Fair which boasted of "trained" palmists, psychic readers, phrenologists, biorhythmic plotters, numerolo-
gists, astrologers, dream interpreters, and tarot card readers
—all of whom were "available for readings, interpretations,
and consultations at the fairs which are held twice a month."[14]

Heather Von Hughes, author of *The Science of Numerology:
Your Life in 3 Dimensions,* said in a full-page color spread in
the *Houston Post* that many people are curious about their
future and need guidance. She explained, "An aura is a psychic energy field which surrounds both animate and inani-
mate objects and produces vibrations. The trained reader
tunes in to these psychic vibrations in much the same way you
tune your radio to find a particular station. After finding what
corresponds to your particular wave length or frequency, the
reader interprets what the vibrations mean about your life."[15]

Unfortunately, those who expect to find out all they need
to know in fifteen minutes for ten dollars or thirty minutes for
twenty dollars (no discount for double time) are looking in all
the wrong places.

Isn't it amazing how many intelligent, well-known people
are discussing what they were in a past life, what they think

they are now, and what they expect to be in the next life. Best known for her occult beliefs is Shirley MacLaine, who promoted the miniseries *Out on a Limb.* This series was based on her best-selling book of the same name and tells of her "spiritual search"—her looking for God—and how she ultimately found him in *herself!* Surprise! Surprise! According to a *USA Weekend* review, "In one climactic scene, the actress celebrates her new found spirituality by shouting 'I am God, I am God.' . . . She's the premier celebrity pundit for the growing New Age movement, a group of people and institutions that want to venture beyond traditional religion into new spiritual realms. They range from major corporations delving into est-like human development seminars to individuals who share MacLaine's further-out beliefs in psychics, out-of-body experiences and extraterrestrial phenomena."[16]

The *USA Weekend,* which gave this review two full pages with color pictures, took a survey and found one out of four people believe in reincarnation and one out of seven in mediums or "channels." Shirley is teaching spiritual seminars for $300 per person and plans to build a spiritual center in Virginia Beach, Virginia, amazingly close to the home of the "700 Club" and Christian Broadcasting Network. But we need not worry because "fervent as her beliefs are, MacLaine insists she wants to converse, not convert."[17] She and her thousands of followers are looking for God but in all the wrong places.

9. MIND CONTROL

Not all psychic activity is "Out on a Limb." According to *Newsweek* in an article titled "Corporate Mind Control" New Age gurus are entering the world of business. "Faced with increasing competition and sluggish productivity growth,

American companies are hiring motivational gurus to change the way their employees think." The article lists some corporate giants who have signed on New Age consultants. "By one estimate, their programs account for about $4 billion in corporate spending each year."[18]

Positive thinking in its extreme, meditation, hypnosis, group agreement, and end-state-vision are means to achieving "organizational health." Gratefully, there is some opposition to this move toward mind manipulation. Yes, "the rush to go touchy-feely is encountering resistance. Some workers say the programs constitute mind control or promote values inimical to their religious beliefs."[19]

◇

10. CHANNELING

Others seek to increase their spiritual dimensions through "channeling"—an idea about 150 years old with a new popularity especially among the affluent, intelligent, well-educated, yuppie population. According to a report on channeling in the *Los Angeles Times* (Dec. 5, 1986), "Channels are mediums who purposefully enter a semiconscious or unconscious trance state to communicate with the unseen 'spirit realm' which is variously considered to be long dead spirits or extraterrestrials or the 'collective unconscious.' Speaking as the 'spirit' in the trance, they may lecture or answer personal questions on past lives, events, romantic, business or health matters."[20]

The NBC "Today" show on March 17, 1987, dedicated a segment to this mystical magic. They showed a film clip of an all-American looking seminar leader casually dressed in a striped T-shirt who sat on a folding metal chair on a bare stage. The audience had paid to watch him moan with his eyes shut seeking spirits who amazingly came out of his mouth with different accents making them more intriguing than plain American spirits.

The commentator explained that "extraterrestrial beings speak through him." These "beings" all seem to have fascinating names like Indira and Bajah.

A woman "medium" explained how she goes into a meditating state with each client and changes her mental levels until she, the individual, and the spirits "match frequencies."

A normal-looking businessman said he goes to "channeling" twice a week to get answers. He wasn't sure how the process worked, but he said he felt better when he left. He was seeking something beyond himself.

Father Greeley popped up for a moment in the "Today" segment to say that 42 percent of the American public have talked to the dead. This appearance of a well-known, if controversial, priest in the middle of a commentary on channeling was made to look as if he, and perhaps the church universal, approved of this metaphysical practice.

Most amazing was an obviously wealthy lady shown in the midst of a glamorous society gathering where the elegant were being led to higher spaces. This woman was hugging a large jagged rock and patting it as she explained it to be an "energized crystal." "I sleep with this every night," she cooed, "and when I wake up I feel love from this crystal."

I guess she's lucky that she's not cut to shreds by morning. Her motto could well be "If your marriage is on the rocks, sleep with a crystal."

The concluding message of this amazing segment of the "Today" show was that once we're freed into a higher consciousness we are able to do our own thing without guilt. The commentator mentioned, "This all shows people's needs for inner spiritual dimensions."

Yes, we're all looking for God but in some very strange places.

Where is God today? Is he in the church coffee hour or the Rotary Club? Is he in a pastor or a priest? Is he in money or the media? Is he in cults, in college, or in "transgressional medication"? Is he in fortune tellers, mediums, and psychics?

Is God in the cards, in a crystal, or in reincarnation? Never have there been so many diverse groups claiming to have kidnapped God and to be keeping him exclusively for their adherents.

If you've been running from place to place in a desperate search for spiritual experience, I've got good news. God can meet you today, just where you are, right now!

A Check List

If you or a friend are at all doubtful about any group or practice you are considering, ask yourself these questions:

✓ In this group, is a certain person, whether living or dead, revered and honored above the Lord Jesus? Someone like Jim Jones, Rev. Moon, the Rajneesh, or some spirit speaking through a human being? "Salvation is found in no one else, for there is no other name under heaven given to men by which we must be saved" (Acts 4:12, NIV).

✓ Does a person or practice exert control over your mind or your money and dictate what you must do or give? "For the love of money is a root of all kinds of evil. Some people, eager for money, have wandered from the faith and pierced themselves with many griefs" (1 Tim. 6:10, NIV).

✓ Is prosperity considered to be a means to or sign of spiritual success? Does the leader promote sacrificial giving and yet seem to live a lavish lifestyle personally?

✓ Do individuals attempt to shift you into a state where they are in control of your bodily movements or emotions? Do you notice any members who seem to be in a trance or dazed condition? Any who are kept apart from the main group for periods of time?

✓ Are there any moral or ethical practices contrary to what you know God would expect of you? Examples: Go out and have an affair; it will lower your stress level. Steal from the rich and give to the poor. The Bible tells us in Ephesians that we are to behave in accordance with the truth that is in Jesus. "Be made new in the attitude of your minds; . . . put on the new self, created to be like God in true righteousness and holiness" (4:23–24, NIV).

✓ Are there books or other printed materials that are considered inspired and held above the Bible in importance? "But even if we or an angel from heaven should preach a gospel other than the one we preached to you, let him be eternally condemned!" (Gal. 1:8, NIV).

✓ Are the rules, practices, preachings, and theories of this group or religion inconsistent with the Word of God? "The things that come out of the mouth come from the heart, and these make a man 'unclean.' . . . evil thoughts, murder, adultery, sexual immorality, theft, false testimony, slander" (Matt. 15:18–19, NIV).

✓ Do spirit and sex seem to go hand in hand? Is any kind of free sex advocated and accepted? Does the leader exempt himself from normal moral principles? "Thou shalt not commit adultery" (Exod. 20:14, KJV).

✓ Is getting drunk, drugged, or high a part of the ritual and considered a sign of spirituality? "And be not drunk with wine, wherein is excess; but be filled with the Spirit" (Eph. 5:18, KJV).

✓ To belong to this group, do you have to change the style of your dress or hair? Do you have to move to some separate area? Forsake family and friends?

✓ Are you encouraged to get in touch with your past lives or dead relatives? "And as it is appointed unto men once to die, but after this the judgment" (Heb. 9:27, KJV).

✓ Do the members use mediums, cards, boards, crystal balls, love crystals, or any other implements or spirits to get close to God? Leviticus 19:31 cautions: "Do not defile yourselves by consulting mediums and wizards, for I am Jehovah your God" (TLB).

If your answers to this check list are yes, I suggest that you locate some respected Christian leader outside of the group you are considering and ask for counsel before you get involved. All kinds of new religions have sprung up and many initially seem to be warm, loving, sincere, Christian groups. We must all be very careful that in our search for God, we don't end up in the wrong places.

> Do not be carried away by all kinds of strange teachings (Heb. 13:9, NIV).

> For the time will come when men will not put up with sound doctrine. Instead, to suit their own desires, they will gather around them a great number of teachers to say what their itching ears want to hear. They will turn their ears away from the truth and turn aside to myths. But you, keep your head in all situations (2 Tim. 4:3–5, NIV).

Throughout our adventure in looking for God we will pause for a time of restful introspection. We will sit by a reflection pool in our spiritual desert. Because so much of life is a race, a mad dash from here to there, we need to "Be still, and know that [He is] God" (Ps. 46:10, NIV). Sometimes we're in such a hurry that if we came face to face with God in a burning bush, we'd not notice and we'd pass him by.

We want to enjoy our journey, but we don't want to skim over the top so quickly that when we get home we have no memories but a few snapshots of Moses.

Pause, inhale, reflect. "If there be any virtue . . . think on these things" (Phil. 4:8, KJV).

THINK ON THESE THINGS

1. What do you remember of the church you attended as a child . . .

The building and style?
Theology and doctrine?
Pastor and teachers?
Outside speakers and evangelists?

2. What did you learn of God in a personal way . . .

From church?
From parents?
From teachers?
From friends?

3. What avenues did you (or your children) take in pursuit
of God . . .

Fortune telling?
Horoscopes?
Other denominations?
Cults?
Bible studies?
Prayer or support groups?

4. Why are people attracted to . . .

Cults?
New religions?
The prosperity gospel?
The occult?

5. Have you committed your life to the Lord . . .

When did you first make that commitment?
What were the circumstances?
Where did it take place?

6. Is there any harm in Christians reading books like *Out
on a Limb* by Shirley MacLaine? What is your opinion of this
for Sunday school material? What does God's Word say about
the occult? See Exodus 22:18; Leviticus 19:31; 1 Samuel
15:23, 28:7; 2 Kings 9:22, 23:24; 1 Chronicles 10:13; Micah
5:12; Galatians 5:19–21.

7. If someone asked you how to find God, how would you
reply?

8. As you see how and where people found God in the Bible and as you progress in your journey, you will find Bonus Stories of how some modern-day people met the Lord. If you are in a group study, after reviewing each Bonus Story, ask if anyone knows a similar situation about themselves or a friend and would be willing to share it. Have someone record these testimonies, and create your own collection of Bonus Stories which you could duplicate and give out to the group members at the conclusion of your study.

Bonus Story

◇ ─────────────────────────────────────── ◇

LOOKING FOR GOD IN GROUP THERAPY

Everyone's looking for God but so often in the wrong places. Recently I spent a week in a home where sixteen-year-old Jennie, a committed Christian, had an eating disorder known as bulimia. This young woman had a pattern of overeating and then forcing herself to vomit. As I questioned her, she explained that a friend had shown her how to do it as an easy way to enjoy food but not gain weight. Initially she had no idea that there was anything wrong with this occasional act, but suddenly she found herself gripped with a need to empty her stomach whenever anything was in it. She quickly developed a compulsive behavior which she hated and which, if continued, would cause damage to the esophagus and deterioration of the teeth.

Her parents had taken her to a psychiatrist who treated her as a sad case and put her in a therapy group where she met with him, eight others with bulimia, and six with anorexia nervosa for three evenings a week. Jennie dreaded going, felt she learned nothing, and was depressed each time she left the group. She began to pray about her problems and discuss them with mature Christian women who encouraged her and counseled her.

By the time I arrived at their home, Jennie had improved, and I tried to give her hope. She felt strongly that the therapy group was not right for her because God was left out of the program completely. The one night she had dared mention her faith, the doctor had smiled benignly and said, "Well, if it works for you, that's fine." Together we decided she would go one last time and hope to be able to contribute something positive before leaving.

Here's what happened in her own words:

> I attended my last meeting and was determined to speak up for once and express exactly the way I really felt about the program. I explained to the girls that the meetings were fine for expressing feelings, but for getting well, there seemed to be NO hope. I spoke about my Christian beliefs and the encouragement God gave me. I told them that God was concerned with every aspect of life, and He especially wants to help with personal problems and show us how to begin to build a personal relationship with Him.
>
> The girls, surprisingly, were fascinated with what I had to say. They seemed to be lost, searching for the fulfillment of that empty space only God could fill.
>
> Since it was my last meeting, the girls wished me luck and told me that I was so fortunate to have a relationship with God.
>
> One mentioned that she did not know much about religion, but she wished she could understand the way I did.
>
> I could see in their faces that they longed to understand and I wanted to shout, "You can all have God! He wants to be in your life and help you, too!"
>
> I waited until the meeting ended; then I was able to witness to two of them. They really wanted to hear "The Good News," and I got their phone numbers so we could discuss it later. They were thrilled!
>
> I felt as though all of the meetings I had attended were worth it if I could help them find God.

How exciting it is that Jennie was able to lead some girls to the Lord in a therapy group for eating disorders. Everyone's looking for God, even in unexpected places.

Part II

————————————◇

Looking for God in All the Right Places

Ten Stops in Our
Search for God

◇ ——————————————————————— ◇

1. IN THE GARDEN

Every rocket needs a launching pad, each board game a square-one, each baseball diamond a home plate, and each journey a beginning. As we pack our bags for our adventure, we find there isn't anywhere to go; but wait, God's making us a world. He's creating heaven and earth; day and night; water, land, and sky; plants and trees; seasons, days, and years; sun, moon, and stars; birds, fish, and animals; man and woman. He's making a paradise for each one of us, and we don't even have to bring a suitcase full of clothes. We're going to the Garden of Eden and meet Adam and Eve. We're going to follow the guidebook: Genesis, "the Beginning."

For God's People in Bible Times

The people in the Old Testament were just like you and me. They wanted their own way, they were pursuing happiness, they liked fine food and fancy furnishings, and they appreciated the beauty of gold and precious stones. Yet, they knew in their hearts they needed God, a God who was close at hand and not far off, a God who had power, a God who spoke to them. In the second verse of Genesis, we see that God, unlike most of us, spoke words before there were any people to listen to him. "And God said, 'Let there be light,' and there was light" (NIV). God spoke; God had power; God could bring about change; God could create. He made trees that were pleasing to the eye and that produced good food; in fact, after he planted this garden in Eden, he even put gold and onyx in the ground to be unearthed. When he created

43

the first couple, Adam and Eve, he put them in the garden to take care of it. They were sure they'd live happily ever after. Isn't that what we all want: to live happily ever after, to find a faith that will make us feel good?

Adam and Eve lived in a perfect garden and had a stress-free existence. Their Father God wanted to walk and talk with them forever, and he gave them only one rule: Don't eat the fruit from the tree of the knowledge of good and evil. I'm sure they were content in this tropical paradise for a season, but the day came when all Eve wanted was the forbidden fruit.

Eve was probably a sanguine[1] lady whose main aim in life was to have fun and whose emotional need was to be praised. She wanted to be the center of attention, but she couldn't find an audience. Phlegmatic Adam never seemed to get excited over anything, including her. He just wanted to be left alone to do his gardening; he wanted to live in peace. This very first couple didn't seem divinely made for each other; they were opposites. Did God make a mistake? If Eve only knew we were available, she'd probably have us over for a garden party. Adam, on the other hand, would want to avoid the crowds. What an ideal candidate Eve was for the wiles of a flattering serpent who told her to pay no attention to what God and Adam had said about "the tree" and about the rules. "Do what you want to do," he encouraged. "Be your own person. Don't you know that when you eat that fruit you will be even more wise than you are right now? This is miracle food." I imagine this feast sounded like a lot of fun to Eve. She had been so lonesome that she probably jumped for joy in finding a friend that understood her and encouraged her desires. And even though she knew God was in the garden, she took a chance he wouldn't notice, and she ate the fruit. She not only partook herself, but she also got Adam involved. Perhaps she wanted to make sure that, if she got in trouble, she wouldn't be alone. Adam being phlegmatic and agreeable didn't think about it or ask God about it; he just ate as Eve instructed. Even though she and Adam knew God personally and were close to him in the garden, they yielded to temptation and disobeyed.

Then the man and his wife heard the sound of the Lord
God as he was walking in the garden in the cool of the day
(Gen. 3:8, NIV).

Besides being disobedient and suddenly becoming aware
of their nakedness, both Adam and Eve were deceptive.
When God came looking for them in the garden, they were
afraid and hid from sight in hopes he wouldn't find them. And
when the all-seeing God asked them if they had eaten the one
fruit that was forbidden, they responded like children caught
with their hands in the cookie jar. Adam tried to avoid responsibility by putting the blame on Eve, "The woman whom
thou gavest to be with me, she gave me of the tree, and I did
eat" (Gen. 3:12, KJV).

Eve wasn't much better. She avoided honest responsibility
by saying quickly and cleverly, "The serpent beguiled
me" (Gen. 3:13, KJV). Can't you just hear her saying "Surely
it wasn't my fault! Shouldn't we always be seeking self-
improvement?" Eve tried to evade the truth by putting the
blame on the serpent instead of saying, "I did it. It's my
fault. I'm sorry."

Because they had disobeyed God and were deceptive,
"Because you listened to your wife and ate from the tree"
(Gen. 3:17, NIV), they were punished and driven from the
Garden of Eden. To protect the entrance to the garden, God
placed the first cherubim mentioned in the Bible as a
guardian.

Because Adam and Eve disobeyed God's simple and clear
command and then tried to cover their tracks in deception,
God expelled them from their place of perfect peace.

God had created Adam and Eve, and they knew him.
What's more important, they knew where to find him. Each
night he had walked and talked with them in the garden.
But because he had given them a free will, a mind of their
own, they were able to make decisions, and they chose to
disobey. This act, referred to as the Fall, caused man to be
separated from God and sent one generation after another
on a perpetual search for the living God. If Adam and Eve

had not fallen, we wouldn't need to be looking for God. If they had not been lost, we wouldn't need to be found. If they had not sinned, we wouldn't need a savior.

When my adopted son Fred was eight years old, he got himself in a little trouble at school. Having listened to my teaching on Adam and Eve, when I questioned him on how it all happened, he replied, "If it hadn't been for Adam and Eve, and that apple, I wouldn't be in this mess today!"

How true.

For Us in Today's World

How about the rest of us? Are we in a mess today? Are we looking for God to bail us out? Are we hoping to find him in some mythical garden? Has someone told us that when we ask the Lord into our life it will become a rose garden?

My favorite hymn as a child was "In the Garden" by C. Austin Miles. Because my father's store in which we lived was set right on the sidewalk and our yard was the cracked cement where the one gas pump had settled in, I always longed for green grass and some flowers. I tried planting things in the dirt next to the side of the store and was grateful that at least the hollyhocks kept coming back each year. Once I tried to transplant some lady's-slippers from the woods near my grandmother's house but they soon died, leaving nary a footprint in the soil. I often pictured living in a garden, and I loved novels where the heroine looked out her window onto manicured English hedges, cool fountains, and magnolia blossoms.

Singing the words "I come to the garden alone while the dew is still on the roses" became a spiritual experience for me, knowing he would walk with me and talk with me and tell me I was his own. As I would sing in church and look out the window to our shabby brown store across the street, I wished for flowers. I wanted to walk and talk with God in a garden where the dew was still on the roses.

A young lady wrote me a touching letter composed in a public Rose Garden. She had serious family problems, so she took her Bible in hand and drove to the garden. As she sat

quietly praying and reading Psalms, a peace came over her
and she felt the presence of the Lord. She could have done
the same thing at home, but for her, removing herself from
the scene of agitation allowed her to look for God in the
garden. And he walked with her and he talked with her and
he told her she was his own. This woman still has unsolved
difficulties, but she knows there is a garden where she can
meet her Lord.

In the beginning God walked and talked with Adam and
Eve in the lush Garden of Eden. He asked simple obedience
and honesty in return for fellowship and food. Given a free
mind, the two made wrong choices. (It seems that being in
perfect circumstances didn't guarantee they would choose
correctly.) Beautiful surroundings weren't enough. Lack of
stress wasn't enough. Being with God didn't make them spiritual. They both disobeyed and were deceptive.

How many of us feel if we could only get our house in
order, if we could get the lawn mowed and the roses to
bloom, if we didn't have to go to work each day, if we didn't
have those children who messed things up, if our environ-
ment were only perfect, if God was walking in our backyard
where we could see him in the cool of the day, we could be
spiritual. We could pray out loud; we could write psalms; we
could sing like the angels.

God doesn't ask for dramas and displays; he wants simple
obedience to his directions and honesty, not deception. Our
circumstances may never be anywhere close to perfection,
but God will create a haven of peace, a garden of rest in our
hearts, when we choose his approval over the temptations of
the world.

Let's not wait for that great day when we get it all together
and have time for God. Let's meet him in the garden of our
heart right now and let him restore our soul.

◇

2. IN THE FIELDS

As we leave the Garden of Eden and catch the last glimpse of the cherubim at the gate and the "flaming sword flashing back and forth to guard the way to the tree of life" (Gen. 3:24, NIV), we find ourselves in barren fields where thorns and thistles grow. Adam, banished to painful toil for the rest of his life, is working by the sweat of his brow with his son Cain while Abel is tending the sheep.

For God's People in Bible Times

In Genesis chapter 4, God called for the first recorded sacrifice from his people. Adam's son Abel, in obedience to God, brought an animal from the firstborn of his flock, and God was pleased. Because choleric Cain, strong-willed and rebellious, brought fruit and did not make the expected blood sacrifice, God was displeased and let him know it. Cain, in his anger at being rebuked, struck out and killed his brother Abel. When God asked Cain directly what had happened to Abel, he avoided the honest answer by deceptively asking, "Am I my brother's keeper?" (Gen. 4:9, NIV). How should I know where he is!

God knew what Cain had done to Abel, and he was disheartened by Cain's deception. God could have killed Cain, but he chose a punishment more severe: God banished Cain from his fertile fields and said, "You will be a restless wanderer on the earth" (Gen. 4:12, NIV).

Cain called out to God, "My punishment is more than I can bear. Today you are driving me from the land, and I will be hidden from your presence; I will be a restless wanderer on the earth, and whoever finds me will kill me" (Gen. 4:13, NIV).

God assured him that he would not be killed, and to set him apart and protect him, God put the "mark of Cain" upon him.

For Us in Today's World

Do we sometimes feel that we are wandering in the wilderness, that God has forgotten us?—if he ever knew us in the first place! He has promised that "he will never leave you nor forsake you" (Deut. 31:6, NIV).

God met with Cain and Abel in the fields where animals were grazing and grain was growing. What better place to be close to God and admire his handiwork than in the fields where God's gardening plan of reaping what we sow is in such clear evidence. We see that mighty oaks grow out of little acorns, and apple trees don't grow bananas. Without God there would be no explanation for how a tiny pansy seed knows it must grow up to be a pansy, and not a petunia; no chance that on occasion a grain of wheat might not become an ear of corn.

Let's stop and think right now. What are we sowing? What are we putting in our minds personally? Are we reading God's Word and Christian literature? Or are we filling our minds with trivia and trash? Garbage in; garbage out. What are we planting in the hearts of our mates and close friends? Are we inserting kind and gracious words that will produce positive responses? What seeds are we placing in the fertile minds of our little ones? How embarrassing it is sometimes to hear our own words repeated back to us out of the mouths of babes. We do reap what we sow—God's principles work in people as well as in the fields.

3. ON A WALK

Many articles are written on physical fitness and the value of exercise. We know that walking and jogging increase our circulation. So no doubt, exercise is a must—for other people, and we plan to join them for an early morning walk—someday. A few of us even buy cute jogging clothes to tuck in our suitcase so that if we get an urge to run while in a distant city, we'll be prepared. How impressed we all will be as we meet Enoch, a man who didn't just do an occasional sit-up but who "walked with God 300 years"!

For God's People in Bible Times

Enoch, the father of Methuselah, was an obedient and godly man. "Altogether, Enoch lived 365 years. Enoch walked with God; then he was no more, because God took him away" (Gen. 5:23–24, NIV).

Enoch walked with God, and because he had obeyed and had not been deceptive, God took him to be with him in paradise without experiencing a physical death.

Although Enoch lived in a society of sinful souls, he walked so closely with God that he was able to be in the world, but not of the world. Because the people feared death, Enoch became a symbol of a positive afterlife.

By faith Enoch was translated that he should not see death; and was not found, because God had translated him: for before his translation he had this testimony, that he pleased God.

But without faith it is impossible to please him: for he that

cometh to God must believe that he is, and that he is a re-
warder of them that diligently seek him (Heb. 11:5–6, KJV).

For Us in Today's World

How about you and me? Are we earnestly seeking God?
Are we walking with God as Enoch did? Are we so close to
God that our very steps are going uphill toward heaven? Are
we so identified with Jesus that God looks down and can't tell
us apart? Could God say of us, "That person is so perfectly in
tune with me I must bring him up to fellowship with me and
seat him in heavenly places"? That's how God saw Enoch, as a
friend so close to his divine thinking that they were two
hearts that beat as one.

Sometimes we have that relationship with another human
being where we know exactly what the other one is thinking.
Our daughters, Marita and Lauren, and I are "tuned in" to
each other. We are of one mind; we walk together. Whenever
they are with me, they can take one look at a meeting room
where I am to speak and see it with my eyes. They put themselves in my position automatically because they've been
close to me for so long. Neither one has to stand and say,
"What would Mother want changed or moved?" They just
take action as I would; they can see with my eyes. When I am
speaking, they sense when I'm too hot, when the room is too
stuffy, or when I need a drink of water. We have joked for
years that, since they have heard my testimony hundreds of
times, if I were to drop dead in the middle of it, either one of
them could step over the body and continue my life story
without missing a beat. We are not just related by blood, we
are close in spirit. We have not only traveled together, we
have "walked" together.

God wants us to have that kind of a fellowship with him. He
wants our relationship to be deeper than just a born-again
experience; he wants us to be of one mind in the spirit—not
just strolling down the path to heaven but walking with Jesus.

I used to tell my Bible classes when they would tend to
elevate me as their leader, "As long as I keep showing up

each week you'll know I'm not yet perfected, for when God sees me as 'like unto himself' he will snatch me up to heaven and no one will know why or how I disappeared. I'll be like a spiritual Mary Poppins floating off into the future."

Enoch was so close to God that the Almighty couldn't leave him here with the rest of us; he translated him, whisked him away. How about us? Are we so in step with the Lord that our feet hardly touch the ground? Are we one wink away from eternity? Do we tread so in tune to God's plan for our life that there's but one set of footprints in the sand?

Bill Bright, founder of Campus Crusade for Christ, calls this process "spiritual breathing," inhaling and exhaling with the very breath of God.

Oswald Chambers puts it so clearly when he says:

> It is a painful business to get through into the stride of God, it means getting your second wind spiritually. In learning to walk with God there is always the difficulty of getting into His stride; but when we have gotten into it, the only characteristic that manifests itself is the life of God. The individual man is lost sight of in his personal union with God, and the stride and the power of God alone are manifested.[2]

Are we in stride with God? Or is he several steps ahead of us? Has he already turned the corner and disappeared from sight? Walking with God is not being cheerfully chummy with Christ but being so close to him that we lay our head on his bosom and breathe in and out to God's rhythm.

How do we get to know Christ that well? The same way we get to know anyone. By spending time with him. When a new neighbor moves in, many times we make our initial judgment on their status and taste by observing their furniture as it comes out of the moving van. But we don't really know them. To get to know our neighbors we have to walk next door, introduce ourselves, and spend some time with them.

It's the same with God; we have to spend time with him. We all want to know him, but we don't take the time to study his Word, to feel the power of his presence, to get in stride with God. Let's get acquainted today so we can walk in stride tomorrow.

Enoch's testimony was that "he pleased God." Let's hope the same can be said of us.

THINK ON THESE THINGS

Read Genesis 1–5.

1. When you were a child what kind of Bible teaching did you receive? What did you learn that has shaped your life? Did you ask questions about God that adults couldn't answer? What questions? What answers did you get? Share any circumstances you remember about your early concept of God.

2. What are some of the major hurts, disappointments, or tragedies in your life? Who or what has helped you the most? What things were said to you that hurt? What have you learned from your experiences that have shown you how to help others? For help in sharing other people's sorrows in a godly manner, read *What You Can Say—When You Don't Know What to Say,* by Lauren Littauer Briggs.

3. Do you have a place of retreat, a garden in your life, where you can go to walk and talk with God? Where is it? How often do you go there? How do you feel when you're there?

4. Do you and your mate have opposite personalities? In what areas are you different? Are you . . .

Sanguine: let's have fun?
Choleric: let's get control?
Melancholy: let's do it perfectly?
Phlegmatic: let's keep peace?

Explain one situation where your differences got you in trouble. For more information on different types of personality, see my book *Your Personality Tree.*

5. Why do you feel people are deceptive? What circumstance last led you to skirt the truth? Do you feel we are born

deceptive? Why was Eve deceptive with God? How do you
handle your children when they lie?

6. Why did Cain say, "Am I my brother's keeper?" How do
you feel about the current philosophy of independence? Is
"doing your own thing" always positive?

7. Do you have another person with whom you are in
tune? How has this understanding developed? Who is it? Do
you have that same feeling with God? How much time do you
spend each day in study? In prayer? How could you improve
your spiritual breathing? How could you get in stride with
God?

For Your Notebook

Genesis means "beginnings." List all the beginnings (the
firsts) that you can find in these verses. For example, 4:26
says that it was during the time of Seth and his son Enoch
when men first called "on the name of the Lord" (NIV).

As we continue our study, take note of each beginning that
you find and add it to your list.

◇

4. IN THE RAIN

From the time I was a child, I knew the story of Noah and
the ark. I knew the animals came two by two, that it rained a
lot, and that a rainbow appeared to end it all. People today
are still fascinated by this story. In August, 1986, former
astronaut James Irwin went to eastern Turkey to climb the
17,000-foot Mt. Ararat in search of the lost ark. Is it there?
Is this story fact or fiction? What does the Bible say? As we
move on in our journey toward God, we come to the land of
Noah. Pull out your raincoat and umbrella. It's beginning
to sprinkle.

For God's People in Bible Times

In the times of Noah, God saw that his creations had become evil. "The Lord was grieved that he had made man on the earth, and his heart was filled with pain" (Gen. 6:6, NIV).

But Noah found favor with God because he, like Enoch, was "a righteous man, blameless among the people of his time, and he walked with God" (Gen. 6:9, NIV). From what I read about Noah in the Scriptures, it seems to me he was a melancholy: deep, thoughtful, introspective, analytical. Whatever he did, he did perfectly.

God talked to Noah and said, "I am going to put an end to all people, for the earth is filled with violence because of them. I am surely going to destroy both them and the earth" (Gen. 6:13, NIV).

God then gave Noah explicit directions on how to build the ark, the vessel that was to be his salvation. "Noah did everything just as God commanded him" (Gen. 6:22, NIV).

The rains came for forty days and forty nights and then Noah sent a dove to see if the water had receded, but the dove returned. He waited seven days and then sent out the dove again. This time the dove came back with a fresh olive leaf. In seven more days, he sent the dove out again. This time it did not return, and Noah concluded it was safe to leave the ark and begin a new life.

The first thing Noah did when he left the ark on Mt. Ararat was build an altar and sacrifice some animals and birds in praise to God for saving him and his family. "The Lord smelled the pleasing aroma" (Gen. 8:21, NIV) and pledged not to destroy the earth by flood again. He made a covenant with Noah—"a covenant for all generations to come"—because he knew he could trust him.

> I have set my rainbow in the clouds, and it will be the sign of the covenant between me and the earth. Whenever I bring clouds over the earth and the rainbow appears in the clouds, I will remember my covenant between me and you and all living creatures of every kind. Never again will the waters become a flood to destroy all life (Gen. 9:13–15, NIV).

Noah walked and talked with God and because of honest obedience he and his family were saved.

For Us in Today's World

I've often thought of how I would have responded if God had told me to go home and build an ark. Would I have done "just as God commanded"? Or would I have argued? "God, you know I can't hammer straight! I've never been good at mechanical things. And it's not even raining. Don't you see I live in the desert of Southern California? Plus what will people think of me? If I start building a big ark in the front yard, the neighbors will be furious. They already made the man next door remove his motorboat from the driveway where he had settled it on blocks for the winter. What would they do if I built an ark?"

Even if I were willing to build the ark, would my choleric nature want to do it God's way? Would I like his instructions? I'm sure I'd have better ideas. "Couldn't we have more windows? I like a view and I get claustrophobia when I can't see outside. Could we paint it blue, give the boat a name, and wallpaper the bathroom? There won't be a bathroom? Then count me out!"

I've never wanted to do anything exactly as someone else had in mind, and naturally I always feel I'm improving on their plans. One night when Fred and I were eating out, he asked me what I was thinking about. I hesitated to tell him I was redesigning the floor plan of the restaurant and unconsciously constructing a wall to hide the dish room which was in my clear view. When I mentioned this dubious talent of mine to my choleric daughter Lauren, she laughed and told me she had just gone to look at a mini-mall still under construction to see if she would like to open a new coin store there. As she talked with the builder, she could see he needed some help in laying out a floor plan that would be more functional. She pointed out some necessary changes and obvious improvements which she felt needed to be done whether or not she rented space. By the time she left, the confused man was reviewing his blueprints and modifying his plans.

What would Lauren and I have ever done if God had told us to build an ark and to use his directions without changing them? But gratefully Noah wasn't like us. Noah was willing to meet God in the rain, to obey his instructions, and to do "everything just as God commanded him." He didn't argue with God or insist on his own way.

"By faith Noah, when warned about things not yet seen, in holy fear built an ark to save his family. By his faith he condemned the world and became heir of the righteousness that comes by faith" (Heb. 11:7, NIV).

Is God asking you and me to build an ark today—to do something we don't understand, to prepare for a future we can't foresee? Is God telling you personally to spend more time now building relationships with your children in order to save your family when the rains come? Is he asking you to prepare for bad weather while the sun is shining? Is he begging to spend time with you, but you're too busy? Do you look up through the clouds and shout, "Don't rain on my parade!"

Noah listened to God in the sunshine and prepared for the stormy weather. And when the rains came, Noah continued to listen to God and remained faithful. Oswald Chambers states:

> At times God puts us through the discipline of darkness to teach us to heed Him. . . . watch where God puts you into darkness, and when you are there keep your mouth shut. . . . Darkness is the time to listen. . . . When you are in the dark, listen, and God will give you a very precious message for someone else when you get into the light.[3]

Let's spend time with God today; tomorrow may be too late. There are no instant arks; they take time to build. Let's get to know the Master Builder so he'll keep us afloat. He's no fairweather friend, but he wants to get to know us NOW!

Shakespeare wrote:

> There is a tide in the affairs of men,
> Which, taken at the flood, leads on to fortune;
> Omitted, all the voyage of their life
> Is bound in shallows and in miseries. . . .
> We must take the current when it serves.
> Or lose our ventures.

> *Julius Caesar*, act 4, scene 3

Don't be one of those Christians who's "bound in shallows and in miseries." Get to know God in the warmth of his sunshine so that you'll be singing in the rain. God wants to save you and me as he did Noah. Don't miss the boat!

Bonus Story

◇ ──────────────────────────────── ◇

LOOKING FOR GOD IN THE RAIN

One summer evening Elaine was scheduled to share her testimony at a friend's poolside supper party. As the guests arrived the skies parted and rain poured onto the patio. Tables and chairs were quickly dragged into the small living room which was so filled with furniture that there was no room for the people.

The resourceful hostess, seeing no change in the weather, decided to move the party and Elaine's performance to the garage. "This was no finished room," Elaine explained wide-eyed. "It was just a dirty old garage with a wheelless Dodge up on jacks. Water was pouring in under the doors and piling up against the far wall. It began to look like an oil-laden swamp."

Elaine stood at a podium that was placed over the drain in the garage floor and told her life story to a sad-looking group who well may have wondered what they were doing listening to Bible verses in a garage with water swirling around their feet.

At the conclusion, the hostess, seemingly oblivious to the dampened spirits and wet shoes, asked all the guests to take off their limp name tags and put an X if they had asked the Lord into their lives. After the guests "swam" out to their cars, Elaine was too embarrassed to look at the tags, but the hostess counted the decisions and found that despite the rain several people had met the Lord.

Because Elaine had been obedient in a bizarre set of circumstances, twelve searching people found God in a garage in the rain.

◇

5. AT THE TOWER

So many of us wish we could have a second start in our life. "If only I could begin again!"

Would we do it all better if we had another chance? Or would we perhaps make bigger mistakes? God the Father gave his people a new beginning. He had created the world and said, "That's good." But he had given Adam and Eve a mind of their own, and even though they walked with him in the garden, they both disobeyed and were deceptive. After viewing several generations, the Father looked at his children in disappointment and had to admit "This is a sorry lot."

If you are a parent, perhaps you've had similar feelings when your offspring made choices that disappointed you. Perhaps at some point you've even wondered how a sane, sober, conservative person like yourself could have produced a child who wears green and pink punk hair and a gold earring, or one who's still in school at thirty-two, or one who has returned home unmarried with a new baby. Even though there is no way to really compare these frustrations with God's disappointment in the days of Noah, perhaps you can somewhat understand God's anguish as he sighed and wished he'd never created us in the first place. Yet, in the midst of all the wickedness on the earth, there was Noah, a righteous man, and God spared him to give the world a second chance. As we leave Noah there on Mt. Ararat with his own personal rainbow curled around his shoulder, we travel through time to a city where we find people with short memories and little gratitude toward God.

For God's People in Bible Times

As with any difficult experience, the impact decreases with the passage of time, so Noah's descendants soon forgot that God desired obedience, honesty, and humility among his people. The leaders settled in the area of Babylon about fifty miles south of today's Baghdad, and as they structured their new civilization one of their first thoughts was to build a monument to themselves to show their power and authority. This tower was not an altar to their God but to themselves.

> "Come, let us build ourselves a city, with a tower that reaches to the heavens, so that we may make a name for our-selves and not be scattered over the face of the whole earth."
> But the Lord came down to see the city and the tower that the men were building (Gen. 11:4–5, NIV).

> So the Lord scattered them from there over all the earth, and they stopped building the city. That is why it is called Babel—because there the Lord confused the language of the whole world. From there the Lord scattered them over the face of the whole earth (Gen. 11:8–9, NIV).

Although Babel means "gate of God," our God knew this tower was not a doorway to his holiness but, instead, a step toward the reverence of humanity.

For Us in Today's World

In my lifetime, I have seen how many godly people with good intentions become overly impressed by their own spirit-uality when surrounded by an adoring audience. The world is looking for a leader to follow, a god to guide them. How easy it is, when sensing the adulation of the crowd, to see one's self as a mini-god and to build a little tower of Babel. But God is still sovereign and his eyesight has not dimmed. When he observes a ministry that has shifted its attention and worship from him to its human leader, he can confuse their language and scatter their ministry right before our eyes.

What a lesson there is in this brief passage of Scripture for those of us who are visible as leaders: we must keep our eyes on the Lord and not on ourselves so that we build ministries for him and not monuments to us.

At the time of the Jim Jones mass suicides, Rabbi Harold M. Schulweis wrote in the *Los Angeles Times* that we tend to "set charismatic leaders apart, idealizing some as saints or condemning others as devils." Often the leaders who were "saints" one day become the fallen ones the next. The Rabbi goes on to say:

> Overnight, leaders who have been raised to the heights are cast to the depths.
>
> We would be less taken aback by such contradictions if we were to follow the wisdom of Biblical monotheism, for the scripture knows the mischief that follows from either idealizing or demonizing God's creatures.
>
> Scripture warns us that "there is no righteous person who does good and does not sin" [Eccles. 7:20]. Its respected tales of flawed patriarchs, princes, priests and prophets illustrate the tragic folly of idolatry.
>
> But we mortals do need heroes; we seek out figures of exemplary strength and wisdom. Yet we must be reminded that the creatures of God are limited, and that adulation often becomes a temptation to mount the tower and assume the power of divinity.[4]

Let us limited creatures be reminded that we aren't God and that we don't have any special license to sin because we've given up so much for God. We must not be tempted "to mount the tower and assume the power of divinity."

◇

6. IN THE WILDERNESS

In my early days of Bible study, I skipped genealogies. I didn't care who begat whom or in what order, but as I became a more serious student, I saw how important it was to follow a family line, to trace their inherited characteristics, both bad and good. During the writing of *Your Personality Tree*, I spent time in reviewing my relatives, revisiting childhood haunts and homes, meditating in the cemetery, and analyzing family personalities from the past. As I became enthralled with my own family background, I had a new desire to trace the traits of God's family and examine their personality tree. As you think about your family tree, come and meet Abram. We'll trace his lineage and move with him through many experiences in the wilderness.

For God's People in Bible Times

From the three sons of Noah came all the nations of the earth. Japheth's descendants spread to many lands and spoke different languages. Through Ham's son Canaan came the Canaanites, and through Ham's son Cush came Nimrod the mighty hunter. Nimrod was blessed of God, and his reign extended to Assyria where he built the city of Nineveh. From Shem, the oldest of the three, came some fascinating names such as Lud and Uz, Gether and Mash. Later Shem's descendants included Nahor, his son Terah, and Terah's sons Abram, Nahor, and Haran (father of Lot).

In about 1921 B.C., God spoke to peace-loving Abram, saying, "Leave your country, your people and your father's household and go to the land I will show you" (Gen. 12:1).

Abram who lived in Ur of the Chaldeans had no desire to move, but God promised him a reward for his obedience, "I will make you into a great nation and I will bless you." God also said he would bless those who blessed Abram and curse those who cursed him.

In the wilderness at Haran. Abram traveled through Mesopotamia to Haran, a place named after his brother. Obedient to God's command, Abram dutifully built an altar of sacrifice and praise to the Lord each time he moved.

In the wilderness in Egypt. From Haran he took his ten-camel caravan to Palestine and later, because there was a famine, Abram decided on his own to go to Egypt with his exciting and beautiful wife. In typical phlegmatic fear that the Egyptians would desire Sarai and then kill him, Abram asked her to say she was his sister. By this deceptive ploy, Abram hoped to save his life. The Pharaoh did take Sarai to his palace and treated her "brother" Abram well "for her sake."

When God inflicted disease upon the Pharaoh and his household because of Abram's deception, the "Pharaoh summoned Abram. 'What have you done to me?' he said. 'Why didn't you tell me she was your wife? Why did you say, "She is my sister" so that I took her to be my wife? Now then, here is your wife. Take her and go!'" (Gen. 12:18–19, NIV).

In the wilderness in Bethel. Abram, who'd only been trying to avoid conflict, left Egypt in shame and went back to Bethel (which means "House of God") where he had previously built an altar. There he fell down before God and worshiped him.

In the wilderness in Sodom and Gomorrah. As Abram and his nephew Lot were in the wilderness together, quarrels broke out between their families. Abram, always the peacemaker, suggested they go in separate directions. Under God's inspiration Abram selflessly gave Lot first choice of the available land. Lot selected the fertile plain of the Jordan settling in near the city of Sodom (Gen. 13:8–13, NIV).

Noah's lessons of God's destructive power over evil had long been forgotten. Because of their unrepentant sins of lust and homosexuality (19:5), the people of Sodom (which means "place of lime") and Gomorrah (which means "rebellious people") were guilty in God's sight and he prepared to wipe out wickedness once again. Abram, wanting to keep peace and avoid any disaster, begged God to spare the cities if there were ten righteous people in them, but God spared only Lot, his wife, and two daughters, and told them to flee to the mountains and not look back. Lot and his daughters obeyed, but his wife, seeing God rain down burning sulphur from the heavens, looked back to her past and, because of her disobedience, she was turned into a pillar of salt.

In the wilderness in Canaan. Abram settled in Canaan, the land God gave him as an everlasting possession for him and his descendants. As patient Abram grew old and still had no children, he became doubtful of God's promise and cried out to God. The Lord made a covenant with Abram—he would be the Father of the Hebrew race, his children would be as plentiful as the stars in the heavens, and they would inherit the land between the river of Egypt to the Euphrates (Gen. 15:5, 18).

In the current Middle East conflict these words from the Bible are still remembered. Quoting from an Arab attending a dialogue workshop, the *Los Angeles Times* says the Jews "see anything between the Nile and the Tigris as fair game."

God also predicted that Abram's descendants would be enslaved in a land not their own for four hundred years before returning to possess their promised land (Gen. 15:13–16—for fulfillment see Exod. 1 and Ps. 105).

As the years went by and Abram and Sarai had none of these promised children, Sarai got impatient and suggested to Abram, who was 86 by then, that he have a child by her servant Hagar. Humanly speaking this seemed to make sense, but it was not God's plan. Hagar was as choleric as Sarai, and when two strong-willed women have to live or work together they either agree, fight, or one gives in and puts on a phlegmatic mask of peace. Because Sarai was the boss, Hagar had played passive. But when Hagar conceived, she dared to look with disdain upon Sarai who in turn lashed out and mistreated her until the maid ran away into the wilderness. As Hagar sat weeping near a spring in the desert, not wanting to accept defeat, the angel of the Lord appeared to her and told her to return to her mistress and as a reward for her obedience, "I will so increase your descendants that they will be too numerous to count" (Gen. 16:9–10, NIV). She was to name her son Ishmael, meaning "God hears" when you cry out to him.

Hagar replied, "You are the God who sees me. . . . I have now seen the One who sees me" (Gen. 16:13).

Hagar met God in the wilderness and because she obeyed, God made Ishmael the father of the Arab nations.

When patient Abram was ninety-nine years old, the Lord appeared to him again to confirm the covenant. The power of God caused Abram to fall flat on his face in abject humility. As a reward God changed his name to Abraham, "father of many nations." He changed Sarai's name to Sarah, princess, and reaffirmed she would have a son. Both Abraham and Sarah laughed at the prospect, and God told them to name their son Isaac, meaning laughter.

For Abraham's side of the covenant, he was to be obedient to God, "Walk before me and be blameless" (Gen. 17:1, NIV). And he was to establish a policy of circumcising each male child who was eight days old (Gen. 17:9–14).

When Abraham, who didn't want to hurt anyone, asked God what was to become of Ishmael, he replied, "I will surely bless him; I will make him fruitful and will greatly increase his numbers. He will be the father of twelve rulers and I will make him into a great nation" (Gen. 17:20). (The present-day Arab people are descendants of Ishmael.)

Abraham was one hundred years old when his son Isaac was born to Sarah and on the eighth day after his birth he circumcised him as God had commanded. Although Sarah had appeared accepting of Ishmael before Isaac's birth, as her own Isaac grew up she became angered by Hagar's child and told

Abraham what to do! "Get rid of that slave woman and her son, for that slave woman's son will never share in the inheritance with my son Isaac" (Gen. 21:10). Isn't it amazing how the thought of sharing an inheritance, then and today, brings out the baser nature in each one of us!

Abraham was depressed because he loved Ishmael so he called out to God who answered him,

> "Do not be so distressed about the boy and your maidservant. Listen to whatever Sarah tells you, because it is through Isaac that your offspring will be reckoned. I will make the son of the maidservant into a nation also, because he is your offspring" (Gen. 21:12–13).

In the wilderness of the desert. The next morning Hagar and Ishmael left. "She went on her way and wandered in the desert of Beersheba" (Gen. 21:14, NIV). As choleric Hagar sobbed in the wilderness because life was out of her control, God called down from heaven and asked, "What is the matter, Hagar? Do not be afraid; God has heard the boy crying as he lies there. Lift the boy up and take him by the hand, for I will make him into a great nation" (Gen. 21:17–18, NIV).

When she looked around, Hagar saw a well of water and knew then that God would provide. Ishmael grew up in the wilderness, became an archer, and married an Egyptian. However, it is easy to see why the rejected Ishmael had little fondness for his favored brother Isaac and the Hebrew people as a whole. No wonder four thousand years later the Arabs and the Jews still have an inborn enmity toward each other.

Currently in the Los Angeles area there are approximately 600,000 Jews and 250,000 Arabs. Of these, a few hundred are meeting "to address themselves to the seemingly endless dispute in the Middle East." Because of the animosity starting with Ishmael and Isaac, the two sides are, as the *Los Angeles Times* headlined, trying to find an "Oasis of Understanding in a Desert of Despair."

In the wilderness of Mt. Moriah. As we go back to where these current problems all began, we find that Abraham dearly loved his passive son Isaac, who was similar in personality to his phlegmatic father. This boy was now his only son, and Abraham must have been shocked when God told him to take Isaac up to Mt. Moriah and sacrifice him as a burnt offering. But Abraham had pledged obedience, and because he loved God so much, he was willing to sacrifice his only begotten son. As he lifted the knife to kill Isaac, who had obediently laid his life on the altar, Abraham heard the voice of God, "Do not lay a hand on the boy. Do not do anything to him. Now I know that you fear God, because you have not withheld from me your son, your only son" (Gen. 22:12, NIV).

Because Abraham had not withheld his son, God reaffirmed his pledge to bless the Hebrew race and make them a very special people.

Abraham walked with God, he talked with God, he visited with God, he obeyed God, and, because of his close relationship with God, he and his descendants were blessed. Abraham, Sarah, and Hagar all found God in the wilderness.

For Us in Today's World

How many of us feel we are wandering around in a spiritual wilderness? We haven't seen God in months. We wonder if he remembers us. We've disobeyed a few things God made clear to us, and who knows how we've done with those things on the fringes. We've been a little deceptive here and there, always for good reason and to save unnecessary confrontation. Why don't we feel close to God? Why are we so lonely in the wilderness?

Elizabeth Dent, a radio personality in Baton Rouge, said to me one day, "I wandered in the Desert of Divorce and I wanted to die." In her time of loneliness, depression, and despair, she, like Abraham, cried out to God.

> The righteous cry out, and the Lord hears them;
> he delivers them from all their troubles.
> The Lord is close to the brokenhearted
> and saves those who are crushed in spirit.
>
> —Psalm 34:17–18, NIV

The Lord heard Elizabeth wandering in the wilderness, and they became close in spirit. As she prayed and studied God's Word, he healed her broken heart. During that time of painful growth, Elizabeth wrote poetry to God—as David did with his psalms. She listened in the darkness so she could give a message to others when she was in the light.

> Lord, thank you for being my GUIDE each day.
> Thank you for teaching me how to pray.
> You're a special friend, Lord, who's always there.
> Help me give to others what you and I share.
>
> —Elizabeth Dent[5]

◇

7. BY THE WELL AND ON THE ROCKS

One of my favorite Bible stories has always been Rebekah at the well. Even as a child, I thought how romantic it would be to stand by a well, or even a bus stop, and have some stranger pick me out and change my life forever—whether it was to be the bride of some rich man far away or a Hollywood star. When I heard that Lana Turner, the glamorous movie star, had been discovered sitting on a stool at a drugstore soda fountain, I practiced looking glamorous while in pharmacies. Since I had none of Lana's assets, I was never snatched up by any prince charming or even one of the local boys.

Let's forget our youthful rejections and travel to the town of Nahor where we can see how Rebekah was discovered, chosen by an angel of God. Perhaps I didn't pray enough!

As we view her love story, her marriage to Isaac, and the birth of her twins, we will see that even a girl hand-picked by God can put life under her own control. She can become deceptive to her husband and pass that trait on to her son

Jacob. Later we will rejoice with Jacob as we watch him meet God face to face on the rocks.

For God's People in Bible Times

In Abraham's old age, he wished to find an appropriate wife for Isaac. So he called his chief servant before him and instructed him to go back to his homeland, Northwest Mesopotamia. He told the servant God would send an angel through the wilderness before him and show him which girl should be chosen. When the servant got to the town of Nahor near Haran, he prayed to God and asked him to have the right girl give him a drink from the well and offer to water his camels.

"Before he had finished praying, Rebekah came out with her jar on her shoulder. . . . The girl was very beautiful, a virgin" (Gen. 24:15, 16, NIV). She went down to the spring, filled her jar, and came up to where the servant was waiting. When he asked for a drink she gave it to him and volunteered to pour water in the trough for his camels. When he asked her name and family, he was amazed to find that God had truly chosen the granddaughter of Abraham's brother Nahor. Rebekah took the servant to her home where he explained his mission. Before asking Rebekah's hand in marriage for Isaac, the servant did as we might have done in a similar situation. He not only established the bloodline, but he told the prospective in-laws of Isaac's wealth—sheep, cattle, silver, gold, menservants, maidservants, camels, and donkeys. After that he explained how the Lord guided him to Rebekah at the well. "Then the servant brought out gold and silver jewelry and articles of clothing and gave them to Rebekah; he also gave costly gifts to her brother and to her mother" (always a good idea) (Gen. 24:53, NIV).

Rebekah must have been a daring and self-confident girl to take off with strangers, and she must have believed God had a plan for her life. The next day when she left with the servant to become Isaac's wife, her brothers gave her a parting blessing.

"Our sister, may you increase to thousands upon thousands; may your offspring possess the gates of their enemies" (Gen. 24:60, NIV).

The servant and Rebekah met God at the well and because they obeyed his plan, he blessed them.

After Sarah's death Abraham married Keturah. They had at least six other sons whom he sent to other lands, leaving the family flocks and wealth to Isaac who was forty when he married Rebekah and sixty when she got pregnant with twins. They "jostled each other" within her, and she called out to God, "Why is this happening to me?" (Gen. 25:22, NIV).

The Lord answered:

"Two nations are in your womb, and two peoples from within you will be separated; one people will be stronger than the other, and the older will serve the younger" (Gen. 25:23, NIV).

The firstborn was red and his whole body was covered with hair, so they named him Esau, meaning "hairy." When his brother came out after him, his hand was upon Esau's heel so he was named Jacob, "He grasps the heel," figuratively, "he deceives." They were so different in looks and personality that each became a favorite of one parent. Phlegmatic Isaac loved choleric Esau, the adventurous hunter, the outdoors man who brought wild game home to his father, who perhaps wished he'd been a little more aggressive during his life. Rebekah doted on her melancholy Jacob, a quiet, submissive young man who preferred to stay among the tents.

One day when Esau came charging home famished from hunting, Jacob had some red stew and hot bread prepared. It was then that Jacob saw his chance to gain some control over his older twin. Before he would give his starving brother food, he made Esau promise to sell him his birthright. Without giving great thought to the future and wishing to satisfy the physical needs of the moment, Esau agreed and sold his birthright for a dish of stew.

While this agreement appears extremely shortsighted, we

might each think of some time in our lives where we made
decisions based on expediency or enjoyment of the moment,
without analyzing the needs of our future or the possible
repercussions.

At this time there came a famine in the land, and Isaac
considered moving his family to Egypt, but the Lord appeared to him and said, "Do not go down to Egypt; live in the
land where I tell you to live. Stay in this land for a while, and
I will be with you and will bless you" (Gen. 26:2–3, NIV).
God then reviewed the covenant he had with Isaac's father,
Abraham, promising to make Isaac's descendants as plentiful
as the stars in the sky if he would obey God's commands. So
agreeable Isaac stayed in Gerar, present-day Gaza, and the
Lord blessed him. "The man became rich, and his wealth
continued to grow until he became very wealthy" (v. 13).

How God delights in blessing those who are obedient to his
will.

When Isaac got old, his eyesight failed and he knew he
would die. So he called for his favorite and oldest son Esau in
order to pass on his birthright and inheritance and give him
the official family blessing. He asked Esau to go hunting first
and prepare him his favorite dish. As soon as he had gone,
Rebekah, who had been eavesdropping, called her favorite
son Jacob and told him of her deceptive plan. She didn't want
Esau to get the blessing and inheritance, and she couldn't
stand Esau's wives. In her choleric way she stated, "I'm dis-
gusted with living because of these Hittite women" (Gen.
27:46, NIV). They were obviously from the wrong side of the
tracks and were driving her crazy. "If Jacob takes a wife from
among the women of this land, from Hittite women like these,
my life will not be worth living" (v. 46).

Adding all these problems together, Rebekah, who had met
God at the well, rationalized that even God would understand her deceptive ploy. She prepared food for Isaac, put
Esau's clothes on Jacob, and put goatskins on his arms so he
would seem hairy like Esau. When Jacob questioned her plan
saying, "I would appear to be tricking him and would bring
down a curse on myself rather than a blessing" (Gen. 27:12,

NIV), Rebekah answered, "My son, let the curse fall on me. Just do what I say" (v. 13).

How many of us have ever put our children up to doing something that we couldn't do ourselves—something even they knew better than to do—and, when they were reticent, said as Rebekah did, "Just do what I say."

Jacob did as she said and deceived his father. When Isaac asked directly, "Are you really my son Esau?" (v. 24), Jacob lied and received the rightful blessing of his brother. When Esau came home from hunting, he went into his father and asked for the blessing. Isaac wept when he found out what had happened and Esau said, "Isn't he rightly named Jacob? He has deceived me these two times: He took my birthright, and now he's taken my blessing!" (v. 36). About this circumstance, Gary Smalley and John Trent in their beautiful book *The Blessing* say:

> When Esau lost his blessing from his father, he was devastated. In fact, when he discovered that Jacob had stolen the blessing, Esau cried out, "Do you have only *one* blessing, my father? Bless me, even me also, O my father!" (Gen. 27:38). For a father in biblical times, once a blessing was spoken, it was irretrievable. In response to his pitiful cries, Esau did receive a blessing of sorts from his father (Gen. 27:39–40), but it was not the words of value and acceptance that he had longed to hear.
>
> Can you feel the anguish in the cry, "Bless me, even me also, O my father"? This same painful cry and unfulfilled longing is being echoed today by many people who are searching for their family's blessing, men and women whose parents, for whatever reason, have failed to bless them with words of love and acceptance.
>
> . . . . the family blessing not only provides people a much needed sense of personal acceptance, it also plays an important part in protecting and even freeing them to develop intimate relationships.[6]

Esau was angry and consoled himself with thoughts of killing his brother the minute their father would die. When Rebekah heard of Esau's plan, she sent Jacob off to her brother Laban in Haran, explaining to Isaac that Jacob must not marry a Hittite woman as Esau had done.

Isaac, accepting his wife's reasoning, gave Jacob a final blessing. Isaac passed down what God had given Abraham to Jacob:

> May God almighty bless you and make you fruitful and increase your numbers until you become a community of peoples. May he give you and your descendants the blessing of Abraham, so that you may take possession of the land where you now live as an alien, the land God gave to Abraham (Gen. 28:3–4, NIV).

How often God's covenant with Abraham is reviewed in the Old Testament, and how alive it is today as Israel constantly scraps to possess and preserve the land God promised through Abraham, Isaac, and Jacob.

On his way to Haran, Jacob, who just days before had no thought of leaving home, stopped for the night out in the wilderness. He took a rock from a pile and used it for a pillow. (That may not sound very comfortable, but I've slept in motels where I'm sure they got the pillows from that same pile!) No wonder he had dreams! He saw a ladder leading up to God in heaven with angels going up and down. God spoke to him and said,

> "I am the Lord, the God of your father Abraham and the God of Isaac. I will give you and your descendants the land on which you are lying. Your descendants will be like the dust of the earth, and you will spread out to the west and to the east, to the north and to the south. All peoples on earth will be blessed through you and your offspring. I am with you and will watch over you wherever you go, and I will bring you back to this land. I will not leave you until I have done what I have promised you" (Gen. 28:13–15, NIV).

When Jacob awoke he marvelled at God's goodness to him in spite of his deceptive acts. "Surely the Lord is in this place, and I was not aware of it. . . . How awesome is this place!

This is none other than the house of God; this is the gate of heaven" (Gen. 28:16–17, NIV).

Jacob made the stone he had slept on into a monument to God and pledged him one tenth of his future income. He named the place Bethel, "house of God," and pledged that if God would bring him home safely and provide for his basic needs, he would choose him as his God forever. Jacob was never the same after he met God face to face on the rocks.

For Us in Today's World

How often we say "the whole thing's on the rocks. It's over. There's no hope." Are you feeling on the rocks today? Look up to God as Jacob did in his wilderness, for wherever you are, this spot may be your gate to heaven. It's an awesome place; surely God is here.

A dear lady named Jill, who had gone through an unwanted and humiliating divorce, wrote me that she and her children had been on the rocks. In fact she said she couldn't "find a rock big enough to hide under or a place on this earth far enough away to stop the pain." She had done all she knew to do to save her marriage, but her husband left her for a secretary in his office. "She needed a daddy for her daughter and she got ours!"

What do you do when you're left alone on the rocks? Jill cried out to God to fill the aching void in her life, and he met her in the wilderness. "I've still had to walk through this time in my life, confronting daily all the uglies surrounding rejection, adultery, separation, cheating, dishonesty, and ultimately, divorce, totally against my will. By God's grace and presence and loving care, I'm still alive. He's walked me through moment by moment. God opened new doors and paved the rocky way to a new life. I don't know why my marriage couldn't have had a miracle cure like others have. I don't want it all to go down the drain and not count. We are surviving triumphantly by his grace. I've lost my husband to the world and its folly, but I've gained a relationship with God that can never be taken away."

Sometimes we have to get between a rock and a hard place to look sincerely for our God, but like Jacob, we too can meet God on the rocks.

THINK ON THESE THINGS

Read Genesis 6–28. For additional reading see *The Blessing* by Gary Smalley and John Trent (Thomas Nelson, 1986).

1. What similarities are there today to the times of Noah? To the cities of Sodom and Gomorrah? What news this week sounds like the end times?

Since God promised he wouldn't send a flood again, what "plagues" is God using today to eliminate blatant sinners, those knowingly disregarding God's will?

2. If God told you to build an ark, what would be your reaction? How do you respond to instructions or suggestions from:

Superiors at work?
Your mother?
Your mate?
Your children?
Your pastor?

3. Give a recent example of a time when you were preparing and/or perhaps delivering suggestions on some project before you were even asked. What was the reaction of those in charge? What is your basic personality type? (See pp. 44, 53, 249—note 1.)

4. Is there some area in your life which you have not, as Shakespeare said, "taken at the flood" and have lost the venture? How has this circumstance left you "bound in shallows and in miseries"? Can you catch this tide again? How have your parents influenced your ability to make decisions? Do you tend to jump too quickly or wait too long?

5. How can a Christian leader lose his initial humility and dependence on God and start building monuments to

himself? What could some of these monuments be? Give some current examples. How are you susceptible to this temptation? Look at the scripture, "Wherefore let him that thinketh he standeth take heed lest he fall" (1 Cor. 10:12, KJV).

6. When have you become impatient, as Sarai did, and pushed for something you regretted later? What were the consequences?

What conflicts have you experienced with two women trying to function in the same house? How did you solve the problem? Did you send one to the desert?

7. Abraham is considered a "type" of God the Father and his son Isaac is a "type" of Christ. What similarities do you see to support this theory? (A "type" is a prophetic representation, one thing prefiguring another. A "symbol" is a representation, one thing standing for another.)

8. If your parents had chosen a mate for you at the well, who would it have been and why? Did they talk about what kind of person you should marry? What traits did they want?

9. What personality trait do you see running through Abraham's family? through your family? through your mate's family? What are you passing on to your children?

10. What is the difference between birthright and blessing? How do you feel your parents either gave or withheld the blessing of acceptance and approval? Are you blessing your children?

11. As Jacob did, can you say of your time on the rocks, "Surely the Lord is in this place. . . . This is the gate of heaven"?

For Your Notebook

Begin a list of obvious personality traits of each Bible character studied.

Keep a record of symbols, one thing standing for another.

SYMBOLS = ONE THING STANDING FOR ANOTHER

Ark	Salvation, something that affords protection and safety
Dove	Peace, Holy Spirit
Rain	Cleansing, revival, refreshment
Rainbow	Seal of God's covenant to not flood the earth Sign of God's presence
Babel	Confused state
Egypt	False refuge, bondage, worldliness
Circumcision	A sign of God's covenant with the descendants of Abraham

Keep a record of types, prophetic representations.

TYPES = PROPHETIC REPRESENTATION

Adam and Eve	Christ and his church, Eph. 5:23–31, Rev. 21:3, John 3:27
Ark	A foretelling of salvation, 1 Pet. 3:20
Abraham	Everlasting Father = God
Isaac	An Old Testament foretelling of Christ Sacrifice of the only son = Christ

Add to all of these lists as you progress.

Bonus Story

◇ ———————————————————————— ◇

LOOKING FOR GOD ON THE ROCKS

About twenty years ago when I was a new-believing Christian and just starting to give my testimony, I was asked to speak at a retreat near Mt. Shasta. When I arrived, I discovered the campgrounds and cabins were extremely rustic with few amenities. Since my idea of camping out is opening the window of a Holiday Inn, I was far from delighted over the circumstances. I soon learned that my opening message was to be given outdoors, in the dark, by a campfire. It had never occurred to me that I wouldn't speak in some kind of a building with some flicker of light, but I found myself out in a field, sitting on a rock. A few bright flames, fanned by the breeze, passed flickering shadows over the faces as the campfire lit up their eyes and the moon reflected off the top of Mt. Shasta. The scene had a friendly glow until the mosquitoes came buzzing out, the moon went behind some clouds, the rocks became hard, the fire died out, and the night chill crept inside our sweaters.

Some voice out of the dark introduced me, and I gave my testimony to what could have been no one. Occasionally the moon would peak out long enough for me to see silhouettes and know there was an audience in the shadows.

At the end, I offered up a prayer of commitment, asking those who had not yet found God in a personal way to ask Jesus Christ into their lives to change them. There was no apparent response. In the following years as I began to speak in bigger and brighter places, I forgot that humbling evening on the rocks.

Eighteen years later I was speaking at a large retreat for women in an elegant hotel when a lovely lady approached me.

"Do you remember sharing your testimony at Mt. Shasta State Park?" she asked. An instant recall zipped into my mind, and I was about to laugh over the bad old days when I noticed a serious look on her face and a moistening in her eyes. "It was that night in the dark that I prayed with you to receive Christ. I'd been looking for God, but I'd never seen him in the light. Somehow the protection of darkness gave me courage, and I dared to ask Jesus into my life without letting anyone know." She then filled me in on the changes in her life including a successful marriage to a Christian leader.

"Thank you for being willing to come to the State Park and speak. Your obedience to God changed the direction of my life."

How unworthy of her praise I felt as I remembered my attitude that night, for, while I had felt a surge of self-pity for my situation, she had found God on the rocks.

8. IN A FOREIGN LAND

With the ease of air travel today, we all look forward to visiting some foreign land. For Jacob it wasn't easy as he wandered through the wilderness in the direction of Haran, hoping to find a wife. How often we think there would be romance if only we were in some castle on the Rhine or lying on the sands of the Riviera or waltzing to "The Blue Danube" in Vienna. Let's follow Jacob as he finds love among the sheep and more wives than he bargained for.

For God's People in Bible Times

After Jacob found God on the rocks, he continued on to Haran—his mother's homeland but a foreign place to him.

Just as Jacob's mother had been discovered at the well, so it was that Jacob spotted the beautiful Rachel, his cousin, as she came to water her father's sheep. He fell in love with her at first sight and rolled away the stone from the well as if it had been a pebble. As her sheep drank, Jacob identified himself. He kissed his cousin and his melancholy nature was so overwhelmed that he cried out loud. As captivating as Rachel was, the opposite seemed true of her sister Leah who is often described as "wall-eyed." Whether this means each eye faced a different wall, I can't tell, but we do know that today she would have "faded into the wallpaper" when compared with Rachel who was "lovely in form." Jacob's complete fascination with Rachel, who could easily have been a candidate for "Miss Haran," caused him to make a pledge to his uncle to work seven years at no wages in order to marry Rachel. Can you imagine such dedication? "But they seemed like only a few days to him because of his love for her" (Gen. 29:20, NIV).

We know that she was well chaperoned and Jacob's love was from a distance, for at the end of the seven years he asked Laban for Rachel. "Give me my wife. My time is completed, and I want to lie with her" (v. 21).

Laban put on a great feast and invited everyone he knew to the wedding. Jacob went to this celebration feast and spent the night with his bride. But when morning came and he opened his eyes, there was Leah! He'd been deceived by his father-in-law. Isn't it amazing how God allows us to reap what we have sown? Jacob had deceived his brother and his father, and now it was his turn.

When he complained in anger to Laban, he replied that it was not the custom to marry the younger daughter off before the older, and he was justified in substituting Leah. "Finish out this daughter's bridal week; then we will give you the younger one also, in return for another seven years of work" (v. 27).

Jacob had little choice, so he kept Leah as his wife, received Rachel at the end of the week, and had to work free for another seven years! Let's hope it again seemed as only a few days because he loved her so much.

Although Leah was neither beautiful nor loved by her husband, she was fertile and produced Jacob's first son Reuben, meaning "See, a son!" and sounding like the Hebrew, "For God has seen my misery." Since this birth gave her an edge over Rachel, she conceived again and produced Simeon, whose name means "one who hears." "Because the Lord heard that I am not loved, he gave me this one too" (v. 33).

She hoped Jacob would become more attached to her than to childless Rachel, so she named her third son Levi, "attached." When the fourth son came she praised the Lord and named him Judah meaning "praise."

Rachel was still at zero in this child-bearing contest, and she cried to Jacob, "Give me children, or I'll die!" (Gen. 30:1, NIV). Jacob attested that he was sure it wasn't his fault, and so she insisted he have a child by her maid Bilhah. How like Sarah, who didn't believe God could produce children by her in her old age and sent her husband into her maid producing the boy Ishmael, father of the Arab races.

When Bilhah conceived, Rachel was relieved. She named this son Dan, meaning "he has vindicated" and suggested another try. This next son in the contest was called Naphtali, "my struggle."

Leah, not to be a loser, offered up her maid Zilpah who produced Gad, "what good fortune." This birth made Leah so happy she sent Jacob into her maid again and named the next Asher, "happiness." She called out to God to give her another of her own, and he answered. Her fifth son she named Issachar, "my reward," and he was followed by a sixth son. She knew Jacob would have to honor her as the winner, so she called him Zebulun, "my honor."

Poor Rachel had given up by now and had confessed to God her disgrace as a barren woman. Isn't it amazing how when we give up striving for what we want and begin to accept our situation, God rewards us! Rachel became pregnant as a miracle and gave birth to her first son. She took that event as a new beginning and named him Joseph, "may God add another."

Once Jacob had a son by his beloved Rachel, he began to think of the boy's future. Laban had deceived and cheated Jacob, and yet Jacob's flocks had been the ones to multiply, infuriating his father-in-law. Jacob wondered what to do, but God told him clearly, "Now leave this land at once and go back to your native land" (Gen. 31:13, NIV).

Jacob gathered together his family, flocks, and possessions and left for home without telling Laban who was out in the fields. When Laban heard of this deception, he pursued him and found the whole family camped in the hill country of Gilead.

Laban called out to Jacob, "What have you done? You've deceived me, and you've carried off my daughters like captives in a war. Why did you run off secretly and deceive me? Why didn't you tell me, so I could send you away with joy and singing to the music of the tambourines and harps?" (vv. 26–27, NIV).

Laban gave the impression he would have thrown a festive farewell party and yet nothing in his past behavior would attest to this possibility.

Jacob answered, "I was afraid."

Isn't that the reason we have for deception? I was afraid. Little children lie when they are caught in disobedience because they're afraid of the punishment. As adults, many of us tell little white lies to escape blame. Some of us pretend to be what we aren't because we are afraid that if anyone knew the real person behind our mask they wouldn't like us. Jacob was just like us and like our children: He was afraid that if he told Laban where he was *really* going, Laban wouldn't have let him go. So fear caused him to deceive Laban, even though God had promised to be with Jacob as he returned to the land of his fathers.

Jacob hadn't been able to accept God's plan for him without taking matters into his own hands and skirting the truth when necessary. Anytime we are not doing what we know God wants of us and we are afraid of being caught, we have the human urge to lie. Disobedience breeds deception in multiple births. Deception ran in Jacob's family.

1. Abraham deceived the Pharaoh of Egypt and King Abimelech of Gerar by saying his wife was his sister because he was afraid of the consequences of telling the truth (Gen. 12:11–20, 20:2–18).

2. Isaac deceived King Abimelech for the same reason, "Because I thought I might lose my life on account of her" (Gen. 26:6–16).

3. Rebekah deceived her husband into giving the blessing to the wrong son (Gen. 27:1–29).

4. Jacob went along with his mother and deceived his poor old father (Gen. 27:18–29).

5. Jacob deceived his brother Esau twice, taking Esau's birthright and blessing (Gen. 27:36).

6. Rebekah deceived Isaac again by pretending to send Jacob away to get a wife when she feared Esau would kill him (Gen. 27:42–46).

7. Laban deceived Jacob into marrying Leah (Gen. 29:22–28).

8. Jacob and Laban deceived each other about their flocks and wages (Gen. 30:25–31:9).

Finally the two deceptive men faced each other and their past behavior. They agreed to be honest with each other and to call a truce. Out in the hill country of Gilead, they pledged to the God of Abraham and made a covenant of peace between them.

Jacob set a stone up as a pillar and the relatives piled rocks around it in a heap. They called the monument Galeed, "witness heap," and because neither one really trusted the other, they called the place Mizpah meaning "watchtower."

As they put up the final stone, Laban called upon God, the only person he knew who was honest, "May the Lord watch over me and thee while we are absent one from another" (Gen. 31:49, KJV).

For Us in Today's World

Each time I read verse 49 in its proper context, two untrusting men asking God to keep a watch on the other, I am amused in recalling the use of that verse in my childhood. Our minister always recited it as his benediction, so I grew up thinking it was a nice way to end a service, a pleasant farewell to the congregation. "May the Lord watch over me and thee while we are absent one from another." Until I had studied Genesis, I never realized that the impact of this verse came only with an understanding of the story of Laban and Jacob—*when we can't trust each other, we ask God to be the watchtower.* How important it is to study verses within their context.

How about your family? Does deception run in the family? Are there some who tell lies as smoothly as telling the truth? Are there some for whom deception is a middle name?

In Psalm 101:7 God says, "No one who practices deceit will dwell in my house; no one who speaks falsely will stand in my presence" (NIV). And in Proverbs 12:22, "The Lord detests lying lips, but he delights in men who are truthful" (NIV).

If we wish to find God in our foreign lands, we must acknowledge that he delights in people who are truthful. Maybe we need to pile up some rocks as a monument to truthfulness, name it Galeed—"witness heap"—and ask God to watch over our tongues to keep them honest. God wants to meet us wherever we are, but no one who speaks falsely will stand in his presence.

For God's People in Bible Times

As we pick up our story of Jacob the deceiver, we find that after he took an oath of honesty before God and his father-in-law he invited his relatives to a meal. The next day Laban returned home, and Jacob went on his way toward Edom and his brother Esau, who years ago had vowed to kill him. Jacob sent messengers ahead to let Esau know he was on his way home. When the messengers returned saying that Esau was coming to meet him with four hundred men, the same fear that had first caused Jacob to flee to Haran gripped him again. He divided his wives, children, and flocks into two groups so if Esau attacked one side the others could escape.

He also sent servants ahead with gifts: two hundred female goats, twenty male goats, two hundred ewes and twenty rams, thirty female camels, forty cows and ten bulls, twenty female donkeys and ten males. Hardly what we'd expect to find under our Christmas tree and certainly more than we could keep in our backyard!

Jacob thought to himself, "I will pacify him with these gifts I am sending on ahead; later, when I see him, perhaps he will receive me" (Gen. 32:20, NIV).

As Jacob lay alone that night in the wilderness, far away from home, across the stream from where he had placed his family, a man came upon him and tried to wrestle him to the ground. Jacob fought with him till daybreak and when the man found he couldn't hold him down, he touched the socket of Jacob's hip and wrenched it. The man asked his name, and when Jacob told him, the man said, "Your name will no longer be Jacob, but Israel [he struggles with God], because you have struggled with God and with men and have overcome" (v. 28). The man blessed him, and Jacob named the place Peniel, "I saw God face to face" (v. 30).

God was gracious to Jacob and caused Esau, founder of Edom, "land of red earth," to welcome him back home after his many years in a foreign land. The prophecy God had given Rebekah before her sons' birth had been fulfilled.

> Two nations are in your womb, and two peoples from within you will be separated; one people will be stronger than the other, and the older will serve the younger (Gen. 25:23, NIV).

God instructed Jacob to settle near Bethel in the land of Canaan and to build an altar on the spot where God had revealed himself to Jacob when he was fleeing from his brother. Before going to Bethel to build the altar, Jacob buried all the foreign gods and statues which his family had brought with them. Later, God spoke to Jacob by the altar he had built and said, "I am God Almighty; be fruitful and increase in number. A nation and a community of nations will come from you, and kings will come from your body. The land I gave to

Abraham and Isaac I also give to you, and I will give this land to your descendants after you" (Gen. 35:11, NIV).

The promise God had given Abraham in his childless old age—the promise that seemed so remote and impossible at the time—was on its way to fulfillment. Before the caravan reached home, Rachel had her second son and died in childbirth. She called him Ben-Oni, "son of my trouble," but after her death Jacob renamed his baby Benjamin, "son of my right hand." Jacob buried Rachel near Bethlehem and made a stone pillar to commemorate her grave.

By the time Joseph was a young man, his father Jacob had established himself in Canaan with his family and was prospering in the land that God had promised his grandfather Abraham.

Joseph was a precocious and gifted child and was clearly his father's favorite son, born in Jacob's old age of the beautiful Rachel. To show his special love for Joseph, Jacob gave him a one-of-a-kind coat of many colors, richly ornamented. "When his brothers saw that their father loved him more than any of them, they hated him and could not speak a kind word to him" (Gen. 37:4, NIV).

How sad it is and yet how true to human nature that petty jealousies split families. It's the same today as it was in the time of Joseph: if one brother turns out smarter, richer, or more talented, many times those less fortunate turn against him and talk behind his back.

Joseph had the natural traits of the choleric personality. He was what would be termed today a gifted child, and he was too young to realize that his open expression and excitement about his abilities would make his brothers feel inconsequential in comparison. As he matured and became closer to God, his brashness was buffered and his leadership qualities ultimately became useful.

Joseph had an additional God-given gift of interpreting dreams which further alienated him from his peers. Worse than having this talent was the fact that all the dreams made him important and his brothers insignificant. Had Joseph realized the deep-seated hostility his brothers had for him, he

might have been wise enough not to share his secrets with
them, but being secure in his father's love and excited about
his unusual talent, he wanted to let everyone know what he
had dreamed.

He told his brothers about one of his dreams where they
were binding sheaves of grain out in the fields. Suddenly his
sheaf stood upright while his brothers' sheaves bowed down
before his in humility. You can imagine how well this idea
went over with his brothers who were already jealous; the
mere thought that they would ever have to bow down to
the younger Joseph in his gaudy coat infuriated all of them.
They must have hid their wrath well, or perhaps Joseph was
so up in the clouds that he didn't notice because he later told
them of his next dream. "'Listen,' he said, 'I had another
dream, and this time the sun and moon and eleven stars were
bowing down to me'" (v. 4).

That was more than they could handle. No doubt at least
one of them mumbled, "If I ever get my hands on the kid I'll
kill him." And eventually they did get their hands on Joseph.
As they were out in the wilderness grazing their sheep, Jacob
sent Joseph to check on them.

"So Joseph went after his brothers and found them near
Dothan. But they saw him in the distance, and before he
reached them, they plotted to kill him" (vv. 17, 18).

Here was their great opportunity to get rid of this spoiled
teen-age brother who was constantly upsetting them with his
visions of grandeur. As Joseph approached wearing that expensive coat, whatever similar thoughts the brothers may
have had caused them to unite against him and enact a punishment far greater than Joseph's innocent pride deserved.

"'Here comes that dreamer!' they said to each other.
'Come now, let's kill him and throw him into one of these
cisterns and say that a ferocious animal devoured him. Then
we'll see what comes of his dreams'" (vv. 19–20).

But Reuben had a slight twinge of conscience and suggested just throwing him in the empty well without killing
him. So that's what they did—and with such little emotion or
remorse that they were all able to sit down nearby and eat

their meal in peace. As they ate their food, they saw a band of Ishmaelites, their camels loaded down with spices, balm, and myrrh, on their way to Egypt. These men had to be descendants of their grandfather's half-brother Ishmael and therefore relatives from the "wrong side" of the family.

When Judah saw this caravan, he said to his brothers, "What will we gain if we kill our brother and cover up his blood? Come, let's sell him to the Ishmaelites and not lay our hands on him; after all, he is our brother, our own flesh and blood" (vv. 26–27). Noble Judah! They pulled Joseph out of the cistern and sold him for twenty shekels of silver, about sixty-four dollars on today's market value.

To cover up their deed they took the hated coat and smeared it with the blood of a goat and returned it to their father. They showed it to him and asked if he thought this could possibly be Joseph's. The poor distraught man cried out, "It is my son's robe! Some ferocious animal has devoured him. Joseph has surely been torn to pieces" (v. 33).

The brothers tried to comfort him, but he vowed to mourn Joseph into his grave. Notice that the brothers didn't really lie; they were just deceptive following in the family pattern of Abraham, Isaac, and Jacob. They allowed their father to make a faulty conclusion relieving them somewhat of their guilt.

For Us in Today's World

How relieved we sometimes feel when people jump to the wrong conclusion without our having to lie about the situation.

There is no evidence that Joseph's brothers had ever had a personal experience with God, but the Bible tells us that Joseph surely had. In spite of being rejected by his brothers, sold for a handful of silver, and bought by an Egyptian official named Potiphar, Joseph kept his eye on the Lord. Having gone from a home where he had servants to being sold as a slave himself, Joseph had every reason to be depressed; yet he knew God was with him even in Egypt. He refused to let his circumstances get him down and as he trusted his Lord in these adverse situations, the Lord blessed him and even made him prosper.

What a lesson to those of us in financial difficulties today or to those of us who have been rejected and are without family support. Joseph didn't waste time on self-pity—thinking how did a terrible thing like this happen to a good person like me—he drew on his choleric strengths and his spiritual reservoir; he got down to the work at hand and thanked the Lord that he was even alive. "When his master saw that the Lord was with him and that the Lord gave him success in everything he did, Joseph found favor in his eyes and became his attendant. Potiphar put him in charge of his household, and he entrusted to his care everything he owned" (Gen. 39:3–4, NIV).

What have we learned as we've traveled with Joseph to Egypt? Have we been walking so close to the Lord that people who have seen us in the desert know we've been with Jesus? When life has dried up and we have been rejected, have we been able to praise God anyhow? Think of Joseph; what an example. Even sold as a slave, he was so close to the Lord that people noticed there was something different about him. Instead of being jealous of Joseph's exceptional spirituality, Potiphar was grateful and left all decisions in Joseph's hands "except the food he ate" (v. 6).

Joseph found God was even in Egypt, a pagan country with golden idols, but so was Satan who is always on the prowl to catch believers in some moment of weakness. Potiphar's wife had observed how well-built and handsome Joseph was, and she set out to have an affair with him. No doubt, she wanted to brighten up her life as one of the idle rich. While we might feel aggressive women are a phenomenon of the '80s, we have only to listen to Potiphar's wife to know they've been around forever. "Come to bed with me," she said clearly to Joseph. What a tempting opportunity to be seduced by the boss's wife. How many godly men have given in to such a taste of forbidden fruit?

But Joseph knew God, even in Egypt, and he refused to

be tempted. He turned her down and explained that her husband had put him in charge of everything but her and that he would not violate this trust! Who can find such a virtuous man? His price must be far above rubies.

Poets throughout the centuries have written of the appetites of unrequited love and know that "Hell hath no fury like a woman scorned." After repeated invitations, all of which Joseph refused, Potiphar's wife gave one more impassioned plea for attention. Joseph turned quickly to get out of her sight. She made a desperate grab at his coat hoping to pull him toward her, not willing to admit that she had been unsuccessful in her bid for love and attention. He fled the temptation, but she was left with his coat in her hands, a limp souvenir of an unfulfilled lust. What an insult that she, the lady of the house, would offer herself to a common slave and be turned down! She'd show him he couldn't treat her that way. She called for her servants and showed them the proof that Joseph had come to molest her and had fled when she'd screamed. All afternoon she held the coat close to her and when her husband came home she lied convincingly, "That Hebrew slave you brought us came to me to make sport of me. But as soon as I screamed for help, he left his cloak beside me and ran out of the house" (Gen. 39:17–18, NIV).

Believing his wife's report and not taking time to investigate the other side, Potiphar threw Joseph into prison. To be sure we don't get into trouble, we'd better stay out of Potiphar's house!

THINK ON THESE THINGS

Read Genesis 29–39 paying special note to examples of deception and rejection.

1. Jacob deceived his father and his brother, then his father-in-law Laban tricked him into marrying Leah when he had worked seven years for Rachel. How did Laban rationalize his actions? Have you ever been deceived or done in

by a friend or relative? What was the situation and how did you react? What has been, or could be, a healthy resolution of your conflict?

2. Do you have a child who has a pattern of lying? Have you probed his underlying reasons? What would God have you do about this situation? Don't let deception become a family trait.

3. Throughout Scripture the names of people and places have special meaning, and nowhere is this more noticeable than in the twelve children of Jacob. Review these names and make a list of words and their meanings for your notebook. As we continue our study, there will be other names to add to this list.

4. Although Jacob had met God on the rocks, there were times he showed a lack of faith in God. He was afraid to face his father-in-law and tell him he was leaving, and he was so fearful about meeting his brother that he divided his family for protection. In what ways are you fearful? Do you recognize fear and worry as a lack of faith in God's plan for your life?

5. Jacob wrestled with God in the night. What wakes you up at night? What struggles do you have when you should be sleeping? What can you do about these concerns? If you had to bury your idols as Jacob did, what would they be?

6. Why was Joseph Jacob's favorite son? Do you have one child who is your favorite? What problems does this cause? What problems did this cause with Joseph's brothers? In retrospect, had Joseph been more mature, what could he have done differently in his sibling relationships?

7. Is there a "wrong side" in your family? a poor group? some snobs? some phonies? some cheats? Is this the truth or a family myth? Are you depriving your children acquaintance with some colorful characters or cousins? As a child, I couldn't associate with my father's family because they were of an unacceptable religion. Where do these biases originate and what can we do to change family attitudes?

8. Joseph was sold as a slave and had every right to be depressed and feel rejected. What reasons from your past do

you have for negative feelings? What kept Joseph above his circumstances? What could help you? What were Joseph's personality strengths and weaknesses? How did these traits both hurt and help him?

9. How did Joseph—an innocent, God-fearing man—get himself into trouble? When did you last take a chance that could have had serious consequences? What lesson can you teach your children from the story of Joseph? How spiritual would you be if unjustly thrown in prison?

For Your Notebook

Find out the meaning of your name. Florence is "blooming flower." Frederick is "peaceful ruler." In our family, I've been blooming while Fred's been quietly ruling. Christian bookstores carry plaques with almost every name and its meaning. Why not find one for each member of your family and tie this action in with your study?

Add to your list of Bible names and places and their meanings, and begin a record of numbers and their significance. For starters, seven stands for perfection and completeness:

> Noah waited seven days each time the dove returned before sending it out of the ark again.
> Jacob worked seven years for Leah and seven years for Rachel.
> Laban pursued Jacob for seven days.
> Jacob bowed down to the ground seven times as he approached Esau.

◇

9. IN PRISON AND IN POWER

If we were in Joseph's position wouldn't we be ready to give up on God? We'd probably be saying, "Here I am a spiritual giant rejected by my family, sold as a slave, living far below my accustomed lifestyle, alone in a foreign land, and now because I was virtuous and refused to be tempted I've been thrown into jail? It doesn't make sense. Surely God has abandoned me here in Egypt. Woe is me."

Haven't we cried out to God in far less harrowing situations? Haven't we given up when we couldn't see God acting in our behalf—right now? "Lord you know I'm a good girl. I pray each day and teach a Bible study. I even put up with the worldliness of my unsaved husband and his boorish friends! And now you want me to move hundreds of miles away from my family and friends? Surely you have abandoned me! Oh, woe is me!"

But that wasn't Joseph's response to this totally undeserved treatment at the hands of a man he had served faithfully and well. Instead he must have said, "I don't understand Lord, but if you've allowed me to be here, there must be some reason, so I'll make the best of it and hope someday to see some good in this bad situation."

Joseph was in the pit once again, but he took an objective look at the jail conditions and began to institute positive reforms. Because the Lord was with him, Joseph was soon put in charge of the whole prison and all its inmates. "The warden paid no attention to anything under Joseph's care, because the Lord was with Joseph and gave him success in whatever he did" (Gen. 39:23, NIV).

As we observe Joseph's behavior, we might ask ourselves,

"Where are we with the Lord today?" Although we are on the outside looking in, are we imprisoned in some way? Does some painful situation have a grip on us? Are we prisoners of our phobias? Joseph walked with God even in jail, and he had success in all he did. Whatever our gifts may be, God can find use for them even in prison. Whatever our fears, God can set us free.

For God's People in Bible Times

While Joseph was there two new men were added to his group, the cupbearer and the baker for the King of Egypt. Each had in some way displeased the king, and they were both dejected. When Joseph questioned them, each man said that he had had a dream but didn't know the meaning.

The cupbearer dreamed he saw a vine with three branches. As soon as the vine budded, it blossomed and immediately turned into clusters of grapes. He squeezed them into the Pharaoh's cup, and he had instant wine.

Joseph explained that God had given him a gift of interpreting dreams. "The three branches are three days. Within three days Pharaoh will lift up your head and restore you to your position, and you will put Pharaoh's cup in his hand, just as you used to do when you were his cupbearer. But when all goes well with you, remember me and show me kindness; mention me to Pharaoh and get me out of this prison. For I was forcibly carried off from the land of the Hebrews, and even here I have done nothing to deserve being put in a dungeon" (Gen. 40:12–15, NIV).

Such a small request for such a positive prediction.

The baker dreamed he had three baskets of bread on top of his head. The baked goods were for Pharaoh, but birds were eating them quickly out of the basket.

Joseph interpreted the baker's dream for him saying, "The three baskets are three days. Within three days Pharaoh will lift off your head and hang you on a tree. And the birds will eat away your flesh" (Gen. 40:18–19, NIV).

On the third day after the dreams, the Pharaoh celebrated

his birthday by restoring the cupbearer and hanging the baker, just as Joseph had predicted. Now you might think the cupbearer would have been so elated at his release and at the accuracy of Joseph's interpretation that he would have immediately brought Joseph's name to Pharaoh's attention. But no, he didn't want to give his time in jail another thought. He was free, and he forgot his promise to Joseph.

For two more years Joseph labored in the prison with little hope of ever getting out. But the Lord was with him, and Joseph was at peace. One night the Pharaoh had two dreams that disturbed him. He sent for his magicians and wise men, but they had no answers for his confusion. Suddenly the cupbearer remembered Joseph. "Today I am reminded of my shortcomings" (Gen. 41:9, NIV). He then explained the situation of the dreams in prison and of the Hebrew slave that had interpreted them correctly. "Things turned out exactly as he interpreted them to us: I was restored to my position, and the other man was hanged" (v. 13).

Pharaoh had Joseph brought to him immediately. And when he told Joseph that he understood that he could interpret dreams, Joseph replied humbly, "I cannot do it . . . but God will give Pharaoh the answer he desires" (v. 16).

For Us in Today's World

It is difficult for me to imagine making such a selfless statement. If I'd been in prison for years and had just been released because of some great gift that I was about to demonstrate and praised because of my abilities, I probably would be taking bows and trying to appear humble as I murmured, "It's really nothing." But Joseph walked with God so closely that his natural response to the Pharaoh's comment was to give God the glory. Don't we wish to be so spiritual that we react in a godly way? Joseph continued his intimate relationship with God while in prison—he walked with God in the darkness as well as in the light.

Are you in a dark place right now? Are you imprisoned by some circumstance? Brother Lawrence, an uneducated lowly member of the barefooted Carmelites in Paris in the 1600s, was assigned to wash the pots and pans for the more learned brothers. Imagine the thought of never leaving the kitchen sink! Dishes day after day. How would you react?

Brother Lawrence is remembered because he walked so closely with God that he could pray, "Lord of all pots and pans and things . . . Make me a saint by getting meals and washing up the plates!"[7]

Brother Lawrence lived so abundantly in the presence of God that he could say, "The time of business does not with me differ from the time of prayer, and in the noise and clatter of my kitchen, while several persons are at the same time calling for different things, I possess God in as great tranquillity as if I were upon my knees at the blessed sacrament."[8]

In the letters that he wrote after his long days in the kitchen, Brother Lawrence taught others how to *practice the presence of God* in spite of adverse circumstances. He wrote:

> We cannot escape the dangers which abound in life without the actual and continual help of God. Let us, then, pray to Him for it continually. How can we pray to Him without being with Him? How can we be with Him but in thinking of Him often? And how can we often think of Him but by a holy habit which we should form of it? You will tell me that I am always saying the same thing. It is true, for this is the best and easiest method I know; and as I use no other, I advise all the world to do it. We must know before we can love. In order when we come to love Him, we shall also think of Him often, for our heart will be with our treasure. This is an argument which well deserves your consideration.[9]

This humble man, in our sight doomed to a life of washing pots, shows us that we can find God anywhere, and that we must discipline ourselves to practice his presence.

Joseph practiced the presence of God. He didn't say, "When I get out of here, I'll go to church" or "If you save me, God, I'll believe in you." Are our circumstances so much worse than Joseph's that we can't trust God to redeem us?

Have we ever been thrown in a pit and left to die? Have we been pulled out only to be sold by our brothers as a slave? Have we been thrown in jail and forgotten?

I met a Southern beauty queen who had married a seminary student and was living "in the pits," the pits being student housing. "My life is so miserable and my apartment so appalling that I refuse to unpack my wedding presents. This place isn't good enough for my dishes. We'll just eat on paper plates 'til I'm let out of this prison."

"How long will you be here?" I asked.

"For four long years."

"Are you planning to be miserable for four years?"

"There's no other choice. But when my husband gets his degree and we have our own church, then I'll be happy."

Will she really? If she practices misery for four years, will a degree change her life? In motivational speaking the motto is, "If you do anything consistently for thirty days, it will become a life-time habit." What are we doing consistently? Joseph and Brother Lawrence practiced the presence of God while in the pits of life. They certainly wouldn't have waited to unpack the dishes. What about you? Are you waiting to unpack the dishes, or have you learned to practice the presence of God, even in the pits?

For God's People in Bible Times

Because Joseph was faithful in adverse circumstances, God rewarded him. Because he used his gifts to interpret the Pharaoh's dream, he was set free. Because Joseph gave God the credit, Pharaoh put him in charge of the whole land of Egypt. Even though Pharaoh was not a believer, he could see that God was with Joseph, and he wanted to be on the winning side.

Perhaps you will recall that Joseph interpreted the Pharaoh's dream of seven fat cows and seven lean cows to mean that there would be seven years of plenty followed by seven years of famine. Joseph told Pharaoh that if Egypt stored up its surplus, it would be able to survive without starvation.

We know that God used the widespread famine to bring Joseph's brothers from Canaan to Egypt to buy grain and to bring Joseph's childhood dream to fulfillment. There Joseph stood in robes of fine linen, with a gold chain around his neck and a signet ring on his finger, while his brothers bowed down before him, their faces to the ground. Joseph recognized them and was so moved at the sight of his long-lost brothers, evil though they had been, that he had to turn his head and weep.

Before he would let them go back home, Joseph told them he'd keep Simeon until they returned with Benjamin, his only full brother. The scene that followed this request from the one they perceived to be the Egyptian ruler would be humorous if it were not so sadly typical of human nature.

These many years the brothers had deceived their father over the circumstances of Joseph's death. Because they had not been caught, they had put their deeds behind them, but the guilt had been resting just below the surface waiting to take control. Isn't it amazing that when we have sinned and even gotten away with it, the guilt is still within, keeping us from the full presence of God.

One said to the other, thinking Joseph couldn't understand their language, "Surely we are being punished because of our brother. We saw how distressed he was when he pleaded with us for his life, but we would not listen; that's why this distress has come upon us" (Gen. 42:21, NIV).

Suddenly they were thinking of Joseph whom they hadn't seen in years. They felt God was punishing them for their sins. Then Reuben, wanting to make sure they remembered his ounce of virtue, stated, "Didn't I tell you not to sin against the boy? But you wouldn't listen! Now we must give an accounting for his blood" (v. 22).

If you'd only listened to me, we wouldn't be in this mess!

Isn't it amazing how quickly we point the finger at others in time of trouble and remind them that this surely was not our fault! This sad, immature, guilt-ridden group had to go home and report their problems to their father who was instantly distraught and depressed. "Everything is against me! . . .

You will bring my gray head down to the grave in sorrow" (vv. 36, 38). This mournful, melancholy message was enough to instill guilt in even an innocent group.

As the months passed and the supply of grain dwindled, the brothers were forced to return to Egypt and take Benjamin with them even though Israel cried, "Why did you bring this trouble on me by telling the man you had another brother?" (Gen. 43:6, NIV).

When Joseph saw Benjamin, his own mother Rachel's son, he was so touched that he went to his room and wept. He never thought he'd look upon his brother again. When Joseph got control of himself, he dismissed his servants and cried out, "I am your brother Joseph, the one you sold into Egypt!" (Gen. 45:4, NIV). As they cowered, terrified before Joseph, he explained what had taken place since they had pulled him from the pit and sold him into slavery. Imagine the guilt as they relived the event from Joseph's point of view. Yet when they thought they would die of shame or possibly at the hands of the Pharaoh, Joseph gave them unexpected relief. Instead of making them squirm in guilt, Joseph—the one who practiced the presence of God even in prison—comforted them by saying, "Do not be distressed and do not be angry with yourselves for selling me here, because it was to save lives that God sent me ahead of you" (v. 5). What his brothers meant for evil, God meant for good.

Joseph became the savior of his family and forgave their sins. How like Christ who, while we were yet sinners, died for us so that we might be saved. Joseph practiced the presence of God when in prison and when in power. Success didn't go to his head. Joseph's family (all seventy of them) settled in the land of Goshen. His father Jacob lived there seventeen years until he died at age 147. His body was then taken back to Canaan to be buried in a cave in the field of Mach-pelah. Here he was placed with Abraham, Sarah, Isaac, Rebekah, and his wife Leah.

As the Jewish people still say, "May the God of Abraham, Isaac, and Jacob bless you, too."

For Review:

As we conclude our journey through Genesis, let's take a moment to review. First we saw God's power as he spoke the creation of the universe—heaven and earth; day and night; sky and water and land; seeds, plants, trees, and flowers; sun, moon, and stars; birds, fish, and animals; man and woman. We learned how God created Adam and Eve, the sacrament of marriage, and the institution of family. We can see in Adam and Eve a foretelling of Christ the bridegroom and his bride the church.

In our walk, we also saw that Noah was the beginning of different nations, the tower of Babel the beginning of different languages. Abraham was the founder of both the Hebrew and the Arab races through Isaac and Ishmael. Abraham, the father, was willing to sacrifice his beloved son Isaac, as later God the Father sacrificed his son Jesus that we might have everlasting life. Jacob had the first spiritual struggle with God and came out a changed man, the founder of the twelve Hebrew tribes. Joseph, Jacob's favorite son, was rejected by his brothers and sold as a slave, and yet he continued to walk with God, forgiving those who wronged him as Christ was later to do with his enemies.

Besides the beginnings and foretellings, we have seen that God gives clear instructions to his believers and blesses those who obey and punishes those who don't. He both blessed and punished Adam and Eve, Abraham and Sarah, Isaac and Rebekah, Jacob and Rachel. He blessed Noah because he was a righteous man, and he took Enoch into heaven because he was a faithful man. He turned Lot's disobedient wife into a pillar of salt and blessed Joseph who walked closely with him, even in difficult human circumstances.

As the sins of the fathers are visited upon the children, so did a thread of deception run through these families. Adam and Eve hid the truth from God; Abraham lied about his wife being his sister; Rebekah encouraged Jacob into deceiving his father and his brother; Jacob was deceived by his father-in-law Laban into marrying the wrong daughter; in turn, Laban was deceived by Jacob when he fled for home without telling Laban. Jacob was deceived by his sons over the supposed death of Joseph, when, in fact, they had sold their brother into slavery. This family was hardly a trustworthy lot!

Through it all, however, they knew there was a God. They kept looking for him in gardens, on walks, in the rain, at altars, in the wilderness and desert, on mountains, at wells, in famines, on the rocks, in foreign lands, in struggles, in dreams, in prison, and in power.

How about you? As we have walked in the wilderness together, has God made a new beginning in your life? Have you obeyed him and been blessed? Have you been deceptive or avoided the truth? Have you been slogging through the rain or struggling on the rocks? Are you and your family still looking for God in all the wrong places? Don't waste another moment in searching, but ask the Lord to come into your life right now. Begin today practicing the presence of God— discipline yourself to walk closely with God.

THINK ON THESE THINGS

Read Genesis 40–50—the life of Joseph.

1. Self-pity is often the basis for depression. How did Joseph handle the unfair treatment by his boss? In what area do you feel self-pity today? Is life fair?

When Joseph was in prison, he assessed his situation. What positive steps did he take? What can you do about your circumstances?

2. What small request did Joseph make of the cupbearer when he was restored? How long was it before this man remembered his pledge to Joseph? How would you have responded in Joseph's place? How did Joseph behave?

3. What does it mean to practice the presence of God? How did Joseph do it? Brother Lawrence? You?

What have you practiced in life, good or bad, that has

become a habit? What habit do you need to break? Can you discipline yourself for thirty days?

4. If you get away with some bad deed, do you have a clear conscience? What happened to Joseph's brothers when they were put under pressure? Whom did they blame for their predicament? How did Reuben respond? Do these same human responses ever come forth from you today? In what circumstances?

5. If maturity is the acceptance of blame and responsibility, where would you rank Joseph's brothers? Joseph? yourself? your mate? your co-workers?

6. How did Jacob respond to the news that Benjamin had to go to Egypt? Why was Benjamin so special to him?

7. If you had been in Joseph's place and had these brothers bowing before you, what would you have wanted to do and say? What did Joseph do? How did he comfort their guilt?

For Your Notebook

Review the chart on the comparison of Joseph as a "type" of Christ (see p. 104). You may wish to copy this in your notebook and add any other ideas you or your group come up with in your study.

Add seven lean and seven fat cows to your list of sevens.

Beginning with Terah make a family tree for your notebook, including all three of his sons—Haran, Nahor, and Abraham and their descendants (Gen. 11–50).

JOSEPH AS A TYPE OF CHRIST

JOSEPH		CHRIST
Genesis 37:3	Well-beloved son	Matthew 3:17
Genesis 37:13	Sent by his father	John 3:16
Genesis 37:5–9	Revealed his future position	Matthew 24:30–31
Genesis 37:19–20	Brothers plotted against him	Luke 20:13–14
Genesis 37:26–28	Sold for silver	Matthew 26:15
Genesis 39	Unyielding to temptation	Matthew 4:1–11
Genesis 39:13–18	Wrongfully accused	Matthew 26:59–65
Genesis 39:20	Put in the place of criminals	Mark 15:27–28
Genesis 41:14, 40	Raised up again	Ephesians 1:19–22
Genesis 41:42–44	Given power	Matthew 28:18
Genesis 47:25	Acknowledged as Savior	Philippians 2:10–11
Genesis 45:1–15	Forgave wrongdoers	1 John 1:9

PATRIARCHAL FAMILY TREE

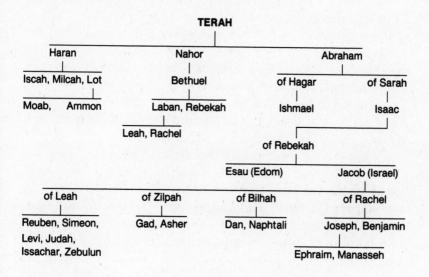

Bonus Story

◇ ————————————————————————————— ◇

LOOKING FOR GOD IN DEPRESSION

"I don't know what I'm doing in this damned place."

I looked up to see a tall girl with her hands on her hips. "I'm Iris. Remember me?"

For a moment I didn't recognize Iris, but as I searched my memory I recalled having met her at a national convention we'd both attended. As I welcomed her to CLASS (Christian Leaders and Speakers Seminars), she reiterated, "I don't know why I'm here. I've been so damned depressed. I've just lost my job, I'm alone, I'm struggling to make ends meet, and the last thing I'm interested in being is a Christian speaker. I don't know what I'm doing in this damned place!"

Nor did I! What sounded like swearing to me was obviously a way of life for Iris. And I wondered how she ever got to a seminar for Christian leaders and speakers. But I didn't have to wonder for long.

"I went over to my friend's house and told her I'd had it! I haven't had a good day in years and I'm ready to quit. I'd be better off dead. My friend handed me your brochure and told me I ought to come to CLASS. I'm here, but I haven't paid yet."

I suggested she just sit down and listen, and if she didn't think our material would help her, she could leave at noon and there would be no charge.

"That sounds like a fair deal," she said. She sat down and we began CLASS.

As I explained the many problems of our world today which are listed in 2 Timothy 3, Iris nodded over the words proud, boastful, disobedient, ungrateful, cruel, greedy, violent, fiercely independent. She looked startled when I told of women who were always seeking, going to new seminars, but never coming to know the truth.

She came up at the coffee break and stated, "I didn't know the Bible said all that stuff about women. It even makes sense. I've been to almost every seminar, seance, and guru and none of them has helped." I noticed she was wearing a name tag, so I knew she had paid and was planning to stay.

Later on I suggested she sign up to see Lana, our counselor. "Do you think I need some help or something?"

While I tried to think of something positive to say, she added, "Well you're right. I do. Where do I sign up?"

Iris and Lana were to meet at 10:00 the next morning. At 10:30 I called a coffee break and sat down for a minute with a lady who wanted to tell me about her wayward son. As we were involved in deep conversation, Iris came and stood over me.

As I looked up, Iris dropped to her knees beside me and grabbed my hand. "Now I know why I'm here. I needed to meet Jesus!"

The other lady watched spellbound as Iris told how Lana had led her to the Lord just minutes before. I'd never seen such an amazing and instant conversion. Iris even looked different. Her tough stance had been gentled, and her talk had a new tone.

Since then, Iris's new life in the Lord has flourished, and we've become friends. In three years, she's gone from being an unbeliever to becoming a Christian speaker, and when you see her, you know that she has been practicing the presence of God.

Iris had been looking for a way out of her pit of depression, and as she cried out to the counselor, she came face to face with the living Lord. In her own words, "I crawled to the foot of the Cross and left my heavy burdens there."

SPIRITUAL Z's

Father,
do I ever glance
at the miraculous—
and yawn?
Do You part
Red Seas
before me,
and I meander through
casually,
kicking small pebbles
with my feet
and lamenting
my distant God?

—Carolyn Jensen[10]

◇

10. IN PLAGUES AND IN THE PASSOVER

As we have traveled together from the Garden of Eden to the land of Egypt, we have observed that the Book of Genesis is about *beginnings*, the Book of Exodus about departure, a *going out*. Genesis shows us the Fall; Exodus the Redemption. Genesis is family history; Exodus is the history of a nation. In Genesis we saw that Jacob's family numbered seventy when they moved to Egypt but grew to over three million by the time God was ready to have Moses lead them out.

As we reflect on our lives, we see that we have each had a beginning, each fallen into some kind of trouble, each tried to find a way out. Just as the Hebrews in Egyptian slavery were trying to escape, so are we seeking solutions for our problems. As they were looking for a savior, so we are looking for a God who'll set us free.

How perfectly the Bible relates to you and me, how beautifully God tells the story of his people, how richly he fills the Old Testament with symbols, types, and predictions which culminate in the person of Jesus Christ, our savior.

When I first committed my life to my Lord and began to study the Bible, I read the New Testament. I had always loved the stories of the Old Testament, but now that I had accepted Jesus I wanted to spend my time with him. Little did I realize in my study that I couldn't understand many of the references to Christ as the lamb, the light, the bread, the high priest, and the passover nor grasp the value of the sacrifice of his life or the power of his shed blood without reading the Old Testament. I believed Jesus had come to save me, but I'd never connected his redemptive act with Noah saving his people from the flood, Abraham saving Lot from Sodom and

Gomorrah, Joseph saving his family from starvation, and Moses saving the Hebrews from slavery.

It was not until I began the Book of Beginnings, that I saw how essential it was to know the history of the Hebrew people and their search for God. This background is necessary in order to have any concept of why Jesus came to earth as a man and shed his blood for me and for you. I'd sung the hymn "There's Power in the Blood," but I had no idea what it meant or how I could ever be "cleansed by the blood of the lamb." Neither thought was either appealing or significant to me, but as I looked into the Old Testament, both Genesis and Exodus gave me God's pattern and the pieces began to fit together. The puzzle I'd been playing with suddenly made sense, and I began to see the whole picture. Let's put the loose pieces of our lives in a big bag and move ahead four hundred years, for I hope to share with you my enthusiasm for God's miraculous plans for our lives and my excitement over finding God in all the right places.

For God's People in Bible Times

In God's covenant with Abraham, he'd predicted his people would be slaves in a foreign land for four hundred years. That prophecy came true in the times after Joseph. Because God blessed his people, "Their descendants were very fertile, increasing rapidly in numbers; there was a veritable population explosion so that they soon became a large nation, and they filled the land of Goshen. Then, eventually, a new king came to the throne of Egypt who felt no obligation to the descendants of Joseph" (Exod. 1:7–8, TLB).

Because he feared their numbers and their prosperity, the Pharaoh made slaves of the Hebrews and put hard taskmasters over them. Amazingly, the worse they were treated, the more they multiplied. Pharaoh instructed the Hebrew midwives to kill all the newborn boys, but because these women believed in God, they couldn't do this. A beautiful boy was born in the tribe of Levi and his parents hid him at home for three months. Then his mother made him a little basket, waterproofed with tar, and laid him in the weeds along the water's edge where he was found by a princess, one of Pharaoh's daughters. She named him Moses—"to draw out"—because she took him out of the water, and she hired his own mother to be his nurse. For forty years Moses lived like a king, but one day, when he saw an Egyptian mistreating a Hebrew slave, he killed him and then, in fear for his own life, he fled the country.

While sitting at a well in Midian, Moses was mulling over his future when seven daughters of the local priest came by. After he helped them water their flocks they invited him home for dinner. Since he was a Hebrew who had run away from trouble in Egypt, he had no home and decided to stay in Midian where he married Zipporah and had a baby named Gershom, meaning "foreigner." Midian was named for one of Abraham's sons by Keturah and is on the eastern arm of the Red Sea in today's Jordan.

The plight of the Hebrews in Egypt became worse and God wanted to fulfill his promise to Abraham: "I will punish the nation that enslaves them, and at the end they will come away with great wealth" (Gen. 15:14, TLB).

When Moses had been in Midian forty years, God appeared to him in a burning bush. God told Moses to take his shoes off because he was standing on holy ground. "I am the God of your fathers, of Abraham, Isaac, and Jacob." Moses hid his face for he had never met God personally before even though his Hebrew background caused him to believe in the traditional God.

Oswald Chambers writes:

> If we have never had the experience of taking our commonplace religious shoes off our commonplace religious feet, and getting rid of all the undue familiarity with which we approach God, it is questionable whether we have ever stood in His presence.[11]

We may be religious and refer to the Lord as our friend, but if we've never been dropped to our knees by the overwhelming power of his majesty, if we've never taken our shoes off because we know we're on his holy ground, perhaps we've never found the real God, the King of Kings. Since Moses wasn't looking for God, he was awe-struck when God said, "I've chosen you to go back into Egypt and set my people free."

There is no one more shocked than a nominal believer, who's been living a good life, when he suddenly hears God speak clearly and give him an assignment. "God, I didn't mean to believe in you that much. Surely you don't mean me."

But God did mean Moses. He had been preparing Moses for eighty years to be a leader. Moses had grown up in the palace and had learned the structure of Egyptian government. After his hasty departure, he had worked for years as a reclusive shepherd. Moses' personality was that of the quiet, deep, introspective melancholy who didn't want to be up front and who had little confidence in his ability to be a leader.

When Moses complained that he wasn't a good speaker, God agreed to include his sanguine brother Aaron in the package as a mouthpiece. No doubt, Aaron loved to talk and enjoyed being the center of attention. Moses knew the Hebrews hadn't been very spiritual during their years in Egypt and some had even worshiped the pagan idols. He wondered what God they'd think he was talking about when he'd say, "I Am has sent me."

To overcome Moses' fear of rejection, God demonstrated his miracle-making power by turning Moses' staff into a snake and his hand white with leprosy, and then returning them both to normal. When Moses saw the power of God right before his eyes, he made the commitment to go back to Egypt and set his people free even though this didn't seem to be a job with much of a future—no health insurance and the land of retirement only a promise.

When Moses and Aaron arrived in Egypt, they went first to the Hebrew elders and performed miracles to establish their credentials as messengers from God. The people, who were worn down from overwork and whose spirits were depressed from servitude and slavery, rejoiced that God had indeed

sent help. There was a way out, an exodus, however it wasn't
an easy route. As God had said about Pharaoh, "I will make
him stubborn so that he will not let the people go" (Exod.
4:21, TLB).

Pharaoh's first reaction to Moses' request to "Let my people go" was to insist on the same production quota for the
bricks the Hebrews were making but to give them no straw.
When the Hebrews couldn't produce the required bricks, the
taskmasters beat them.

Suddenly Moses didn't look like a man from God any more.
Moses tried to review the plan, but they wouldn't listen. He
lost heart himself and cried out to God, "Why did you ever
send me, if you were going to do this to them?" (Exod. 5:22,
TLB). "My own people won't even listen to me any more; how
can I expect Pharaoh to? I'm no orator!" (Exod. 6:12, TLB).
Moses often reviewed his weaknesses to himself and God.

How often do we get excited over some plan God has for us
and then, when it doesn't seem to work out easily and we have
to face more adversity than we expected, we cry out, "Why
did you do this to me? Why didn't you send someone else?
I'm not even any good for this. I have no talent!"

God grieves over this kind of wailing from his people so he
told Moses how to approach Pharaoh and what to have Aaron
say. He even discouraged Moses by telling him it wouldn't be
easy. God wanted the Exodus to show his almighty power and
be a happening that would never be forgotten.

Poor old Moses was eighty years old when he began the
fight with Pharaoh. God sent him to perform miracles which
the court magicians were able to duplicate, but with an important difference. When Aaron's rod became a serpent, so
did the magicians', but Aaron's serpent ate up theirs. Pharaoh
was not impressed then or later when Moses turned the rivers
into blood or when the palace was filled with frogs. But when
the dust turned into lice, infesting the people and the animals, and when swarms of flies infiltrated each room in every
home, Pharaoh began to weaken, saying the Hebrews could
go worship their God if Moses would get God to stop the

plague. But each time God called off the plague, Pharaoh would not keep his promise to let the Hebrews go. Then God caused the flocks of the Egyptians to die while keeping the animals of the Hebrews well. Although Pharaoh saw this was true, he wouldn't give in—not even when boils broke out on all the Egyptians. Neither a hail storm that was the worst in history nor a swarm of locusts that covered the face of the earth and blotted out the sun could convince the Pharaoh. Three days of darkness—while the Hebrews stood in light—caused the Egyptians to cry out to their Pharaoh for relief, and he offered to let Moses and his people leave without their flocks and herds. "All or nothing at all" was Moses' reply as he prepared his people for flight. God instructed them to ask their Egyptian neighbors for gold and silver jewelry and to get ready for their Exodus, thus fulfilling the prophecy that they would leave with much wealth after their four hundred years in slavery.

As a child I had memorized the ten plagues put upon the Egyptians, and as an adult I knew of the Passover as a Jewish holiday, but I had never seen any of these events as significant to me or as a part of any great plan of God for his people. Once I began to study the Old Testament with spiritual eye-sight, I was in awe of the miracles God did in spite of the human reactions of his cast of characters. Melancholy Moses was frequently depressed and angry while his people were contentious, complaining, and ungrateful. Although they were initially thrilled when Moses arrived to set them free from slavery, after a year of plagues and punishment, they were angry with Moses and had somehow shifted the blame for their problems onto him. When he announced that God was about to kill the firstborn in every Egyptian home, even the firstborn of each animal, unless Pharaoh let the people go, the stubborn ruler refused his request, and the Hebrews wondered how God would know their homes from those of the Egyptians.

Once again it was up to Moses to explain God's plan of provision to the people—God's way of salvation for those who would believe. In Exodus 12, we read of God's detailed instructions to Moses. As we have already seen with the story of Noah, God the Father gives specific steps to follow. He never says "Go do your own thing" but "Do it my way and be blessed." Noah built the ark to code and became the savior of his family and preserved the human race. God told Abraham to build an altar and sacrifice his beloved son. When Abraham did as God required, God spared his son and provided a lamb as a substitution. God blessed Abraham as the father of both the Hebrew and the Arab races. Now it was Moses' turn to be the savior of his people to bring them from slavery into freedom.

Even though God had been the moving force in sending the plagues and sparing the Hebrews, these descendants of Abraham, Isaac, and Jacob were looking for God in all the wrong places. They couldn't see God's hand in amongst the flies and frogs, the locusts and lice. They wanted a god in high places, a god like Pharaoh. They weren't looking for God in the common place. So it was not until God was ready to perform a miracle—a miracle so great it is still celebrated today—that they heard his voice. They found God in the Passover and followed his clear instructions as Moses explained them.

Each Hebrew father was to *provide* a year-old lamb, a perfect lamb without spot or blemish, for his family.

He was to kill this lamb and *place* the blood of the lamb on the upper door frame of the house. He was to take a cluster of hyssop (a common weed), dip it in the blood, and strike it against the lintel above the door and on each side. Just draining the blood into the basin was not enough; it had to be applied, placed where it could be seen. God said, "When I *see* the blood I will pass over you and I will not destroy your firstborn children when I smite the land of Egypt" (Exod. 12:13, TLB).

Each father was to *present* the roasted lamb to his family for their evening meal, being careful not to break the bones of the animal. If any of the lamb was left it had to be burned. Nothing was to be saved for the next day. He had to provide the lamb, apply the blood, and then eat for nourishment and strength.

The bread for the meal was to be prepared with no leaven (yeast being a symbol for sin) that the family might *purge* themselves from unrighteousness. They also were to eat bitter herbs as a sign of suffering.

Before partaking of the meal, each family member was to be dressed in traveling clothes with their bags packed, ready for the journey. They were to eat hurriedly while standing and *prepare* to go into the wilderness.

The people believed Moses and were amazingly cooperative. At midnight there went up a cry from each Egyptian home as God caused each firstborn son to die. By morning there was much grief throughout the land. This time Pharaoh insisted the Hebrews leave, and the Egyptians gave them gold jewelry, clothing, and riches as a farewell present. The sons of Jacob had been in this land for four hundred and thirty years when Pharaoh finally said, "I'll let the people go."

God wanted his people to remember this event each year, so he set aside a time of celebration—"The Feast of the Passover."

All Hebrews were to commemorate this miracle with a seven-day celebration. No yeast was to be used or even possessed in the home during this seven days. This permanent law is still obeyed today in faithful Jewish homes about the last week of March as they remember how God passed over their homes and saved them from destruction.

As the Hebrew people looked up to God that night and did as he instructed that they might be saved, so can we look to him for salvation today.

For Us in Today's World

God has *provided* his son Jesus as our perfect sacrificial lamb. You are redeemed "with the precious blood of Christ, as of a lamb without blemish and without spot" (1 Pet. 1:19, KJV).

"For Christ, our Passover lamb, has been sacrificed" (1 Cor. 5:7, NIV).

As God has made provision for our salvation through the shed blood of his son, we must take hold of this offering and apply the blood to our lives. The blood alone didn't save the Hebrews until they *placed* it on their homes and their hearts. Just head knowledge of God's plan wasn't enough; they had to act upon it, apply it, *place* it, make it a part of their lives. So it is with us that just knowing there is a God is not enough to save us.

As God provides the sacrifice and we apply his son's blood, we are then to *present* his Word as food for our souls. "Just as the living Father sent me and I live because of the Father, so the one who feeds on me will live because of me" (John 6:57, NIV). We must feed on God's Word so that we will never hunger.

If we are to find God and fellowship with him, we must search our lives and root out the hidden sin. "Be on your guard against the yeast of the Pharisees and Sadducees" (Matt. 16:6, NIV). Paul explained to the Corinthians who were believing Christians, but who had not yet *purged* out their old habits and natures, that they had to take action. "Don't you know that a little yeast works through the whole batch of dough? Get rid of the old yeast that you may be a new batch without yeast—as you really are. For Christ, our Passover lamb, has been sacrificed. Therefore let us keep the Festival, not with the old yeast, the yeast of malice and wickedness, but with bread without yeast, the bread of sincerity and truth" (1 Cor. 5:6–8, NIV).

As we *purge* that old leaven—the yeast of sin—from our lives, we can remember the bitter herbs the Hebrews ate that night and realize that the Christian life is not without heartache and suffering.

"Endure hardship as discipline; God is treating you as sons" (Heb. 12:7, NIV). God disciplines us for our good, that we may share in his holiness. "No discipline seems pleasant at the time, but painful. Later on, however, it produces a harvest of righteousness and peace for those who have been trained by it" (Heb. 12:11, NIV).

Christ suffered for us and drank the bitter cup of death that we might have everlasting life; yet he, like the passover lamb, had none of his bones broken. "These things happened so that the Scripture would be fulfilled: 'Not one of his bones will be broken'" (John 19:36, NIV; see also Ps. 34:20, NIV).

In order to respond to God when he calls, we must be ready to move. We are not to sit idly by, waiting for some bolt of lightning to jolt us into action, but we are to be *prepared.* The Hebrews had no proof that God would spare them, some had even been worshiping Egyptian gods, but they took him at his word and got ready. They stood up while eating, they had on their walking shoes, they were ready to go. Are we ready to go? When God calls on us will we say, "Here am I, send me." Oswald Chambers says, "When God speaks many of us are like men in a fog, we give no answer. . . . Be ready for the sudden surprise visits of God. A ready person never needs to get ready. Think of the time we waste trying to get ready when God has called."[12]

The Hebrews had been looking for God to save them from slavery and set them free, and he did. He passed over each home marked with the blood of the lamb and told them never to forget what he had done. "Again I say this celebration shall identify you as God's people, just as much as if his brand of ownership were placed upon your foreheads. It is a reminder that the Lord brought us out of Egypt with great power" (Exod. 13:16, TLB).

As God's mark was on the Hebrews in the past it will be on all believers in the future. In the Book of Revelation, we read that harm was to come only to those who do not have "the mark of God's seal on their foreheads" (9:4, TEV).

As we believe in God's power today and accept his salvation, we are marked in God's sight. "When you heard the true message, the Good News that brought you salvation . . . You believed in Christ and God put his stamp of ownership on you by giving you the Holy Spirit he promised" (Eph. 1:13, TEV).

"The Spirit is God's mark of ownership on you" (Eph. 4:30, TEV).

Although we can't see this mark on each other, God can. His all-seeing powerful eyes look down on us, and he knows those who are his. The shepherd knows his sheep.

If you enter Disneyland, your hand is stamped. You can't see it, but if you wish to leave and return again, the guard places your hand under a special light and "the stamp of ownership" appears before your very eyes. So it is with God. He has his mark on us and his special light shines down and shows up his saints.

As a further encouragement to the people he had saved, God led them in a cloud by day and a pillar of fire by night giving tangible evidence of his abiding presence. Don't we often feel today, "If only I could see God or some sign of his reality, I could believe." The Hebrews could see proof and at first this excited them, but as they plodded through the wilderness carrying everything they could manage, plus the bones of Joseph, they got weary and began to cry to Moses.

"Have you brought us out here to die in the desert because there were not enough graves for us in Egypt? Why did you make us leave Egypt?"

Isn't it amazing how quickly they lost sight of God, took their minds off his miracles, and began to cry, "poor little me! Oh, for the good ol' days in Egypt."

As Pharaoh and his armies pursued them, the Hebrews headed straight for the Red Sea. If dying in the desert looked bad, drowning in the depths looked worse. Moses called out to the Lord for a new plan of salvation and God answered, "Quit praying and get the people moving! Forward march!" Has God ever had to say that to you as you sat weeping and wailing over the deep waters you were in? "Quit praying and get moving. It's easier for me to push you if you're already in motion!"

The people had little faith that God in his cloud could save them, but they had no alternative plan so they headed into the sea. That night God placed his pillar of fire between the pursuing Egyptians and the Hebrews, blinding the Egyptians and giving warm light to his people. In the morning, Moses stretched his rod over the sea, and the Lord opened up a dry path with high walls of water on each side.

Do you look for God when you're in deep waters? Are you often out to sea or—as my mother used to say—in a boat without a paddle? God does the most amazing things when we believe in him in unbelievable situations. Not only did he save his people, but he drowned their enemies! Now that's a God who sees the mark of ownership upon his people—one who separates the saints from the sinners.

Many of us wander around in our deserts waiting for God to lift us up to a mountaintop experience. Surely the murmuring and disputing Hebrews, still longing for the good ol' days of Egypt, were ready for some excitement. They had wandered through the Sinai Peninsula for three months when God called Moses to the mountaintop and offered him a new contract. As always, God wanted to give some clear instructions and have the people obey. If they would follow his commandments, he would make the Hebrews a kingdom of priests, a holy nation—a special people.

Moses went down from the mountain to prepare the people to meet God face to face. They even washed all their clothes so that they would be clean before a righteous God. On the morning of the third day a huge thunderstorm rolled in, a big black cloud settled on the mountain, a ram's horn blasted, the whole mountain shook, and God spoke in a deep voice calling Moses to the mountaintop.

Surely the people would be positive, accepting, faithful believers after meeting God on the mountain.

THINK ON THESE THINGS

Read Exodus 1–15. Pay special attention to the miracles of God, the spirituality of Moses, and the humanness of the people.

1. When do you remember being so in awe of God's presence in your life that you took off your spiritual shoes and said, "This is holy ground"? Do you agree with Oswald Chambers that if you haven't felt this way "it is questionable whether we have ever stood in his presence"? How does this feeling of awe compare with people talking of having a spiritual experience?

2. What plan has God ever revealed to you personally? What steps have you taken? How easy or difficult were these steps? When did you cry out "This is too hard, send someone else"? Do you see that when the way is easy God gets no credit?

3. What have you or some member of your family been a slave to? Have there been addictions or compulsions? Did you find a person like Moses to set you free? a prescription or human plan to release you? a spiritual victory beyond human ability? What healings have you experienced?

4. Can you think of some people who are never content? What have you tried to do for them that has failed? What occasionally robs you of your joy? How do you apply the strength of Christ to your moments of discouragement?

5. Are you ready to leave your Egypt? your place of bondage? your past life? your emotional pain?

For Your Notebook

Write down the five steps of the Passover and then answer the questions for yourself.

Provide: Have you accepted Jesus as your sacrificial lamb which God has provided for your salvation?

Place: Have you placed God's plan into your life—have you applied it?

Present: Do you present God's Word to yourself and others?

Purge: Are you willing to let God purge you of past problems and bad habits?

Prepare: Are you preparing yourself to know God in a more personal way this year than ever before?

Add seven daughters of Midian to your seven list.
Start a list of forties, the number of probation and testing.

It rained 40 days and 40 nights (Gen. 7:12).
Isaac was 40 years old when he married Rebekah (Gen. 25:20).

Esau was 40 years old when he married his Hittite wives (Gen. 26:34).

Moses was on the mount 40 days and nights (Exod. 24:18).

The Israelites ate manna for 40 years (Exod. 16:35).

(It was D. L. Moody who said: "Moses spent 40 years in a palace thinking he was somebody, 40 years in a pasture knowing he was nobody, and 40 years in the wilderness learning what God can do with a nobody.")

For a Pause That Refreshes

Before we move on let's check our map. We want to make sure we have followed our scheduled route and not made a wrong turn along the way. Let's pause by an oasis in the desert and reflect on our personal progress.

During our journey from the Garden of Eden through the Red Sea, we have seen several principles which have been repeated often enough to catch our attention.

God doesn't ask a lot of us. He's not unreasonable, but he does expect obedience and honesty.

When God's people follow his clear directions, he blesses them, provides for them, and saves them.

When God's people disobey or are deceptive, he punishes them, teaches them, and forgives them.

What simple truths! What wonderful principles to use in the raising of our own children.

We have visited some of the right places where people in the Bible and in today's world look for God. We've become acquainted with some of the heroes of faith, great men and women with human personalities, strengths, and weaknesses called out by God to lead and save their people.

1. We started in the lush Garden of Eden where Adam and Eve walked and talked with God. We saw that Eve had everything she could possibly want, yet she reached out for something more. She knew God's one rule clearly, and yet she disobeyed. She was easily beguiled. She knew she was wrong,

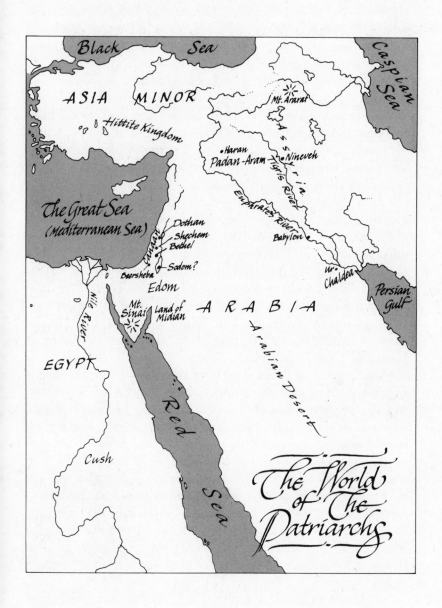

Black Sea

Caspian Sea

ASIA MINOR

Mt. Ararat

Hittite Kingdom

Haran
Padan-Aram

Nineveh

A s s y r i a

The Great Sea
(Mediterranean Sea)

Euphrates River

Tigris River

Dothan
Shechem
Bethel

Babylon

Canaan

Sodom?

Beersheba

Ur-
Chaldea

Persian Gulf

Edom

A R A B I A

Nile River

Mt.
Sinai

Land of
Midian

EGYPT

Arabian Desert

Red Sea

Cush

The World
of The
Patriarchs

yet she tried to deceive God. Her husband knew right from wrong, but he went along with her ideas to keep peace.

How about you? Are you content with what you have until God provides more? Do you know when you are being tempted or beguiled? Do you know at least one area of your life where God is disciplining you into obedience? Are you willing to put aside any deceptive ploys and stop compromising your standards to go along with the crowd?

If your answers are all positive you may move ahead. You can't leave the garden until you've learned to be obedient to his simple directions for your life.

2. As you stroll out into the fields you will remember meeting Cain, a strong-willed and rebellious man who wasn't about to obey God. He had not learned the lesson of the garden. He wasn't interested in fostering family relationships, and he surely didn't want to be responsible for his brother. Think for a moment about your life. There may have been a few times in the past when you wanted your own way. Perhaps you're always the one who has to give in and take care of other people. In frustration, have you ever said as Cain did, "Am I my brother's keeper?"

When you read these sentences do you see some need for improvement in your attitude toward others? Are you willing to look for opportunities to be of assistance to your brother? Are you willing to be pleasant to someone you don't even like? Knowing the principle of reaping and sowing, are you ready to evaluate what you are planting in the fields? "The one who sows to please his sinful nature, from that nature will reap destruction; the one who sows to please the Spirit, from the Spirit will reap eternal life" (Gal. 6:8, NIV).

As you review these questions, decide if you are ready to move on in your search for God or if you need to stay out in the field to improve the quality of your seeds before planting again.

3. If you've learned to obey God and care for your brothers, you are ready for a long walk with Enoch. Not much was written about Enoch, perhaps because he was a godly man who caused no trouble. Decent people don't make good

press, but Enoch impressed God so much that God didn't wait for him to die, he translated him into heaven to be with him. How about you?

Are you breathing in and out with God? Are you in stride with God? Do you exercise with him each day? Do you need to spend more time in God's Word to get to know him?

There's no hope in looking for God if we have no time to walk with him when we find him. If you're not satisfied with your stride, pause and pray until God gives you some insight on the closeness of your walk with him.

4. Now that you are breathing in harmony with God, you are ready to review the lessons learned from Noah, another godly man, who was obedient to the Father's instructions down to the last gangplank and pigeon. He built an ark when there was no rain, and he had faith that God knew what he was doing, even when there was no evidence. He was patient for those forty days in the ark, and the minute he got free he built an altar to worship God. Noah was surely a righteous and blameless man, and one we should think about each time we see a rainbow of promise.

As you think about Noah, how does his dedication and obedience compare with yours?

What's the longest you've been cooped up in one place? How did you react? Do you need to learn some patience?

When you finish an arduous task, do you stop to worship God? Do you make your prayers full of thanksgiving?

How does your faith compare to that of Noah, a man who was willing to be ridiculed in order to obey God's instructions?

What kind of an ark is God asking you to build? Are you ready? Don't move until you're sure or you might drown in the big flood.

5. Now that your faith has been strengthened and the waters have receded, you can look again at the tower of Babel. God the Father had brought up his children well, provided them with gardens and rainbows, and still they didn't give him any respect, credit, or praise. He'd created their talents and endowed them with ministries, and yet they got so

caught up in their own successes that they went out to build themselves a monument. It could have been a prayer tower to God, but that thought never crossed their minds.

How often do you give God credit for the intelligence and abilities he's bestowed upon you? Have you ever followed a person instead of God? What lesson does God have for you personally in the tower of Babel? What confusion is in your life right now that needs to be healed before you move on? What monuments have you been building to yourself?

6. Now that you've taken down those mental statues of yourself, you are able to focus your attention on God.

When Abraham heard God's call, he packed up everything and started to move even though he didn't know where God was guiding him. It's always easier for God to give us momentum when we're already moving. Because Abraham trusted God and had faith in his directions, God forgave him when he was deceptive and later made him the father of all nations. Abraham was so obedient to God's directions that he was willing to kill his favorite son on the altar as a sacrifice to God.

How in tune are you to God's voice? What was the last instruction that you knew came from God? How did you react? Do you need to take some time to practice your faith and build your trust in God? Aren't you glad God forgives? Tell him right now why you need forgiveness—confess any of your actions that are displeasing to God.

Before you can move forward in your search for God, you have to bolster up your faith and check again on your obedience and honesty. Are you in the wilderness right now? Do you not know which way to turn? Is the lure of Egypt calling you?

Remember Abraham; he didn't move until he heard God's voice. But the minute Abraham got the call, he headed off, trusting God to direct his path. God asks us to believe in him and not lean on our own understanding. Are you ready to pack if God gives the call?

7. How would you like to be named "the Deceiver" and then live up to your title! Jacob just seemed to attract trouble.

His mother, Rebekah, manipulated his life and kept him around the house. We can be grateful that he ever grew up and got married.

Do you still have a parent who has emotional control over you? Do you have parents or in-laws who use you as a pawn in their games? Have you sometimes been deceptive and worked one parent against the other?

In Genesis God tells us when we marry to leave and cleave, both emotionally and physically. He doesn't want adult children still tied to their parents. If you have a parent problem, pause and ask the Lord for direction. As an adult, Jacob still did what his mother told him to do even though it violated a clear ruling of God; he just went along to save confrontation. How often we see someone compromise what they know to be God's standards in order to avoid a potential problem. Don't be a victim of the easy way out. Listen to God's plan for your life.

Jacob was forced to leave home because of his deception. But God knew he was a good man, and so he met Jacob on the rocks face to face in an awesome place. If you're on the rocks today, look up. This could be a new beginning for you. This could be your "gate of heaven." Move on!

8. For Jacob it was love at first sight when he met Rachel, and he was willing to do anything to get her for his wife, including working fourteen years for no money. During the time Jacob lived in his father-in-law's land, he and Laban both deceived each other. There must be a reason that we become so easily deceptive. Think back to the last time you told a "white lie." Why did you do it? How do you feel about it now?

What could the church do to increase awareness of the need for honesty and integrity? Is there someone right now to whom you need to go and straighten out some past problems?

Remember God's words, "No one who practices deceit will dwell in my house; no one who speaks falsely will stand in my presence" (Ps. 101:7, NIV).

Does someone have a grudge against you that you need to repair?

It is so easy for Christians to look good in church while harboring ill will toward one another; it is so natural to see our side of a situation and not be willing to take the first step toward healing.

Jesus himself said, "I tell you that anyone who is angry with his brother will be subject to judgment. . . . Therefore, if you are offering your gift at the altar and there remember that your brother has something against you, leave your gift there in front of the altar. First go and be reconciled to your brother; then come and offer your gift" (Matt. 5:22–24, NIV).

Today could be a turning point in your human relationships. Be the one to take the first step.

9. With all the problems that Joseph had as a teenager, it's a miracle he grew up to be a balanced and godly man. Before you walk on toward God, check your past. Were you rejected, molested, unloved, or deprived as a child? Do you have some emotional weights of the past that you need to shed? Seek out a trusted friend or counselor and begin to deal with these past pains. For additional help read my book *Lives on the Mend*, Jan Frank's *Door of Hope*, or David Seamands's *Healing of Memories*.

Chances are you haven't been in jail, yet you may be a prisoner in some other set of circumstances. You may be locked in an alcoholic home, you may be suffering in a difficult marriage, you may be serving time for some emotional pains of the past. Many of us are in the chains and fetters of financial burdens that keep us from enjoying the freedom the Lord promises.

"Then you will know the truth, and the truth will set you free" (John 8:32, NIV).

When Joseph went to prison for a crime he did not commit, what did he do? He didn't run and hide. He didn't deny he was there and sink into a false world of unreality. And he didn't wallow in self-pity. Instead, he faced the facts, undeserved as they were, and refused to waste energy on hatred and bitterness. He thanked God that he was alive and developed a plan of how to make the best of an unexpected tragedy. Here was an innocent man persecuted for his exemplary behavior.

Does his situation sound at all like yours? Not all punishment is deserved, and those of us who are victimized in any way have to make a decision whether to sit and cry, hating those who have done us wrong, or whether to formulate the best possible plan, praise God, and move on. We can focus either on the prison bars on the windows or the sky beyond.

Are you in a prison today? Is some guard trying to whip you into shape? Take a realistic view of your options, decide if you need some counsel, and move a few steps toward the door. Practice the presence of God whether in prison or in power. The truth will set you free.

10. Moses had been trained in the Pharaoh's palace for a position of leadership, but as you will remember, he'd gotten himself in trouble and left town to escape the consequences. Starting a new life, he'd soon settled into the safety of the status quo, where he was leading nothing more complex than a flock of sheep. Moses knew about God, but he hadn't been actively seeking to know God in a personal way. His basic needs in life were being met, and he had no urgency to seek spiritual direction.

Does any of this have a familiar ring? Are you a good person who's content to stay out of trouble and tred the middle line? Do you have some talent you're not using? Does God see you as a potential leader? Perhaps he is ready to call you as he did Moses. Will you also say "Who me? You must have the wrong person. Find someone who can really speak." Will you be as surprised as Moses when God taps you to go and save his people?

In CLASS we often find participants who don't know why they've come. They don't really want to be leaders, but somehow they find themselves there and realize they're beginning to hear God's voice faintly in their minds.

Each one of us can be a leader in the area of our own experience. Those of us who have suffered and have triumphed over tragedy can use our trials to give hope to others. Remember, the God of peace comforts us not so we'll become comfortable, but so we will comfort others.

What potential for leadership do you have? Are you available for training so that you'll be ready when God calls? Don't just sit around with the sheep. Stand up and say, "Here am I. Send me."

In reviewing these ten stories based on the lives of Old Testament people, we've had a chance to examine our personality, our attitudes, our character, our patience, our honesty, our obedience, and our willingness to heed God's call. Now that we've looked at who we are and have felt the touch of God, we're ready to take those steps necessary to stand in the very presence of God.

The Lord delights in the way of the man whose steps he has made firm; though he stumble, he will not fall, for the Lord upholds him with his hand (Ps. 37:23–24, NIV).

Bonus Story

◇ ——————————————————————— ◇

LOOKING FOR GOD AT THE RIVER

When I spoke at an international business conference in Amsterdam, I met an Englishman named Reginald. He identified himself as a Christian and told me how he had found God. During World War II, his battalion was trained to cross the Rhine and invade German-held territory. They practiced swimming through gunfire and removing their backpacks quickly when thrown into the water.

They were young, brash, and confident, and they could hardly wait to get into action. As the day approached when they were called into battle, Reginald came down with a high fever and was put into a Dutch hospital for treatment. He couldn't believe after all his training that he was going to be left behind. The troops went out in their boat to bravely cross the Rhine, but when they were in the middle of the river, their boat was blown up. There was no time to shed the packs and swim; they all sank and drowned.

Reginald told this story as we stood on the banks of the Rhine in Arnhem at the very spot where his friends had been killed. Tears filled his eyes as he recalled, "I lay on that bed and said, 'Thank you God for sparing my life. I'll give it back to you and do whatever you want me to do.'"

Somehow our cruise on the Rhine that day was more serious and spiritual than we had expected it to be as we looked into the water that had engulfed Reginald's friends. "I'm the only one God saved."

Although the troops Reginald had trained with had drowned in their Red Sea, Reginald had been passed over, spared, saved to give his testimony to others. Reginald found God at the river.

Part III

——————◇

Finding God Face to Face in the Right Place

Ten Steps into the Presence of God

◇ ———————————————————— ◇

1. LEAVE EGYPT
—AND FOLLOW THE CLOUD

As I travel around to different places, people give me souvenirs of their city. I have collected such diverse mementos as a wooden cutting board carved in the shape of Texas, a gallon of home-grown honey from the Rio Grande Valley, a bag of rice and special pralines from Louisiana, hand-crafted silver jewelry from New Mexico, and a blue Delft plate from Amsterdam. I've been given so many luscious fruit baskets that at the end of one long trip I got on the plane with two baskets of goodies hanging on each arm, looking like little Red Riding Hood.

What have you and I collected so far on this trip through Genesis? Did you bring back an apple from the Garden of Eden, a map of Enoch's 300-year walk with God, a wooden replica of Noah's ark complete with pairs of little animals? Did you purchase a miniature pillar of salt, a replica of the ram in the thicket, a statue of Abraham, or a bottle of water from Rebekah's well? Did you try on a coat of many colors? Do you have some "bitter herbs" from the Passover laminated into a bookmark? Have you put all the souvenirs of your search for God into a basket replica of Moses' bed in the bulrushes?

What have you gathered up so far? No trip should be without memories, without pictures of those we've met, without recollections of the steps we've taken, the mountains we've climbed, the lessons we've learned. But our trip isn't over yet; we've still ten more stops before we reach our destination, before we come into the presence of God. We have a perfect plan to follow; we don't need to wonder or wander in the wilderness. We don't need to look for God on the plain, in the rain, on a walk, or on a rock. We are within sight of our destination. We will now prepare ourselves for the most exciting part of our journey, the ten steps to finding God.

We will follow the same plan God gave to Moses, we will make the same moves the Hebrews took when they left the slavery of Egypt and headed for the Promised Land. Let's start with their Passover decision. They had to make a choice.

For God's People in Bible Times

Before God could catch the full attention of his people, he had to get them to leave Egypt, an idolatrous country where they were slaves to sin but where little was asked of them spiritually. The Book of Hebrews tells us "By faith Moses, when he had grown up, refused to be known as the son of Pharaoh's daughter. He chose to be mistreated along with the people of God rather than to enjoy the pleasures of sin for a short time. . . . By faith he *left Egypt,* not fearing the king's anger; he persevered because he saw him who is invisible" (Heb. 11:24–25, 27, NIV).

Moses knew the invisible God who appeared in the form of a burning bush to send him back to Egypt to save the people. At first, Moses was a hero rescuing the Hebrews from four hundred years of slavery. But when God sent the plagues as demonstrations of his power to Pharaoh, there were many who weren't sure they wanted to leave Egypt that much. They knew *of* God, but they didn't *know* God, and so they had little faith to call upon. The night when God "passed over" each Hebrew home and spared their children became a moment of decision. Would they do what Moses said and eat their dinner lamb while standing up in their walking shoes ready to leave their homes behind and head for the unknown wilderness before them? What guarantee would there be that they would escape the Pharaoh's wrath? Was there in fact this Promised Land that the God of Moses offered those with faith? Each family had to decide that night whether to take a chance on God or stay in Egypt.

When you haven't practiced the presence of God in your life, when you haven't walked and talked with him in the garden, it's not easy to take that step of faith.

> When our fathers were in Egypt,
>   they gave no thought to your miracles;
> they did not remember your many kindnesses,
>   and they rebelled by
>   the sea, the Red Sea.
>
> —Psalm 106:7, NIV

For those who made the right decision, the Exodus was not an easy trip, but God met their every need and provided miracles along the way for encouragement. Those who obeyed his instructions were blessed because they were willing to *leave Egypt* and try God.

For Us in Today's World

What does this mean to you and me today? Is there some Egypt that we are unwilling to leave behind us? Have we never been close enough to God to trust him for tomorrow? For those of you who have never committed your life, your present and future, to the Lord, here is your first step in finding God: being willing to *leave Egypt* and trust God, being willing to leave the known for the unknown in faith.

In retrospect the writer of Hebrews said of Moses: "He regarded disgrace for the sake of Christ as of greater value than the treasures of Egypt, because he was looking ahead to his reward" (Heb. 11:26, NIV).

Are there some treasures of Egypt that you can't bear to leave behind? Would you rather take your basket of souvenirs and go home? God is calling you from your present world and offering you a reward in the future. Are you willing to make a choice?

Perhaps you've been trying to get close to God, but you

haven't *left Egypt*. Perhaps you have some destructive habits that you are unwilling to give up. Perhaps you have some "secret sins" that no one knows about so you haven't been disciplined to change. Perhaps you're too busy with the pleasures of Egypt to spend any time with the Lord.

I never knew I had to make a choice because I'd always been a good churchgoing girl. I assumed if someone got too religious God would send down stone tablets saying "Thou shalt not have any more fun!" But once I'd made the decision to follow Jesus, I found God didn't drop directives, but he did begin to change my desires.

Shortly after Fred and I became believing Christians and before we had any idea God was much more than a reason to go to church on Sunday, we went to the Country Club one Saturday evening. This was not just any old country club, but the one in which we'd been founding members. Fred was the tennis champ, I was the bridge winner, and the girls were on the swim team. The club was the center of our social life, and we always attended the weekend parties and formal dances. This one evening we were sitting at our usual table with our usual friends when suddenly I saw them as if for the first time. The conversation seemed pointless and the people pathetic. I realized they had all been drinking too much and weren't even making sense. Since we had always been considered squares because we didn't drink, we had tried to be the life of the party and go along with their behavior no matter what it was. This charade had never bothered me because I wanted so much to be an accepted part of the club elite, and Fred's ability to bring tennis trophies back to the club made him a valuable member.

I can picture that evening with Fred looking movie-star handsome in his tuxedo and me in one of my many gowns. The man next to me, whom I knew well, had his arm around me and was noisily kissing my shoulder. Suddenly he looked pitiful, and I had an urge to push him off his chair. I glanced across at Fred, and a voluptuous, tipsy woman was hanging on him and batting her false eyelashes up and down in his face. These flirting actions were probably the same that night as they'd been many times before, but I saw them with new eyes. I had no idea why things looked different to me at that time, but as I listened to the same music and stared at the same walls, I wanted to run. I said to myself, "What in the world are we doing here." In the car going home I sighed to Fred, "Do you know what thought went through my head tonight?" Before I got any further he added, "Let me guess because it might be the same as mine. I looked around at the people and the place and said to myself 'What in the world are you doing here!'" I screamed in excitement over our identical thoughts, and if the Angel Gabriel had suddenly appeared on the hood of our car, we could not have been more spiritually moved. God had spoken to us both at the same time with the same message. He'd told us to get out of Egypt and head for the Promised Land. On the way home we agreed not to return to the club, and we never went back again.

This story doesn't mean you should quit your clubs or give up tennis, but it shows that God knows what Egypt is for each one of us. He didn't forbid us from going there or burn the club down, he just changed our desires, and for us that was a spiritual experience. Within a matter of months, we were called as new staff to Campus Crusade for Christ headquarters, and we left Connecticut to live in the desert of Southern California.

Oswald Chambers in his book *My Utmost for His Highest* says:

> God is not with our natural life while we pamper it; but when we put it out in the desert and resolutely keep it under, then God will be with it; and He will open up wells and oases, and fulfill all His promises for the natural.[1]

Is God calling you out of Egypt into the desert where he can get your attention? Is he trying to change your desires, but you're not responding? Are you fearful of what unknown place he might send you or what treasures and pleasures of your Egypt he might strip away? Give him a try; make a decision, for *leaving Egypt* is the first step in finding God.

"Out of Egypt I called my son" (Matt. 2:15, NIV).

"The word of God came to John son of Zechariah in the desert" (Luke 3:2, NIV).

When the Israelites in Egypt made the choice to leave their homes, their shaky faith in a God they didn't really know needed some help. They wanted to view this God and know he was real, so God came to them in the form of a cloud they could see.

How many of us feel if we could only touch God, if we could witness a miracle, if we could see him part the Red Sea, if we could follow his cloud, if we could observe some tangible sign of his presence, *then* we would believe?

We live in a society that doesn't want to believe in anything it can't touch, eat, possess, drive, or enjoy. We are realists; what you see is what you get. We're afraid to trust people, so we don't dare have faith in God. Yet the Bible tells us "without faith it is impossible to please God, because anyone who comes to him must believe that he exists and that he rewards those who earnestly seek him" (Heb. 11:6, NIV).

"What is faith? It is the confident assurance that something we want is going to happen. It is the certainty that what we hope for is waiting for us even though we cannot see it up ahead" (Heb. 11:1, TLB).

"Faith is the substance of things hoped for, the evidence of things not seen" (Heb. 11:1, KJV).

How do we get faith?

"Faith cometh by hearing, and hearing by the word of God" (Rom. 10:17, KJV).

For us who haven't seen the parting of the Red Sea, we gain faith by studying the Word of God and reliving the times of the Old Testament heroes. For the Hebrews they had only to listen and obey. They had evidence of things we have not seen.

Would we really have been any different if we'd been there with Moses? Would we have experienced that certainty of God's presence if we could have heard his voice or seen him in a cloud?

God had already put his people to the test. They had lived

through the plagues, observed the Passover, and left Egypt! To reinforce their faith in him, God chose to appear before them in the form of a cloud. He was right there for them to see. They could wake up in the morning and have evidence that their God was alive and well. Yet their faith was weak. The cloud that had so impressed them originally had become ordinary after a month in the wilderness. They didn't believe God, and they were sure they were going to die in the desert.

Even though their faith had been amplified by visual aids, God had to prove himself to them over and over again. God came to them in three ways: as a cloud of defense, a cloud of dwelling, and a cloud of direction.

For God's People in Bible Times

Cloud of defense. God first showed his physical presence to his people in the form of a cloud as they fled from the Egyptians. He led them in the day and provided both warmth and light for them in the night. He stood between them and their enemies as a wall of protection. Even though God had said he would lead them from slavery to the Promised Land, they whimpered and wailed in unbelief. They could never sustain their faith for long, and so he went from the front of their group to the back and became the rear guard.

"The pillar of cloud also moved from in front and stood behind them, coming between the armies of Egypt and Israel. Throughout the night the cloud brought darkness to the one side and light to the other side; so neither went near the other all night long" (Exod. 14:19–20, NIV).

God, in the form of a cloud, became their defense and protected them from the enemy. God is still our defense today, and he prepares a table for us in the presence of our enemies. He provides shade from the sun of day and covering from the cool of night (Ps. 121:5–8).

Cloud of his dwelling. Because people had been looking for God from the time of Adam and Eve, because they refused to believe in his reality if they couldn't see him, God came to earth in a form they could follow. As they lifted up their eyes from their own self-pity, they could see God above them. He dwelt among them in the cloud. When Moses walked from the people to meet with God, he entered into the holy presence and was enveloped in the cloud of glory. The people saw Moses disappear into the hiding place of God. Later when the tabernacle was built and God took possession of his first designated home on earth, "the cloud covered the Tent of Meeting, and the glory of the Lord filled the tabernacle" (Exod. 40:34, NIV).

When Solomon dedicated the first temple, patterned after the floor plan of the tabernacle, the people again saw evidence of God's presence.

> When the priests withdrew from the Holy Place, the cloud filled the temple of the Lord. And the priests could not perform their service because of the cloud, for the glory of the Lord filled his temple (1 Kings 8:10–11, NIV).

How often have we today been so filled with the presence and glory of God that we have been unable to move? Have you ever been stopped in your tracks by the overwhelming power of our Lord?

Cloud of direction. Not only did God use his cloud as defense and as his dwelling, but as direction for his people. In their wanderings to find him, they were never obedient for long and were constantly deceiving both God and man. So when God made his physical presence known in the form of a cloud, he established himself as their leader once again. When he stood still, they were to stand still; when he moved, they were to follow. His decisions tested their ability to obey; they had to keep their eyes lifted up to him in order to know his will. "At the commandment of the Lord" they traveled, they pitched tents, they rested.

For Us in Today's World

Since God does not stand before us today in a visible form, where do we find our direction? Is there a godly guide for us?

How grateful we should be that we have the travel plan, God's rule book for our lives. Faith comes from hearing God's Word.

Let's look together at God's direction for our spiritual vision in Psalm 121 (KJV):

> I will lift up mine eyes unto the hills, from whence cometh my help.
> My help cometh from the Lord, which made heaven and earth.
> He will not suffer thy foot to be moved: he that keepeth thee will not slumber.
> Behold, he that keepeth Israel shall neither slumber nor sleep.
> The Lord is thy keeper: the Lord is thy shade upon thy right hand.
> The sun shall not smite thee by day, nor the moon by night.
> The Lord shall preserve thee from all evil: he shall preserve thy soul.
> The Lord shall preserve thy going out and thy coming in from this time forth, and even for evermore.

In this Psalm God tells us to lift up our eyes, not to keep our heads down in discouragement and worldly disappointment. He affirms that our help and direction come from him, the Great Creator. As he watched over Israel and was their defense, so he will keep a watchful eye over us. Although we don't see his cloud, he promises he will shade us from the heat of our daily activities and protect us from harm. As we choose to dwell in him, he will preserve our comings and goings for evermore.

What a comfort to know that God is real and that he is our *defense,* our *dwelling* place, and our source of *direction* when we lift up our eyes to him. He watches over us by day and by night; he neither slumbers nor sleeps.

As you and I take step one toward God, we leave whatever Egypt is for us and follow the cloud that leads us to a place of rest and peace. We are no longer going to sit on the fence of indecision; we are going to make a choice. We're going to gather gold jewelry from our Egyptian neighbors and take a souvenir brick to put in our basket. We'll fill a bottle from the Red Sea and take a rock of remembrance from the shore. We don't want to forget that leaving Egypt has changed our life.

Follow that cloud!

THINK ON THESE THINGS

Read Exodus 1–19.

1. What unusual souvenirs have you brought home in the past? How have they helped you to recall your trip?

2. What is Egypt to you? What habits have you already changed with God's power? What do you see in your life that needs to be left behind or eliminated?

3. Read Hebrews 11 in your favorite version. What is the theme that runs through these Old Testament reviews? What is your definition of faith? Compare this with verse one. Using your own and the Bible's definition, how would you evaluate your faith?

4. Look at John 20:24–28. What was Thomas's level of faith? How do you relate to Thomas? What was Jesus' attitude to him and whom did he say he would bless? How can we increase our faith?

5. Psalm 121 teaches us to lift up our eyes. What is significant in the physical position? Why do we also bow our heads in prayer?

To make God's word become real to you, write out Psalm 121 and insert your personal translation after each verse—first the verse and then what it means to you. This method of Bible study is a great way of personalizing Scripture so that it comes alive for you.

◇ ———————————————————————————— ◇

LOOKING FOR GOD IN THE HILLS

Living in our family store on the town square, we had only one hill to look up to—a gradual rise behind our local church across the street. While it wasn't Mt. Sinai, when we lifted up our eyes, we saw the parsonage and, for our childish minds, the place where God lived. Rev. Orville Ullom was the only God we knew. He was a kindly man who spoke softly and donned his god-robes on Sunday, long black gowns with velvet stripes often adorned with an assortment of what appeared to be colorful scarves. He had red velvet for Christmas time, deep gold for autumn, and purple for Easter. Our God dressed up for special occasions, and when church was over he walked up the hill from whence he came. He ascended into the heavenlies.

From my childhood on, I've always associated lifting my eyes up to the hills with seeing God. When I look at a mountain with a big cloud covering its peak, I know that God is at home and all's well with the world.

In the early '70s, Fred and I bought a home in the foothills of the San Bernardino mountains. The house jutted out over a deep canyon and looked into the national forest, vast hillsides that had few trees. My kitchen window faced bare mountains, and at first I thought there was no beauty in hills that produced little but mustard weed. Having grown up in New England where everything was green, I felt these stripped down mountains looked naked.

Yet as I watched throughout the seasons these hills, like Rev. Ullom, changed scarves. Winter brought a white bow of beauty that snowed its way around the top of the peaks and wrapped up the crests for Christmas. As the snow melted in the spring, a green belt surrounded the hills, and by June, bright polka dots of yellow mustard weed burst forth. The scorching heat of summer then burned up the bushes which, by fall, broke off at the base and began to roll across the hills in the Santa Ana winds—tumbling, tumble weeds bounced across my backyard leaving their prints on the brown background.

In November 1970, the Big Bear Burn raged through our hills. We looked up transfixed as a wild wall of flames crested our hills and marched down the mountains toward our home. Hurricane winds propelled the lighted tumble weeds like flaming balls and the olive trees burst like fireworks as each little, oil-laden leaf became a mini torch against a blackened sky.

My son Fred, six years old at the time, called the family to prayer as the firemen stood with hoses poised surrounding the house. He handed me a Bible and said, "Mother, read us something that will tell us God won't let our house burn." Was God with us on the mountain that night? Was he awake and not slumbering? Would he save our home if we looked up to the hills?

God did deliver us from the forest fire flaming furiously around our home. When the inferno hit our deck, the winds shifted. Half the fire went on one side of us and half went over the house and down the other side of the hill. It was our passover. It was God parting our Red Sea. It was Moses holding up his rod for a miracle to take place. We met God face to face on our mountain that night, and he has preserved our "going out" and our "coming in" ever since.

He even brought several neighbors to himself that night and one teen-ager prayed to receive the Lord while holding a hose on our roof.

When our fire had passed over us, we found one charred post that God had left as a reminder of the reality of the flames, lest we might forget. Later I hung a little plaque at the front door for each visitor to read and for me to see each day. It was that verse I'd loved as a child, but with new meaning for me and my family.

> I will lift up mine eyes unto the hills,
> from whence cometh my help.
> My help cometh from the Lord,
> which made heaven and earth.
>
> —Psalm 121:1–2, KJV

Don't wait until the fire comes before you look for God.
He's on the mountain waiting for you right now.

2. LISTEN TO GOD
—AND OBEY HIS COMMANDMENTS

One summer when I was speaking at the Bible Conference
in Lake Okaboji, Iowa, an elderly and sprightly gentleman
gave the evening message on the Ten Commandments. On a
table before him were ten tall vases of different shapes and
colors. He explained these would represent the Ten Commandments as he taught them. He then told the story of a
person who knew what he should do in life but didn't. When
he got to the first violation, the little man picked up a huge
mallet and whacked the first vase with every ounce of
strength he had. The thing smashed instantly and pieces flew
out into the audience. Everyone screamed in surprise. Had
there been any dozing souls in the audience, there weren't
anymore. Each person was sitting up straight and alert,
awaiting the other nine commandments. As he would say,
"And he broke the Third commandment," he would break
another vase and the audience would duck and cover their
faces. There may have been better speakers that summer, but
I can't remember them. However, I will never be able to
forget the man with the mallet merrily breaking the Ten
Commandments.

When he was finished, a pastor next to me told me this

same gentleman had spoken at his church. In the morning service he had asked the ladies of the church to bring vases he could use in his evening message. He obviously had not communicated what he was going to do with the vases because in true female style, they all brought lovely items worthy of display in front of the entire congregation as representative pieces from their families. You can imagine the response as the man raised his mallet and smashed the first vase. The pastor said nine ladies rose from their seats, ran up the aisle and grabbed their vases off the table while the first lady whose vase was destroyed sat shocked and sobbed out loud. The whole program stopped and the group sang hymns while the elders searched the church basement for old vases knowing that the show must go on. I'm sure no one in that church will ever forget the breaking of the Ten Commandments.

How about you? Is there anything about these commandments that has stayed in your mind over the years? God has always been a God of order, and he expects us to obey his clear instructions and not exceed the limits. God gave commandments, not that he expected any one of us to be perfect, but so we would have an ultimate standard by which to judge our own behavior. When we set rules for our children, we know they won't happily do everything we want, but they will know their limits.

In our present society, we have rebelled against any restrictions, and we have cried out for our rights. We want to be free and "do our own things." The most liberal thinker would have to agree that our moral standards have disintegrated as we have proclaimed, "If it feels good, do it."

For God to give us rules seems old-fashioned—something that we had to obey as children, but now that we are mature, we can behave as we wish; we can enjoy the "good life." Some of us remember a pastor who taught us rules in such a heavy manner we were sure the Christian life contained nothing but "don'ts." Some of us may picture Moses as we saw him in our Sunday school books: a stern, unloving old man in a white dress holding what appeared to be a tombstone. Some of us may see him as Charlton Heston, his rich voice rolling out the Ten Commandments like poetry.

Whatever our past views of Moses, a man God chose to save his people, we tend to feel these rules don't relate much to us today. However, some of us may be looking for God and not finding him because we've not listened when he spoke to us, we've rebelled against his Law, and we haven't examined his precepts with an open mind.

Let's look for God in his commandments, listen to what he has to say and try not to break the vases!

1. *Worship no other God* (Exod. 20:3).

The word *worship* means "to honor, to revere, to pay respect." In contrast to other cultures who had many gods for all seasons and all reasons, our God made it clear right from the beginning that he is the one and only God and that he alone is to be worshiped. The believing Hebrew was to stay true to Jehovah; the Creator; the Great I Am; the Father of Abraham, Isaac, and Jacob; the one who brought them out of Egypt; the Lord God. If we wish to know God personally, we must first establish him as the only object worthy of worship and fall down before him in a spirit of reverence. How much time do we spend praising God for who he is? A great way to get acquainted with God is to start calling out to him in honor and in worship and to listen when he answers. We won't be able to resist the Great I Am.

2. *Don't bow to images or idols* (Exod. 20:4).

We who have grown up in a Christian church have perhaps not thought of "other gods," but the Hebrew people, fresh from four hundred years in a land of idolatry and heading for the Promised Land which was populated by Baal worshipers, needed to be warned against bowing down to pagan images.

Do we need to heed this rule today? Do some of us put faith in statues, plaques, relics, saints, and visions? Do some worship wealth, position, big homes, wall-to-wall carpeting, or drapes? Do some of us idolize parents, pastors, children, or celebrities? Do we become addicted to drugs, alcohol, food, or gambling?

When we put our focus on any activity, person, thing, or compulsion to such a degree that we are worshiping it, being mentally consumed by it, we are bowing before something other than God. We may not be creating a golden calf, but we are not practicing the presence of God, a God who wants to possess us and who will not only punish us when we disobey, but will carry this punishment down to our children to the third and fourth generations. Just because we have chosen to ignore many of God's laws does not mean that he has removed the rules or the retribution. His laws are for our lives, for our own good, and as a father, he will reward those who obey.

3. *Don't use God's name irreverently* (Exod. 20:7).

God's name is never to be used as a swear word, and how quickly we must explain to our children the seriousness of taking the Lord's name in vain. Don't just say don't, but show them that they are hurting God the Father, their Creator. Don't let them watch TV programs where the "good guys" use God's name in vain as if it were a sign of manliness to do so.

I once went to a movie for the sole purpose of seeing my brother Ron who had a role in it. Right from the beginning the handsome actors were swearing, and I would have left except that I hadn't found Ron's part yet. Upsetting as the profanity was, after an hour of it, I was hardly hearing it. What this miserable example showed me was that if you hear something offensive long enough it loses its shock value. If any of us watch or listen to anything we know we shouldn't, we become somewhat accepting of it sooner or later.

Using God's name irreverently or using it as an oath to swear something we know is not true is not honoring to the Lord.

4. *Observe the Sabbath as a holy day of rest* (Exod. 20:8).

Because God created the world in six days and then rested on the seventh, he commands us to do the same. Work is a necessity of life, but God wants us to rest from our pursuits one day a week and worship him. I remember how important our day of rest was when I was a child. There was never a question of whether we felt like going to church or whether it was convenient; we all got ready and went. Worshiping the Lord came first without a question. After church we had our biggest meal of the week; it was a time of celebration. In the evening, my mother would lead us into our little den behind the store where I would play the piano, Ron the trumpet, and Mother the violin. Jim would lead the singing and Father would stand in the doorway "keeping an eye on the store." Grandma MacDougall had made it clear we were to do no unnecessary tasks on Sunday, and once when I used the treadle sewing machine against her warnings, I ran the needle through my finger. As I cried and bled on the fabric, she said piously, "That's God's punishment to you for sewing on Sunday." I learned to keep the Lord's Day holy!

5. *Honor your father and mother* (Exod. 20:12).

As I grew up it never occurred to me or any of my friends to be rude or disrespectful to our parents, but this commandment needs to be brought out of the archives and freshened up for today's youth who seemingly have never heard it. In times when courts will award children money because they don't feel their parents did the best they could in raising them and when insecure parents have followed media suggestions to not damage their progeny by discipline, we have bred a generation of young people who are brash and disrespectful.

Since God commands that we honor our parents, is there any hope that we can fellowship with God and know his power if we are not showing honor to our parents and are allowing our own children to be disrespectful toward us?

I remember once when our son made some fresh comment to me in Fred's presence. Fred grabbed him quickly, picked him up off the floor, and said, "Don't ever let me hear you speak to my wife like that again!" He set the stunned child down, and I never had trouble with him from that moment on. He learned he was to honor his mother.

"The rod of correction imparts wisdom, but a child left to itself disgraces his mother" (Prov. 29:15, NIV).

6. *Don't murder* (Exod. 20:13).

Although this is a rule we may not ever need personally, we are living in times when a high school boy shot his teacher because she gave him a low grade and when a commentator reported on the impossibility of keeping guns out of the hands of elementary school children. "If you don't get your own way, shoot someone. It's your right." What a pitiful, ungodly attitude—an attitude that naturally follows when children are allowed to be disrespectful of their parents. If you have no spirit of honor for your parents and you aren't taught differently, you have no respect for life. Couple this attitude with the amount of TV violence most children view, and it is understandable why homicide and suicide are the top causes of teen-age death. Thousands of women who wouldn't kill a fly or trap a mouse go for legal abortions each year. One doctor was sued for malpractice when the fetus he was aborting lived!

7. *Don't commit adultery* (Exod. 20:14).

Here is seemingly an old-fashioned rule, if we read any current fiction, buy a copy of a women's magazine, or watch a television soap opera. According to new word usage, married people no longer commit adultery, they have extramarital affairs, and the unmarried just become "sexually active." Unfortunately this is not just a worldly violation, but a very real problem in the Christian church. Because God's clear statement gets cloudy in our minds, we rationalize that even God himself couldn't stay faithful to this sad excuse for a mate. A radio commentator, bemoaning the epidemic of AIDS (Acquired Immune Deficiency Syndrome) transmitted in this country primarily between homosexual partners, cautioned his listeners to engage in "safe sex." He then added, "It's almost as if we should only have one partner." God's old rule is a new idea in America today.

One morning I watched spellbound as Oprah Winfrey interviewed three prostitutes as if they were schoolteachers. Each told how she got into the "business" and then described a few "clients." One aggressive example even had a beeper so if her services were needed while she was out shopping, she wouldn't miss a call. When asked if she could earn her living a nicer way, one responded, "I was a secretary and took home $180 a week, but I can earn more than that in a couple hours so I'd be stupid to return to an office."

One of the three was religious and when asked if she thought what she did was a sin, she was shocked and quoted Jesus in her defense, "The Lord approved of prostitution," she stated, "for didn't he let the adulterous woman go by asking those without sin to cast the first stone?" The audience responded well to this logic. They assumed that Jesus must have been a free thinker, not knowing that after he forgave the woman he said, "Go, and sin no more" (John 8:11, KJV).

We can always find a verse which out of context seems to support a pattern of loose living, but God will never bless an adulterous relationship because it is against his clear commandment.

8. *Don't steal* (Exod. 20:15).

In an age when people take towels from hotels and ash trays from restaurants, it's difficult to teach children not to steal. In times when the police are too busy with *big* crime to respond to petty theft, ordinary people can grab what they want and probably get away with it. My son-in-law Randy has a store that sells gold coins and jewelry. It is in a large enclosed mall with a paid security staff. One day when a suspicious looking individual was lurking around, Randy called the guard who reprimanded Randy for summoning him *before* anything was stolen. The suspect, who was extremely tall, left, but that same evening Randy looked up to see the same man running into the store. He leaped over the counter, grabbed all the gold chains that were hanging on the far wall, jumped back over the counter, and was gone before Randy could get to the phone. There was nothing to be done; it was all over, and he had to suffer the loss.

Not one of us is going to do such a blatant thing, yet we will run off copies of Christian music to save our church money and feel virtuous. We will use funny lines or good examples from books or other speakers without giving credit and hope no one happened to have read the book this week. Often we Christians feel exempt from worldly restrictions because we're doing it "for the Lord" who if he happens to notice our little theft will forgive us when he sees what a blessing we've been to the budget.

9. *Don't lie* (Exod. 20:16).

When we recall how deception was a family trait starting with Adam and Eve and how Jacob was named "the deceiver," we see how important it was for God to let his people know that lying or covering up or misleading someone is a sin. "Don't lie," he told Moses, who delivered the word to the people. God feels telling the truth is important and teaching our children to be honest is a necessity if we wish them to become adults pleasing to the Lord.

Honesty is a very difficult principle to teach if we're not living it ourselves. If a child reports to you who's on the phone and you say, "Tell her I'm not home," you are lying and teaching your child to lie also. If you brag about what you got away with in your taxes, or say one thing about a friend behind her back and another thing to her face, you are dishonest.

As Paul said to the Ephesians, "No more lying, then! Everyone must tell the truth to his fellow believer, because we are all members of the body of Christ" (Eph. 4:25, TEV).

10. *Don't covet* (Exod. 20:17).

For those of you who may have been perfect on the first nine commandments perhaps even you may have a problem here. We are told not to desire, long for, or crave something (anything) that belongs to someone else. When I first read this commandment with meaning, I realized I coveted everything I saw. I wanted it all. Coming from a childhood without curtains or even a scatter rug, I longed for drapes and carpeting. I could rationalize that I deserved them, especially if *you* had them. Even though I know better today and I realize that greed is a form of idol worship, if I come to visit you and you have new monogrammed towels, I'll want them.

God knew where to catch us when he told us not to be envious of other people's houses and possessions. He told us not to wish we were married to the man next door, for the grass is always greener, but there may be no roots. We are not even to be grabby for the cleaning lady or the boy who cuts our neighbor's lawn, or for their poodle or Siamese cat, or for their Mazda or Mercedes, or for *anything* that belongs to our neighbor.

Coveting is such a subtle sin that most of us don't confess it or even dignify it with a plea for forgiveness; yet, wishing we had more than we have (sometimes misnamed goal-setting, especially when the desire is to possess what our neighbor has) is a sin of great significance to God.

Are these rules, given to Moses by God so long ago, of any significance to us today? Is the order in which they were given of any importance? As I have studied them and applied them to America today, I think they give an explanation to an otherwise unexplainable society. Keeping in mind the commandments we've just reviewed, let's look at how quickly a whole nation can go downhill when those rules are forgotten—when we abandon God.

1. Our country was founded on biblical principles and the desire for freedom from religious persecution. Our leaders were godly men, our government was based on the Judeo-Christian ethic, and our colleges had religious affiliations. "In God we trust" was put on our money, church attendance was an accepted way of life, and those who violated the laws were punished. We were a nation who worshiped God.

2. Our reputations were important and our families were the foundation of our culture. We were normal people, worshiping one God, in different kinds of churches. But in the 1900s things began to change. With advances in modern science, God no longer seemed relevant and church attendance declined. On April 8, 1966 *Time* declared on its cover "God is Dead" and slowly people began to believe it. Young people strayed into strange cults and flower children wilted on street corners.

3. If there was any doubt about the existence of God, then taking his name in vain hardly mattered. Crudity

became acceptable and later even a sign of masculinity or self-importance.

4. When you're not even sure there is a God, going to church seems unnecessary. Leave it to the older people who aren't quite with it anyway or those who are weak and need a crutch. Why not take the whole weekend off now that we have no obligations? Why not use those days to pursue pleasure and give ourselves some of the fun we never had when we were hung up on church? And besides, it's not good to force children to attend anything that doesn't apply to their current lifestyle. They can always find God later when they're able to make sensible decisions.

5. If you don't have much honor for God then why respect your parents. You didn't ask to be born and most of your problems are their fault. They're both working so hard to get enough money to buy all they covet that they're never around anyway. As one young girl said to me "I end up being responsible for my little brother and for getting dinner. That shouldn't be my job. I have rights, you know."

6. When you spend a lot of time watching TV, it's not hard to get ideas you might not have thought up alone—stabbing, shooting, drugging, drinking, molesting, or maybe murder. These are often used by characters on TV as solutions to their problems. If there isn't a God, there's no heaven or hell so you might as well live it up while you're here.

7. Some decided it's time now to throw out old Victorian frigidity and religious morals that have damaged our psyches and kept us inhibited. We've been held down too long by our old beliefs, let's loosen up and have some fun. If religion is just a list of don'ts, let's do them. Let's eat, drink, shoot up, experiment with sex, for tomorrow we may die—whatever that means.

8. If God's no longer looking at our lives, what difference does it make if we take something that's not ours or if we cheat on our exams or our income tax.

9. When there's no standard for truth, no yardstick of honesty left, then there's no black and white, all becomes gray, anything goes. Deception becomes a close friend.

10. Now that we're no longer hung up on rules, we can spend our time freely doing the things that make us happy without any restrictions or guilty conscience. We can buy all those items we've been coveting for years, and won't the neighbors be jealous! We can lust after a different mate a week and not feel guilty.

Isn't it amazing that when we remove God, consider him dead, and seek our own ways, morals and human decency soon come tumbling after.

Is there any need for the Ten Commandments today? Paul said the Law "was added in order to show what wrongdoing is" (Gal. 3:19, TEV). "The Law was our schoolmaster to bring us to Christ" (Gal. 3:24, KJV).

If we have no tape measure, we don't know how far away we've strayed. Recently reports have been made that the only way to curb teen-age pregnancy, abortions, and illegitimate births is to provide birth control clinics on high school campuses to dispense information and contraceptives, each without parental permission. I was literally stopped in my tracks one afternoon when I turned on the TV just in time to hear Phil Donahue ask a crowd of teen-agers on spring break in Fort Lauderdale if it was true that the hotels were putting free condoms in the same drawers with the Gideon Bibles. As I stared in disbelief, the boys cheerfully waved the evidence before the cameras.

A new opinion, crying out like John the Baptist in the wilderness, is "Just Say No." You don't have to make love to every Tom, Dick, and Harry. You don't have to have herpes to be happy. At the pharmacy counter, I recently saw a display of "Just Say No" buttons for $1.98 a piece. I wonder if they'll catch on.

This startling proposal of abstinence has been received with high humor by the press who consider it too much of a long shot to be worth a second thought. Rules for the teens? Ridiculous.

One commentator on TV said, "The sexual revolution has gone too far to think a few nos in the crowd would make much difference."

Another added, "There's no point in making rules when you know no one will obey them."

One morning on the "Today" show, Dr. Art Ulene gave a surprising plea for abstinence outside of marriage. He gave facts and figures of current problems and said there's no such thing as "safe sex." Bryant Gumbel, who was interviewing Dr. Ulene, asked, "Aren't you being a bit unrealistic to think the kids will say no?"

The doctor won my respect when he said, "We don't eliminate morals because people don't obey the rules. I tell my kids what's right, and if they get in trouble, it's not because I didn't warn them."

We don't wipe out the speed limit just because few observe it.

If you've been looking for God in a few wrong places, perhaps you should review the commandments and see if you've been playing in the gray area—not *too* bad but not quite in line with God's laws. With God it's "All or nothing at all." Half a love isn't enough for him.

You might say, "I could never be good enough for God. If he's looking for perfection, I'm not the one." That's probably exactly the way the Israelites felt when they saw God come down on Mt. Sinai. When Moses received the Commandments from God, he came out from the cloud that hid him. The people had seen the lightning and the smoke and had heard the thunder and the trumpet blast and they were afraid. I'm sure they were feeling insecure and wondering if they could ever be good enough for God. Moses calmed them by saying, "Don't be afraid, for God has come in this way to show you his awesome power, so that from now on you will be afraid to sin against him" (Exod. 20:20, TLB).

Not *afraid of him* but, knowing his power, *afraid to disobey him.*

God then gave instructions on how to build altars to him; they must be simple, founded on good earth, made of uncut stones. "I will come and bless you there" (Exod. 20:24, TLB).

God doesn't ask you to be a theology student, but to be a simple altar to him with your feet planted on solid ground.

You don't need to be fancy. "Don't chip or shape the stones with a tool, for that would make them unfit for my altar" (Exod. 20:24, TLB). God wants us to come to him as we are, in our natural state. "Just as I am, without one plea but that thy blood was shed for me."[2]

If you've been waiting until you are perfect to try to find God, come to him today as an uncut and unpolished rock, just as you are, and he will come and bless you. Listen to what he has to say to you. God speaks to us through his Word, through our prayers, and through our minds as we quiet them before him. It's hard to act upon something which we haven't heard, so listen to God and obey his commandments.

THINK ON THESE THINGS

Read Exodus 20–24.

1. Do you have any vivid memory of an outstanding message you once heard? What was the point of it? What did the speaker do to cause you to remember? What would you have done if the speaker had raised a mallet over your vase?

2. Why did God give us commandments that he knew few people could ever obey? What is your opinion of rules? What do you feel abut the modern thought that anything's all right as long as it doesn't hurt anyone else?

3. What is your understanding of worship? How could the "worship service" at your church be brought closer to what God desires of us?

4. What idols do you have in life? What is the difference between an idol and a role model? When do things like alcohol, drugs, eating, and gambling become idols?

5. Has swearing ever been a problem in your life? If so, how did it come to your attention and what steps did you take to overcome the habit?

6. What do you remember about Sundays as a child? Was church attendance expected? Was dinner special? In your present situation is Sunday any different from another day? In what way?

7. How were you taught to honor your father and mother? How was this method effective or ineffective in results? What is your definition of discipline? Using a concordance, find out what God's Word says about discipline, training, and punishment.

8. What is your view on capital punishment? What does the Bible say? (Exod. 21:12, 14). What do you feel has caused the increase of murders and violence in this country? What can be done to change the direction? How do you feel TV influences young people in their behavior?

9. Name some TV shows in which "free sex" is a normal part of the program. What does watching soap operas do to an impressionable young mind? Are you aware that more than 50 percent of teen pregnancies are conceived in the bedroom of one of the participants in the afternoon while watching love scenes on TV? What do you feel about talk shows where prostitutes, lesbians, gays, and live-in companions are interviewed as average U.S. citizens? What do you feel the church should do when knowing of an adulterous situation? What does Leviticus 20:10–24 say about sexual violations of God's laws?

10. What is the connection between the drug culture and the rise in thefts? If you found a stolen item in your child's room, what would you do about it? Have you even taken things from hotels or restaurants which you felt you deserved? What was it and how do you feel about it now?

11. What lie can you remember telling as a child? What was done about it? Why do you feel the issues of disobedience and deception are so prominent in the Bible? How do you handle these two problems when they arise in your home? Give specific examples which would help others in training their children.

12. What was the most recent thing you coveted? What intangible such as prestige or honor have you wanted that someone else received? How do selfishness and covetousness relate? What does Paul mean when he says, "Greed is a form of idolatry" (Col. 3:5, TEV)? What new perspective have you gained on the Ten Commandments?

For Your Notebook

Start a list of tens. Ten is the number of law and government.

God gave us ten commandments.

Start a list of twelves. Twelve is the number of divine order.

Ishmael was the father of twelve Arab tribes.
Jacob was the father of twelve Hebrew tribes.
God gave us twelve months to organize our year.
Jesus chose twelve men for his disciples.

◇

3. MAKE A HOME FOR GOD
—AND VISIT HIM OFTEN

As we travel along with the Israelites, we have left Egypt
and followed the cloud of God's presence—comforted in the
thought that he is our defense, our dwelling place, our source
of direction. We've seen the miracle of the Red Sea parting so
that we could walk across on dry ground. We've watched
Moses disappear into a cloud as he went to listen closely to
God, and we've watched him return with the Ten Commandments. Now that we have left Egypt to follow God, now that
we have listened to his voice and reviewed his laws, what's our
next step?

We must do more than observe, more than trust and obey,
we must make a home for God and visit him often. How does
one build a house for God?

For God's People in Bible Times

After the Israelites had received the Ten Commandments
they were momentarily impressed with God.

"The Lord said to Moses, 'I am going to come to you in
a dense cloud, so that the people will hear me speaking
with you and will always put their trust in you'" (Exod. 19:9,
NIV).

"On the morning of the third day there was thunder and
lightning, with a thick cloud over the mountain, and a very
loud trumpet blast" (Exod. 19:16, NIV).

God got their attention with his clouds, his voice, thunder
and lightning, and a loud blast on the trumpet!

When Moses came down and read the rules to the crowds

they answered in unison, "We will obey them all!" To celebrate their obedience Moses built a simple altar and surrounded it with twelve pillars, one for each tribe of Israel. He took the blood from the sacrificial animals; half he poured on the altar and half he splashed toward the people saying, "This blood confirms and seals the covenant the Lord has made with you in giving you these laws" (Exod. 24:8, TLB).

As the Hebrew people watched Moses go up to God on the mountain, they were overwhelmed with the sight. "Under His feet there seemed to be a pavement of brilliant sapphire stones, as clear as the heavens" (v. 10).

"Those at the bottom of the mountain saw the awesome sight: the glory of the Lord on the mountaintop looked like a raging fire" (v. 17).

The people had received the Ten Commandments from the mountaintop; they had learned to lift up their eyes unto the hills from whence cometh their help.

Then Moses disappeared one more time into the cloud on top of Mt. Sinai and was there for forty days and nights while God gave him new instructions.

Up to this point the people in the Old Testament have been looking for God in all kinds of places, but now God tells Moses he wants him to build a home—a heaven on earth—so that God might live among his people and they would know specifically where to find him.

In spite of the obvious evidence of God's presence the Hebrew people didn't all believe that God was real, and some looked back with fond memories on the good ol' days in Egypt when they worshiped idols they could see. For the first time in history, God decided to come down from on high and settle in with his people, his chosen race. He told Moses on the mountaintop, "I want the people of Israel to make me a sacred temple where I can live among them. This home of mine shall be a tent pavilion—a tabernacle. I will give you a drawing of the construction plan, and the details of each furnishing" (Exod. 25:8–9, TLB).

For forty days Moses listened to the directions for God's home here on earth. Had I been Moses, I would have been flattered to be selected as the builder. Instantly I would have pictured a grandios palace with enough wings on it to fly away. My plans would include high walls for security, a draw-bridge over the moat, and a huge gate of heavy wrought iron. The mail box would be atop a stone pillar and in simple Hebrew script would be painted the one word GOD. I can see it all now. Knock, knock. Is the Lord at home?

If you were to design a house for God, what would come to your mind? Perhaps a Southern plantation with columns out front? A castle with turrets, a formidable fortress, a secluded monastery? Or would you be more spiritual and sketch out a fluffy ethereal haven in the heavenlies with St. Peter at the golden gate surrounded by cheery cherubims? .

If God called you to a mountaintop experience and said, "Child of mine I'm going to come and live with you," what would your reaction be? "Who me? Surely you must be speak-ing to someone else. You haven't seen my house. It's just not big enough for you. There's not even a guest room, and we couldn't put God in the basement."

Would you perhaps react in the same way you might if your mother-in-law decided to move in? Or your mate invited the new pastor to stay with you until his home was ready? Or Billy Graham and the Pope chose your house for their first ecumenical meeting for a TV mini-series, "Communion with the Simple Folk of America"?

When Moses asked the Lord where he intended to live, God replied, "*You* are going to build me a home." How sur-prised would you have been? Where would you have chosen to build? As I think of the possibility, I recall a large lot I've had my eye on for years. It's on top of a rolling hill in Red-lands with a 360-degree view of the surrounding orange groves bordered by tall palm trees, the desert valleys below, and the majestic snow-capped mountains. The city of Palm Springs sprawls silently on one side and the natural formation of an arrowhead points to the healing mineral baths of Arrowhead Springs on the other. I'd like to build a house there, so I know God would love it: trees, deserts, mountains, cities, and springs. What more could he want?

"You don't want a house—you want a *tabernacle?* Well that puts a whole new slant on it, because this lot isn't zoned for churches. But there's a beautiful spot by the freeway that's already been approved by the city for a Christian school that couldn't raise the money. Would that be a good place for your tabernacle, God? It has easy freeway access and it's on the right side of town."

If I'd been Moses that's probably how I'd have talked with God. I always want to be helpful and give creative suggestions, but God wasn't asking for help, and he is the Great Creator. All he wanted was a willing man to follow his clear instructions. He didn't want some structure similar to the Mormon Tabernacle in Salt Lake City or the Crystal Cathedral in California or even St. Peter's in Rome. I would have chosen one of them, but all he asked for was a tent—a very special tent.

"Be sure that everything you make follows the pattern I am showing you here on the mountain" (Exod. 25:40, TLB). God was clearly saying to Moses "Don't get creative. I have the blueprints. Just do as I say."

The Hebrews had spent years making bricks in Egypt, but God had other materials in mind. In brief, God's instructions were to:

—"Make the tabernacle-tent from ten colored sheets of fine-twined linen, forty-two feet long and six feet wide, dyed blue, purple, and scarlet, with cherubim embroidered on them" (Exod. 26:1, TLB).

—"Make fifty golden clasps to fasten the loops together so that the tabernacle, the dwelling place of God, becomes a single unit" (v. 6).

—Make the roof of eleven goat's hair tarpaulins each forty-five feet across and six feet wide topped with a layer of rams' skins dyed red and a layer of goatskins (vv. 7, 8, 14).

—Frame the tent in acacia wood set in silver bases (vv. 15–25).

—Make two rooms: the Holy Place and the Holy of Holies separated by a veil of blue, purple, and scarlet cloth with cherubim embroidered on it (vv. 31–33).

—Behind the veil put the Ark of the Covenant containing the Ten Commandments. Make the lid of the Ark, the mercy seat, of pure gold, 3 3/4 feet long and 2 1/4 feet wide with two cherubim on top facing each other (Exod. 37:1–9).

—In the Holy Place make a table of showbread, a lampstand of pure gold with seven shafts, and an altar of incense. Use pure olive oil in the lamps and keep them burning continually, forever (Exod. 26:35, 27:20).

—In front of the tent place the laver of washing made from the women's bronze mirrors and the altar of sacrifice made of acacia wood and bronze with a horn at each corner (Exod. 27:1–8, 38:1–8).

—Surround the tent and courtyard with white linen curtain walls 150 feet long, 75 feet wide and 7 1/2 feet high (Exod. 27:9–18).

—Make one gate in the fence and cover it with a colored embroidered curtain attached by silver hooks onto posts imbedded in bronze bases (Exod. 27:16–17, 38:18–19).

From this abbreviation of God's instructions we can see that he was specific in measurements and materials. He left nothing to chance. He combined bright colors with drab goat skins. He desired bronze fittings in the courtyard, silver in the Holy Place, and gold in the Holy of Holies. God cares about quality and details. As an added challenge, God told Moses to make the whole tabernacle and its fittings portable so that it could be carried through the wilderness and set up whenever they settled down.

While melancholy Moses was on the mountaintop meditating with God in the cloud, his sanguine brother Aaron was having a party. He and his friends had made a golden calf to worship. They had forgotten God that quickly. Out of sight; out of mind. In an orgy, later depicted by Cecil B. De Mille, Aaron led the people astray. When Moses came down and saw what was going on, he threw down the tablets on which God himself had written and called Aaron to task. "What in the world did the people do to you . . . to make you bring such a terrible sin upon them?" (Exod. 32:21, TLB).

Aaron, shocked at being caught in the act, recovered

quickly and replied, "Don't get so upset" (v. 22, TLB). The King James version gives a dignified, "Let not the anger of my Lord wax hot!" In other words, cool it Moses. Then in a sudden shift of blame, Aaron alibis, "You know these people and what a wicked bunch they are?" (Exod. 32:22, TLB). "They are set on mischief" (KJV). Since you were gone so long "They said to me, 'make us a god to lead us for something has happened to this fellow Moses who led us out of Egypt.'" (Exod. 32:23, TLB). While the cat's away the mice will play.

I'm sure that many pastors today must feel as Moses did then. Can't you just hear them. "What's the use! They listen to me on Sunday, they seem to care, they thank me for my message, they say 'Bless you brother, Praise the Lord!' and the minute they're out of my sight they do whatever they please. Where are you God? Have you forsaken me?"

Aaron explained creatively how he had asked the women to bring their gold jewelry for some sort of a party game, not dreaming how much they'd bring. To maintain his detachment from the blame, he told how he just threw the gold into the fire and out came a calf. "It's surely not my fault."

My five-year-old grandson Jonathan dropped a Christmas ornament and as it smashed on the tile floor he quickly quipped, "It's not my fault, it just broke automatically."

From the time we're tiny, we know enough to run from responsibility and blame. For a child, this avoidance is understandable but for Aaron? For you? For me? Oh, Lord, help us to grow up and be able to say, "It's my fault, and I'm sorry."

God punished his children for their disobedience in worshiping an idol, and he purged the camp of all who were not on the "Lord's side." Moses took two stone tablets and went up Mt. Sinai again to commune with God who defended him, dwelt with him, and directed him from the cloud. "I am Jehovah, the merciful and gracious God . . . slow to anger and rich in steadfast love and truth" (Exod. 34:6, TLB).

God made a new contract with Moses. God would do miracles and drive out all enemies; the people would obey all his commandments and never compromise with the enemy; they would break down heathen idols and worship no other gods; they would not intermarry with other races; and they would celebrate the Feast of Unleavened Bread, "the Passover."

When Moses came down the mountain after forty days, his face glowed from being in the presence of God. He called a meeting to explain the church building program and to lay out the blueprints before them for their vote of approval. Since the plans had been drawn up by the original architect, the same one who designed the Garden of Eden and Noah's ark, there were no "Nay" votes. Moses explained that they would volunteer their labor for six days of each week and rest on the seventh and worship their God. They were to do no work on the Sabbath under penalty of death.

Even today in Israel the Hasidim (Pious) ultra-Orthodox Jews keep the Sabbath holy and will not let traffic through their neighborhoods on the Holy day. When I was in the Jerusalem Hilton, I was shown a sign that is put up every Friday pointing to the "Shabbat Elevator" programmed to stop at every floor so that Hasidic guests would not have to "work" by pressing a single button on the Sabbath.

Moses asked those with generous hearts to bring as free-will offerings: gold, silver, and bronze; blue, purple, scarlet, and white linen cloth; tanned rams' skins and goatskins; acacia wood and olive oil; spices for oil and incense; onyx and semi-precious stones; gold jewelry and rings. People volunteered to weave, spin, embroider, and sew; to build, carve, forge, and construct.

As the gifts were brought to Moses, he chose, by God's appointment, a man named Bezalel as the general superintendent of the project. Soon the workmen told Moses they had enough materials for the job and that no more donations were needed. In total the people had contributed 3,140 pounds of gold, 9,575 pounds of silver, and 7,540 pounds of bronze.

Moses took God's clear instructions, inspected the work as it was being done, and did not add any clever touches of his own. Because of his obedience to every tiny detail, Moses was blessed by God and the project progressed rapidly.

"On the first day of the first month, in the second year, the Tabernacle was put together" (Exod. 40:17, TLB). It was ready as the residence of God, set for him to move in. "Then the cloud covered the Tabernacle and the glory of the Lord filled it. . . . The cloud rested upon the Tabernacle during the daytime, and at night there was fire in the cloud so that all the people of Israel could see it" (vv. 34, 38). If the cloud did not move, they stayed until it did. This continued throughout all their wilderness wanderings.

For Us in Today's World

God's home on earth was completed and the cloud, the sign of his presence and protection, was evident to the twelve tribes of Jacob encamped wide-eyed around it. The physical setting of the tabernacle surrounded by the tents of the tribes might be compared to the early New England towns where the church was placed on the village green and the houses grew around it. The House of God was central to their daily life, and they were never far from their spiritual source of power.

Did having God so close make a difference in their daily lives? Would you behave better if God lived across the street?

After the "dwelling place" had been completed and God's symbolic cloud was in residence, what were the people to do? The excitement was over; the challenge had been met. Perhaps you've been involved at some time in a church building program of high enthusiasm only to see the spirit drift away when the construction was completed. Having a lofty sanctuary doesn't guarantee spiritual growth. Having God live next door doesn't make much difference if you don't know how to get in to see him or don't even try. Our Lord never leaves us stranded, he always has a plan for us where we may practice the presence of God.

In the New Testament Paul tells us, the believers, that we are God's building and that Jesus Christ is the foundation. "Don't you know that you yourselves are God's temple and that God's Spirit lives in you?" (1 Cor. 3:16, NIV).

Paul lets us know that we don't have to go out in the desert and build a tabernacle, for we are the home of God and Jesus is the cornerstone. "In him the whole building is joined together and rises to become a holy temple in the Lord. And in him you too are being built together to become a dwelling in which God lives by his Spirit" (Eph. 2:21–22, NIV).

How exciting for us to know that we are God's building and that he lives in us. As we make a place for him in our heart, we must live according to his commandments and stay out of Egypt. We must make a home for him and visit with him often. We must listen to what he has to say as we pray.

"I pray that out of his glorious riches he may strengthen you with power through his Spirit in your inner being, so that Christ may dwell in your hearts through faith" (Eph. 3:16–17, NIV).

THINK ON THESE THINGS

Read Exodus 25–40.

1. If God asked you to build him a tabernacle in your town, what location would you choose? What style would you select for the building? What specific features would you be sure to include? Read Hebrews 9:1–10.

2. When I talked to a friend about my study of the tabernacle, she said in surprise, "I had no idea God cared about all these details. What difference did it make how big things were or what color they used?" What would your response have been to this comment?

3. What reason would you give for the specific use of bronze in the outer court, silver in the Holy Place, and gold in the Holy of Holies? What would the price of these pounds of metal be on today's market (cost per ounce given daily in the newspaper)?

4. For further study read about David's plans for the first temple (1 Chron. 22:5–16; 29:2). See how and why Solomon built the temple (1 Kings 5, 6; 2 Chron. 6:12–13, 7:3). In the back of your study Bible look for the floor plan of Herod's

temple in Jesus' time. What are the similarities in the tabernacle and the two temples?

5. What scripture gives the basis for modern Jewish families to celebrate the Passover and send their children to Hebrew school? Why do you feel Israel has survived against overwhelming odds?

6. Why do you feel Aaron and the people turned from God's clear law so quickly and began to worship a golden calf? What golden calves do we have today? What sometimes happens when we put our focus on a person, perhaps our pastor, and lift him up as God on earth?

7. Do you know anyone so close to God that the person's face glows? What attributes does that person have that set him apart from others?

For Your Notebook

If you are in a group study, make a large floor plan of the tabernacle to use in tracing the steps we will be taking as we enter God's house.

Suggestion. Visit a local Jewish synagogue or temple and take a tour of the facility, paying special note to items that compare with those of the tabernacle and the following temples. Be sure you have a guide who is familiar with the history and the uses of such items as the gold candlesticks, and who can explain the Torah.

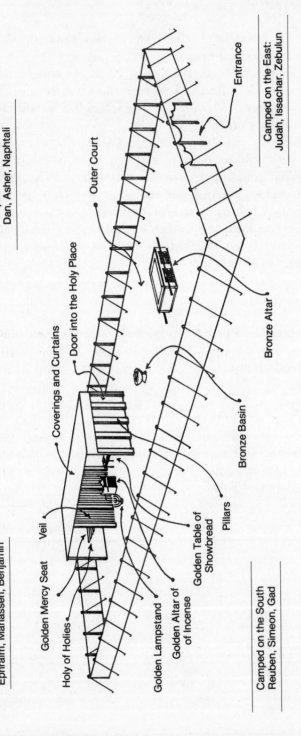

THE TABERNACLE

Camped on the North:
Dan, Asher, Naphtali

Camped on the East:
Judah, Issachar, Zebulun

Entrance

Outer Court

Coverings and Curtains

Door into the Holy Place

Bronze Altar

Bronze Basin

Camped on the West:
Ephraim, Manasseh, Benjamin

Golden Mercy Seat

Veil

Holy of Holies

Golden Lampstand

Golden Altar of of Incense

Golden Table of Showbread

Pillars

Camped on the South
Reuben, Simeon, Gad

◇

4. DWELL IN THE DESERT
—AND BE CONTENT

During the construction of the tabernacle, the Israelites continued to live in the desert. There wasn't much choice. When you leave Egypt, there's nowhere to go but desert.

Psalm 78:52 states: "He brought his people out like a flock; he led them like sheep through the desert" (NIV).

For God's People in Bible Times

At first they were so excited over their deliverance at the hand of God that they sang songs of praise, played timbrels, and danced before the Lord. It was "happy ever after time" until they got dry in the desert and yelled to Moses, "Must we die of thirst?" (Exod. 15:24, TLB).

If you were God, wouldn't you get tired of these people? Nothing made them happy. They'd been passed over and passed through. God moved above them in a visible cloud by day and settled in with them as a pillar of fire at night. What more did they want!

God gave them water, and they cried for food.

He gave them manna from heaven, fresh each day and they got greedy.

He sent quail until they were stuffed with it, and still they complained.

Are there some people who are never satisfied? Are there some who want whatever they don't have? Are there those whom even the Lord himself couldn't please?

God had a whole desert full of them, three million murmuring Hebrews crying out for the good ol' days in Egypt. In

173

spite of their fears, God provided for all their needs. Later
Nehemiah reviewed this period when he called to God,

> Because of your great compassion you did not abandon
> them in the desert. . . . For forty years you sustained them
> in the desert; they lacked nothing, their clothes did not wear
> out nor did their feet become swollen (Neh. 9:19, 21, NIV).

For Us in Today's World

How about you? Have you learned to keep your head above
water? Are you satisfied with quail and manna—or without
either one? Can you say with Paul, "I have learned, in whatsoever state I am, therewith to be content. I know both how to
be abased, and I know how to abound: every where and in all
things I am instructed both to be full and to be hungry, both to
abound and to suffer need" (Phil. 4:11–12, KJV).

Can you also conclude, "I can do all things through Christ
which strengtheneth me!" (v. 13).

Looking for God takes more than an hour on Sunday. It
requires disciplined dedication and the desire to be content
in the desert.

Does God have you in the desert? Sometimes on our way
out of Egypt he lets us live awhile in the desert. So many
Christians I talk with were only churchgoers until they lived
awhile in the desert of divorce, of poverty, of loneliness, of
unforgiveness, of grief, of addictions, of depression, of rejection, of self-pity, of fear, or of disease; but God didn't let them
die in the desert. He met their needs, although not always
their desires.

Many of us don't take that step of spiritual commitment
when our barns are full.

> When your herds and flocks grow large and your silver and
> gold increase and all you have is multiplied, then your heart
> will become proud and you will forget the Lord your God,
> who brought you out of Egypt, out of the land of slavery
> (Deut. 8:13–14, NIV).

When God called me out of Egypt, he literally sent me to the desert of San Bernardino. In retrospect, I see that if he had left me in Connecticut with my big house and prestige in the community, I might have played around on the shores of the Red Sea, dabbling in the good ol' days of Egypt. Instead, he picked us up and moved us from one end of the country to the other and placed us in Bungalow One. While the grounds at Arrowhead Springs were like the Garden of Eden, Bungalow One was hardly paradise. Built in the '30s as a motel, it was like a train going around a curve. Each of the five rooms had a door opening onto a patio and to go from one end to the other you had to go outdoors and cross the cement. The ceilings were falling in, the rugs were down to the nub, and there was no kitchen. As I cooked on a hot plate on the porch, I cried out, "God when I sang 'I'll go where you want me to go' I didn't mean Bungalow One!"

But God did mean Bungalow One, for he knew I needed to spend some time in the desert to shake the Egypt out of me. It was while living in Bungalow One that I started studying the Bible seriously, attending lectures and classes taught by evangelists and theologians, and writing Sunday school lessons. There in the desert, Fred and I created our first marriage class for a local church which led to couples seminars and years later became our book *After Every Wedding Comes a Marriage.* When God wants to get us out of Egypt and into his tabernacle, sometimes he lets us live for a while in the desert.

Surviving a desert experience demands some realistic appraisal of ourselves, for it strips us of pretenses, pulls our props out from under us, and lets us see that we can't do it on our own. We need some outside help that's bigger than we are. Whether your time in the desert is from a broken marriage, a loss of income, or living two years in Bungalow One, whatever the cause, physical or emotional, it is a humbling, perhaps humiliating series of events that can make you bitter for life or cause you to reach for a God who is real.

When Hagar lay crying with her thirsty son in the desert, God knew she had given up just before reaching water. She had quit one step too soon but "The Angel of the Lord found Hagar near a spring in the desert." And he saved her. God will do no less for you and me. When we cry out in the desert he will save us.

David, in depression, wanted to "flee far away and stay in the desert" (Ps. 55:7, NIV). He could see no way out, but God saved him. As a child Jesus "grew and became strong in spirit; and he lived in the desert until he appeared publicly to Israel" (Luke 1:80, NIV). "The word of God came to John . . . in the desert" (Luke 3:2, NIV).

When Paul met the Lord face to face he had such a startling conversion experience, a total change of drive and motives, that he was eager to become an instant Christian leader, but God sent him to the desert for a time of seasoning lest he cause more harm than good. "I went immediately into Arabia and later returned to Damascus" (Gal. 1:17, NIV).

That's what the Lord did with Fred and me. Excited as we were to evangelize the state of Connecticut, he picked us up from those lush green hills and set us down in a desert far away from our Egypt. He closed the Red Sea behind us, we passed the point of no return, and he said, "Sit here in the desert until you're emptied of self and ready for use." Yes, "he humbles those who dwell on high" (Isa. 26:5, NIV).

In these days of financial insecurity, many people I know are having to adjust their standard of living. This step down can put the family in the desert of depression, but the sooner we accept our situation and put curtains up in Bungalow One, the sooner God will move us on. Your "desert [will become] a fertile field" (Isa. 32:15, NIV).

So if you're in the desert today, rejoice; the spring is just ahead. You will become "like streams of water in the desert and the shadow of a great rock in a thirsty land" (Isa. 32:2, NIV).

Don't for a minute think that God has forgotten you. He knows where you are and what lesson he wants you to learn. You may be in the desert, but he's preparing a place for you right now!

Bonus Story

◇ ———————————————————————— ◇

LOOKING FOR GOD IN THE HOSPITAL

When Fred and I were in Baton Rouge we met Gary Hendry. He had always been a good person, a member of a wealthy family, an example to the community, a man who did all the right things. He attended a prestigious church and entertained his friends lavishly expecting nothing in return. He knew who God was, but he'd never spent much time getting to know him. Suddenly he had severe headaches and tests showed he had a malignant brain tumor. Gary went from the pleasures of Egypt to the desert of disease and despair. With the surgery and excruciating treatments that followed, he lay on his back for months knowing he might not live. In his lucid moments, he began to seek the Lord. He asked for relief from the chemotherapy which caused him to remain in bed and promised to spend time encouraging other patients who were in their own peculiar deserts. The doctors wanted him to continue treatments that kept him unable to move, but he decided being immobilized was worse than death. He abandoned the prescribed program and did all he could to build up his energy. He studied God's Word seriously and soon started visiting cancer patients in hospitals.

"Everyone's looking for God," Gary said. "When they find out their disease is terminal, the first question they ask me has something to do with religion."

He told me of one man who wondered if Gary was a minister. "You must have been sent by God. No one else has come to see me."

Another asked him what church he attended and if you could join while in the hospital.

A patient who had just received the bad news of his malignancy and who didn't even know who Gary was begged him to sing old-fashioned hymns, the only touch with God this man could remember. Gary stood beside him and sang while the man cried and clutched his hand. Visitors and nurses paused in the doorway to listen as he led the man to "just a closer walk with thee."

Medically speaking, Gary doesn't have a good prognosis, but as long as God sustains him, he'll provide streams of living water in the deserts of disease.

◇

5. SEEK THE LORD
—AND ENTER HIS GATE

As God prepared a path in the desert for the Hebrew who was sincerely seeking his presence, so he gives us a plan. God could have made the search easier by placing himself in full view of the people, but instead, he fenced his yard and provided only one way to get inside. Why did he make it so difficult for anyone to find him? He wanted each person to care enough to search. Are you willing to follow his plan and take another step toward finding God? Let's move out of our tents and seek the Lord where he may be found.

For God's People in Bible Times

Not every Hebrew who had left Egypt and dwelt in the desert cared enough to seek God and enter his gate. Some were bitter that Moses had settled them down in the wilderness, some still longed for the good ol' days of Egypt, and some didn't want to worship any God who would build his home in a dry desert far away from any civilization. Many remembered the miracles as mere coincidences and were dubious about their traditional God. They'd seen the Pharaoh in his palace surrounded by possessions and they wanted a comparable leader, a God on a throne, one with a royal diadem that they might crown him Lord of Lords.

Instead of their dream of the Promised Land, they were detained in a desert and had only inflated memories of the pomp and circumstance of Egypt. They probably thought, "If there really were a God he surely wouldn't have brought me to a place like this. How could a loving God do this to a good person like me?"

"How often they rebelled against him in the desert and grieved him in the wasteland" (Ps. 78:40, NIV). How quickly they forgot his miracles and how often they murmured and complained over their barren desert experience. "They forgot the God who saved them, who had done great things in Egypt, miracles in the land of Ham and awesome deeds by the Red Sea" (Ps. 106:21–22, NIV).

So God chose to come to earth and dwell among his people, these same people who were wandering in the wilderness wondering what to do. Once his tabernacle had been completed, God asked his people to seek him out. He did not wish to live alone but to fellowship with his neighbors.

We don't find God by living next door to a church, we have to get up and go to him. He wants us to "seek the Lord while he may be found; call on him while he is near" (Isa. 55:6, NIV). He was as near to the Hebrews encamped around his dwelling place as their next-door neighbor, yet "they grumbled in their tents and did not obey the Lord" (Ps. 106:25, NIV).

Imagine how discouraged God must have been with these thankless people who just stayed home and complained. He'd chosen to settle into their midst, he'd excited them with his building program, he'd created a House of God in the desert sands out of materials they'd brought with them from Egypt, and he'd put himself in a visible cloud that hovered white by day and bright by night, but they grumbled in their tents and did not obey the Lord. They wouldn't get up, move toward God, and enter his gate.

For Us in Today's World

How about us? Are we grumbling in our tents, or are we looking for the gate? Are we so full of self-pity that we can't go on? Do we say as they did "If there were really a God why would he leave a nice person like me alone in the desert?"

Moses said, "When you are in distress and all these things have happened to you, then in later days you will return to the Lord your God and obey him" (Deut. 4:30, NIV). He also said you will find the Lord "if you look for him with all your heart and with all your soul" (Deut. 4:29, NIV).

God himself said, "You will seek me and find me when you seek with all your heart" (Jer. 29:13).

Are you ready to seek for God with all your heart and all your soul? If you are, the Bible has exciting news for you and for me. It tells us that the Old Testament tabernacle is a symbol of God's presence in us. It is a shadow of things to come; it is a silhouette of Jesus. "The Word became flesh and lived for a while among us" (John 1:14, NIV).

God takes "The natural elements of creation and transforms them into a symbolic language to depict eternal truths. The tabernacle becomes God's secret code for revealing truth to the sincere and yielding seeker after God . . . the tabernacle is God's flannelgraph."[3]

How grateful we should be that we don't have to go to the Sinai Peninsula to find God. We don't even have to build a tent; for the New Testament—the new covenant—gives us the right to find God in the person of Jesus Christ who says, "When I am lifted up from the earth I will draw everyone to me" (John 12:32, TEV).

"I and the Father are one" (John 10:30, NIV).

"Understand that the Father is in me" (v. 38).

"Anyone who has seen me has seen the Father" (John 14:9, NIV).

As a shadow points to that which casts it, so the God of the tabernacle foreshadows Christ our Lord. As Adam was first man, Christ is First Man. As Isaac was to be sacrificed by his father, Jesus—the only begotten son of God—gave his life for us and became our sacrifice. As Joseph was despised by his brothers, so Christ bore the taunts and jestings of the crowd. And as Joseph forgave his brothers, so Jesus said, "Father forgive them they know not what they do." As Moses was the savior of his people when he led them from bondage to the Promised Land, so Jesus wants to free us and lead us into eternal life when we believe in him. "Everyone who calls on the name of the Lord will be saved" (Acts 2:21, NIV). "Salvation is found in no one else, for there is no other name under heaven given to men by which we must be saved" (Acts 4:12, NIV). In the Old Testament, God came to man in his tabernacle. In the New Testament, and for us, God comes to man in his Son.

When I first found that Jesus was the link between the old and new covenants, suddenly the whole Bible came together and made sense. Jesus wasn't a latter-day idea, but the embodiment of the Old Testament signs and symbols. The tabernacle wasn't just an old tent in the desert, but the figure of our everlasting home in the heavenlies.

"We know that if the earthly tent we live in is destroyed, we have a building from God, an eternal house in heaven, not built by human hands" (2 Cor. 5:1, NIV).

What a comfort to know, as we have left the bondage of Egypt, dwelt in the desert, and begun seeking the Lord, that he is right here, this is the right place. He lives among us and we become temples of his Holy Spirit (1 Cor. 6:19–20). He's not leaving us in a dry thirsty desert, but he's preparing a place for us. And when we are ready to seek him with all our hearts he will come and receive us: that where he is we may also be (John 14:3).

Don't worry about what you've left behind in Egypt. "Seek ye first the kingdom of God, and his righteousness; and all these things shall be added unto you" (Matt. 6:33, KJV).

For God's People in Bible Times

As the Hebrew sought God in the desert, he soon learned he couldn't drop into the tabernacle empty-handed. There was a price to pay to enter into the gates. He had to bring a sacrificial lamb, stop his grumbling in the tents, and "Enter into his gates with thanksgiving and his courts with praise; give thanks to him and praise his name" (Ps. 100:4, NIV).

Let's assume this cheerful Hebrew carrying his lamb headed for the house of God to seek forgiveness. He'd seen the cloud of God's presence and knew God was home. As he approached, he saw a white linen fence in contrast to the black tents where he and his neighbors lived. The fabric fence was too high to look over and too heavy to look through. He had to find some way to enter into the courts of the Lord.

The fence was a barrier to man's ability to reach God, and to get inside he had to be willing to search for the gate with all his heart. He walked around the fence and finally on the east side he found an opening. It wasn't a wrought iron gate or a heavy wooden door; it was a curtain thirty feet wide and woven of blue, purple, scarlet, and white fine-twined linen.

This curtain, custom-designed by God himself, was not of coarse fabric as one might use to make an awning, but of fine-twined linen, the symbol of righteousness. "Fine linen is the righteousness of saints" (Rev. 19:8, NIV). God specified the colors to be used: blue standing for heaven (God's eternal home), purple representing royalty, and scarlet signifying the blood atonement and sacrifice for man's sins on earth.

As we remember our grammar school lessons on color, we can recall that both blue and red are primary colors and that when we blend the two we get purple. Twenty-four times in the book of Exodus these three colors are mentioned in this same order. Since we know God's words are not dropped down by chance, there must be some significance to the sequence; since we know the tabernacle is a foreshadowing of things to come, let's consider how these colors might relate to our Lord Jesus.

Heavenly blue foretells Jesus as Son of God. Earthy scarlet foretells Jesus as Son of Man. And combination purple points to the time when the glory of heaven and earth was united in one person, our Lord Jesus Christ. Jesus is both God and Man, the only religious leader to come to earth as a man, live as both God and Man, do miracles as God, be crucified as a man, and resurrected to be seen both as a man and as God. He had the feelings and hurts of a man with the depth and power of God. His name is "Wonderful, Counselor, Mighty God, Everlasting Father, Prince of Peace" (Isa. 9:6, NIV).

The WORD was made flesh and dwelt among us!

Supporting the thirty-foot-wide curtain of richly woven fabric were four posts, pillars of acacia wood. The hooks of silver held the folds of linen and the bases for each post were of bronze. Once inside the gate, the only entrance to the courtyard, the sinner knew he was saved. His acceptance had nothing to do with how important he was in the world or what good works he'd done, but only upon his decision to enter the gate into the courtyard with his sacrifice in his arms, his commitment to finding God.

As surely as the Red Sea had shut Egypt out of the Hebrew's life, so the curtain that had kept him outside the courts of God now shut him inside close to the very presence of God.

Remember how David sang, "A day in thy courts is better than a thousand. I had rather be a doorkeeper in the house of my God, than to dwell in the tents of wickedness" (Ps. 84:10, KJV).

For Us in Today's World

In our quest for God we have to come to that same decision the Hebrew made: I want to enter into his gates. In our search for an opening to spiritual truth, we often look in the wrong places. I know one lady who has gone to seminars in every possible mystical field including Zen Buddhism, EST, T. A. (Transactional Analysis), B'hai, and Confucianism. She told me, "I want to cover all my bases so no matter what way is *the way* to heaven, I'll be sure to get there." If only she'd known God's Word, for Jesus said, "I am the Door, by me if any man enter in he shall be saved" (John 10:9, KJV). "I am the way, the truth, and the life: no man cometh unto the Father, but by me" (John 14:6, KJV).

As there was one way into the courts of God in Moses' time, there is today one way, one door, into the presence of God. "Verily, verily, I say unto you, He that entereth not by the door . . . but climbeth up some other way, the same is a thief and a robber" (John 10:1, KJV).

The Hebrew in his search came up against a wall and so do we. Somehow we think we're going to make it on our own and suddenly we hit a wall. Their white fence represented the righteousness of God while their surrounding black tents portrayed the sinfulness of man. For sinful man to enter into the presence of God, he had to choose to come through the one gate which, by God's design, faced East in the light of the rising sun. There's no sneaking in to God the back way in the dark; he wants us to be out in the open about our commitment to him.

As we start coming out of our desert experience and start seeking God, we must realize there is a barrier between us and God. But God has provided an open entrance: Jesus Christ the Way, the Truth, and the Life. There is no back door to God, but a wide gate in a bright light waiting for us to enter his courts with praise.

Many of us, however, stand around the door knowing that it's there, but not quite wanting to go in. We eye the door as some kind of a fire-escape; when the flames come we know where to run. For those of us who have been pulling ourselves out of Egypt, wandering in the wilderness, and hoping to find God, just knowing where the door is and what it looks like and perhaps touching the doorpost is not enough. We have to make a decision. Do we want to go inside or not? Are we ready to make a commitment to the Lord Jesus? He is our door, our gate, our way. Have we come this far to turn back? Are we content to be an outsider? Are we going to hover around the door and make a run for it at the last minute?

Let's not wait. Let's make that commitment to our Lord now so that we can enter into his courts with praise.

"Commit your way to the Lord; trust in him" (Ps. 37:5, NIV).

Here is a sample prayer of commitment.

Dear Jesus, I've been looking for God in some odd places and now I'm standing at your door. I see that I'll never get near to God until I pass through this door. I accept that you are the way, the truth, and the life and that I can't come to God except through you. I make a personal commitment to you and ask that you will open the gate that I might come in to the very presence of God.

I pray this in the name of Jesus. Amen.

Bonus Story

◇ —————————————————————————————— ◇

LOOKING FOR GOD IN COMMITMENT

Larry was an extremely attractive businessman who conducted seminars on success. He brought me in to one of his groups that met once a month to teach them about Personality Plus. Before I spoke, he gave the members their "word of the month." He explained they should write down the word *commitment,* read it every morning, and use it often in conversation. As they focused on this word, they would begin to understand "commitment."

They all listened to his instructions and dutifully wrote down their "word of the month."

The next morning Larry called me and said he had to talk with me: would I go out to lunch with him and his wife? As we sat in a corner booth, Larry looked me in the eye and asked, "How do you find God?" For a moment I was stunned; I'd never been questioned quite so bluntly or quickly.

He continued, "I've always been a good person; but my wife just had a mastectomy, and while she was in the hospital and I was faced with the fact that she might die, I had nowhere to turn. I realized I didn't know God. How do you find him?"

By then I had regained my composure, and I started with his teaching of the night before. "Remember how you told everyone to concentrate on the word *commitment*? Commitment to what?"

He hesitated and then answered, "Commitment in general."

"You'll find God when your commitment is specific. A general commitment is an intellectual exercise, but when you commit your life to Jesus, you will come face to face with God."

"I've been committed to good works," he replied, "but somehow when the chips are down, that's not enough."

I then explained that good works are commendable, but they don't bring you into a personal relationship with the Lord. I shared a verse from Ephesians: "For by grace [God's gift] are ye saved through faith [belief, commitment]; and that not of yourselves [not from your earnings and strivings]: it is the gift of God: not of works [no matter how impressive yours may have been], lest any man should boast [or take the credit]" (Eph. 2:8–9, KJV).

"But I'm a self-made man who's committed to excellence."

"There's nothing wrong with good motives, but you won't find the peace of God until your commitment is to Jesus. You have to give up your own will and present yourself as a living sacrifice to the Lord."

I had to assure Larry that a commitment to Jesus was not a weak thing to do, but that it took a strong man to recognize he needed a power beyond himself. I explained that Paul, a man's man, was not ashamed of being a Christian. "I know whom I have believed, and am persuaded that he is able to keep that which I have committed unto him against that day" (2 Tim. 1:12, KJV).

"He'll only keep that which you have committed, Larry. Can you sacrifice your will and commit your life to Jesus?"

Larry was looking for success in life in a word; that day he found meaning to life in The Word!

◇

6. PAY THE PRICE
—AND BE SET FREE

We've all heard the expression, there's no such thing as a free lunch. Somebody has to pay. Whether we go to a concert or fly on a plane, we need a ticket. We have to pay the price. So it was for the Hebrews who wanted to enter the gate and get near to God. Even though they were out in the desert and had no available bank, they had their own currency and a system for using it.

During the forty years the Israelites wandered in the wilderness, the "shekel of the sanctuary" was their medium of exchange and was always looked upon as a divinely ordained coin. Each Hebrew personally paid half a shekel of silver on his twentieth birthday as a ransom to the Lord for his soul. In other offerings, each person gave according to his ability, but in the matter of atonement—making one "at one" with God— all were considered alike. The amount of silver was set low enough so everyone could pay, showing that God didn't accept a person's name for the Book of Numbers or the Book of Life according to his wealth. By paying his atonement money, the Hebrew was declared "not guilty" and the silver represented redemption. Later, after arriving in the Promised Land, the Jews began to use the local Canaanite currency and the "holy shekel" was discontinued until recently.

"After an absence of nearly 2000 years, the shekel— Israel's oldest monetary standard—arrived in Jerusalem early in 1980. Greeted like an archeological find or a returning war hero, it captured newspaper headlines and prime-time television." So stated Bernard Hoenig in an article for *Christian Life* (August, 1983).

"While the *shekel* may not have effectively reduced the severe inflation in Israel," wrote Hoenig, "it has moved the nation closer to its biblical origins, fulfilling a quest that one may recognize in the resurgence of religious faith and a preoccupation with archaeology."[4] Yes, even in Israel today, people are still looking for God, moving closer to their biblical origins, and recognizing the resurgence of religious faith.

For God's People in Bible Times

Not only did the Hebrew of old have to pay his atonement half-shekel, he had to bring an offering to his God. Since the ritual of the tabernacle was new and they had never made sin offerings before, Moses had to educate his people and teach them how to approach God with a gift in hand. As the Hebrew entered the courtyard and brought his sacrifice, the first thing he saw was the altar—the focal point and the center piece, literally "the killing place." He could not step around it, he had to go straight to it. There was no access to God without first making a sacrifice. Sin could only be forgiven by the substitution of an animal for the sinner himself—an innocent animal had to die in place of the guilty man.

The altar of acacia wood overlaid with bronze was a square 7½ feet wide and 3 feet high (Exod. 27:1, TLB). This was no holy hibachi, but a huge bronze altar with a horn on each corner used to bind the victim over the fire. "Bind the sacrifice with cords even unto the horns of the altar" (Ps. 118:27, KJV). The four horns represented the four sides of the fence where the tribes were in tents and also the four corners of the world showing that everyone could come to be forgiven. This altar was a place where God's authority passed judgment on the sinner and his substitutionary lamb.

The fire in the altar was never allowed to go out, showing God's constancy to be available at all times to forgive sin. Before the Hebrew could take one further step toward God, he had to satisfy the demands of the altar. A blood sacrifice is where a walk with God begins.

There were five types of offerings that could be brought: the trespass offering, the sin offering, the burnt offering, the meal offering, and the peace offering.

The *trespass offering*—forgive us our trespasses as we forgive those who trespass against us—was to make atonement and receive forgiveness for sins knowingly committed, to remove the guilt from sins of the past. It was not so much the person as the evil deed that was the focus of this offering. As one comes close to God, he begins to realize, perhaps for the first time, that things he did in the past were sins in the sight of God.

The *sin offering* was to make restitution for sins committed in innocence or ignorance, those unknown things that produce a concerned conscience and need to be purged. "If a soul sin . . . though he wist it not, yet is he guilty" (Lev. 5:17, KJV). Ignorance of the law is no excuse.

From his own flock, the Hebrew brought his sacrificial animal without blemish or spot. He was to bring God the best he had to offer, not some poor sick lamb that was about to expire. As he brought the animal to the altar, it would "be accepted for him to make atonement for him" (Lev. 1:4, KJV). Atonement meant a "covering over"; the blood of the animal stood in for and covered over the guilty man who laid his hand on the animal's head identifying with it, becoming "at one" with it. He then killed it himself. Two substitutions took place: the animal was a substitution for the sinner; then the priest took over and substituted for the sinner by completing the ritual. When the blood was poured out upon the base of the altar, the sinner was forgiven and free, cleansed by the blood of the lamb. "Blessed is he whose transgressions are forgiven, whose sins are covered. Blessed is the man whose sin the Lord does not count against him" (Ps. 32:1–2, NIV).

The other three offerings were called sweet savor offerings given in thanksgiving. The *burnt offering* or ascending offering was presented to God for his pleasure and delight resulting in a feeling of acceptance for the one presenting it. "The Lord taketh pleasure in his people" (Ps. 149:4, KJV).

The offering was not begging for forgiveness, but asking for acceptance; it was not based on the individual's merit, but upon God's mercy.

The *meal offering* was food for the priest made of fine flour that had not been sifted or bruised, showing God's perfection and holiness. Oil, the symbol for the Holy Spirit, was poured on it and frankincense, meaning purity and fragrance, was added. The hotter the fire got, the more beautiful the aroma. No leaven (which represented evil) was to be used and no honey (which represented human sweetness, easily turned sour under fire). Salt was added for flavor and as a preservative.

The *peace offering* was shared by Jehovah, the priest, and the individual and was a prototype of our communion. The offering satisfied God, and the priest was at peace with the one who brought it and was free to share, minister, break bread with the forgiven sinner.

For Us in Today's World

As man approached God in the Old Testament tabernacle at the altar, we can come close to God in only one way through his son Jesus Christ—"He that hath seen me hath seen the father" (John 14:9). To go beyond the Gate of the Christian life and step toward the presence of the Father, we must pay the price, bring an offering, make a sacrifice. Although many churches and evangelists put an emphasis on the need for money, God doesn't require even half a shekel from us in order that we be acceptable unto him. Our salvation is a free gift costing nothing. "For by grace are ye saved through faith; and that not of yourselves: it is the gift of God: Not of works, lest any man should boast" (Eph. 2:8–9, KJV). If we could buy our way to heaven by money or openly work to achieve greatness, then only those with wealth or talent would be acceptable and able to find God. As in the Old Testament, the door is open to each one of us to come face to face with God, but for us the door is Jesus, and he has

already laid himself on the altar for us. "Ye were not redeemed with corruptible things, as silver and gold. . . . But
with the precious blood of Christ" (1 Pet. 1:18–19, KJV).

By following in the steps of the Hebrew as he searched for
God, we have left our Egypt behind. Some of us have wandered in the wilderness, and some are still dwelling in a
desert. We've realized we can't go on in our own power, and
so we've been looking for God in all kinds of places. I found
the Lord in a restaurant. Fred found him in church, Lauren in
Pioneer Girls, Marita in the hospital before having her tonsils
out, young Fred in Campus Crusade Nursery School, one of
Fred's brothers in front of a TV, and another one on a park
bench while contemplating suicide. *We can find God anywhere when we seek for him with all our hearts.*

Many of us have come up against a wall of trouble. We've
tried to go over it, under it, around it, or ignore it; but eventually we have to go through it. Suddenly there is a way, one
way. A gate so wide all can enter; "I am the door." When we
present ourselves at the ticket booth, we find our way has
already been paid. We don't have to put up even a half-shekel,
but we do have to offer up a sacrifice of our own free will.

Does that mean we must bring a lamb without spot or
blemish to church with us every Sunday? How do we lay our
gift on the altar?

We must first realize that the actual shedding of the animal's blood did not physically change the life of the sinner; it
was an outward sign that he was willing to confess to God and
give him an offering to represent his inner nature so that his
guilt might be relieved. Every time he sinned he was to
present himself to God for absolution, and there was never a
time when he'd paid the price completely.

For us, God sent his perfect son, the Lamb of God who
takes away the sins of the world. He becomes our substitute
as the lamb became the substitute for the Hebrews. No
longer do we have to trudge to the altar with a lamb; Christ
has paid it all.

I had heard all these terms as a child. But until I understood the pattern God gave at the tabernacle, I had no idea

why Christ was called a lamb, why he'd paid it all, why we were cleansed by the blood. Things that sounded demeaning, almost offensive, suddenly made sense. The tabernacle was a foretelling of what Christ was going to do for you and me. Now I could understand why John said, "Behold the Lamb of God, which taketh away the sin of the world" (John 1:29, KJV). Now I knew why Peter explained we are redeemed by "the precious blood of Christ, as of a lamb without blemish and without spot" (1 Pet. 1:19, KJV). Why Paul said, "God made him who had no sin to be sin for us, so that in him we might become the righteousness of God" (2 Cor. 5:21, NIV).

The trespass offering for us. One of the first things that happens to the new believer as he seeks fellowship with God is his overwhelming awareness of sin in his life. White lies (previously explainable acts), rebellious attitudes, loose morals, swearing, critical words, and other patterns of behavior that had appeared above average in the ways of the world, suddenly are seen as sin.

Fred and his family had been steeped in the tenets of a cult that had taught them they were God's perfect children and there was no such thing as sin. Lovely as these lines were (and much to be hoped for), these beliefs were in direct opposition to the Bible's "all have sinned, and come short of the glory of God" (Rom. 3:23, KJV). When Fred committed his life to his Lord and entered into his gates with thanksgiving, he immediately saw himself in a new light. He looked in a bright, spiritual mirror instead of the "glass darkly" and came face to face with God and himself. As he says, "I didn't like what I saw."

Although he'd always been a moral person, suddenly he felt guilt and shame and he didn't know how to deal with it. He saw "No trespassing" signs on every corner. I can remember wondering how to handle the new Fred who was morose, depressed, and guilt-stricken. I'd spent fifteen years with his self-confident perfectionism, and I'd learned to put on a phlegmatic mask and feign obedience. What was I to do now? A repentant spirit was frightening.

We went from Connecticut to Arrowhead Springs, California, to a Lay Institute for Evangelism, and the first night Bill

Bright had us go to our rooms and write down all our sins. Sinless Fred wrote and wrote. I was dying to see what he'd found to confess, but before I could peek, he did what he'd been instructed to do: he ripped up the list and threw it away. He'd laid the sins that God had brought before him on the altar. He'd made a trespass offering.

"You were dead in sins, and your sinful desires were not yet cut away. Then he gave you a share in the very life of Christ, for he forgave all your sins" (Col. 2:13, TLB). Our Father who art in heaven forgives us our trespasses.

The sin offering for us. As we become aware of the misdeeds, which we have perpetrated upon ourselves and others, and confess these trespasses to the Lord, he forgives us of these specific acts. But our second awareness comes when we realize that our whole nature is self-centered and that we continue to sin in spite of our good intentions. We find that we must continue to bring our sin offering to the Lord and confess our rebellious attitudes as well as our overt acts. As the Hebrew people did, we, too, must bring a sacrifice for our sins of ignorance. We are not to sit in ignorance forever, using that as an excuse to test God's grace, but we are to study his Word in a personal effort to become aware of what we formerly did while unaware.

We are, as Paul says, to put off the old man with his deeds, our old nature, and put on the new man "renewed in knowledge after the image of him that created him" (Col. 3:10, KJV). To change takes a step of action. We are not to sit in our sins, saying, "If God wants me to be different, he knows where to find me."

The sin offering was to be without blemish so that eliminates us and any animal we might find, but we can rejoice for Jesus is our Lamb without blemish or spot. We can never be good enough to get to heaven on our own merit, but we don't have to.

But now God has shown us a different way to heaven—not by "being good enough" and trying to keep his laws, but by a new way (though not new, really, for the Scriptures told about it long ago). Now God says he will accept and acquit us—declare us "not guilty"—if we trust Jesus Christ to take away our sins. And we all can be saved in this same way, by coming to Christ, no matter who we are or what we have been like. Yes, all have sinned; all fall short of God's glorious ideal; yet now God declares us "not guilty" of offending him if we trust in Jesus Christ, who in his kindness freely takes away our sins (Rom. 3:21–24, TLB).

Yes, Jesus has paid it all, but God wants a personal sacrifice from each one of us, and it doesn't involve building an altar in the backyard and killing a spotless lamb. David, who understood and practiced the Old Testament ceremony of sacrifice, finally caught the spirit of the ritual after his sin of adultery with Bathsheba. When he realized he had violated one of the commandments he taught to others, he cried in repentance to God: "You do not delight in sacrifice, or I would bring it; you do not take pleasure in burnt offerings. The sacrifices of God are a broken spirit; a broken and contrite heart, O God, you will not despise" (Ps. 51:16–17, NIV).

David says, "I know the rules and I have the money. I could give you the best bull and the whitest lamb you've ever seen and say, 'Here it is Lord, forgive me.' I could buy my way to salvation, but that's not what you want of me. You want a repentant heart, a broken spirit. You want me to accept the blame for my sin and give you not animals but a genuine contrite heart. Wash me with your blood and make me, a sinner, white as snow" (see Ps. 51).

What does God want of you and me? A farm full of fluffy sheep? No, a broken and a contrite heart. If you've been pulling out of Egypt, dwelling in a desert tent, seeking God, and standing at his gates, perhaps what you need to do is to present yourself to God—offer him your contrite heart as a sin offering.

When I first gave myself to God, I prayed to receive Christ through Romans 12:1–2. I even taught the meaning of these verses to others and many were won to the Lord through the faithful use of this scripture, but only when I studied the tabernacle did I come to a useful understanding and practical application.

Paul "beseeches" us, begs us, pleads with us—knowing that it won't be easy for many—to present our "bodies a living sacrifice, holy, acceptable unto God, which is [our] reasonable service" (Rom 12:1, 2, KJV). In light of what I now know about the tabernacle, I understand that Paul is asking us to lay ourselves on the altar as Abraham laid Isaac, as the Hebrew laid the lamb, and as Jesus laid himself. We are to present our bodies as a living sacrifice in contrast to the death of the lamb. He does not want you and me to sign some death pact and commit suicide. He wants us to stay very much alive, but to give up our strong self-will; he wants us to give our "control panel" to him. This "giving-up" of self is a holy act, much like that in which the Old Testament Hebrew gave up his offering. When we understand that he wants us, not an animal, doesn't that become a "reasonable service"?

God asks us to "be not conformed to the world," but to be "transformed." He wants to renew our minds, erase the old guilt, sharpen up our thinking so that we can begin to get a glimpse of his good, acceptable, and perfect will for each one of us.

How gracious of God to send his son as savior, substitute, and sample of how we should present ourselves—body, mind, and spirit—as living sacrifices. Jesus has paid the price that we might have the free gift of eternal life.

Oswald Chambers sums it up so well:

> God pays no respect to anything we bring him: there is only one thing God wants of us and that's our unconditional surrender. . . .
> The natural life is not spiritual and it can only be made spiritual by sacrifice. If we do not resolutely sacrifice the natural, the supernatural can never become natural in us. Beware of refusing to go to the funeral of your own independence.[5]

The burnt offering for us. This offering had little to do with sin but was praise given to God for his pleasure. It was presented as if to say: I know I'm not a perfect person, but I love you and I want to be accepted as your child, identified with you. I'm presenting myself as a living sacrifice, hoping to be holy and wanting to be acceptable in your sight.

How exciting it is to finally come to the realization that Christ stands in for me. I can never be good enough on my own, but when I am totally identified with Christ, I become worthy and acceptable. I can't stand before a holy God on my own, but as Jesus increases in my life and we become one in spirit, I am no longer a lost sinner, looking for God, I am there in his presence and he approves of me! Christ gave "himself for us an offering and a sacrifice to God for a sweetsmelling savor" (Eph. 5:2, KJV). He stood in for you and me, and God the Father is pleased!

The meal offering for us. This food presented for the priest was a representation of the Lord Jesus, perfect man, who said of himself "I am the true Bread from heaven; and anyone who eats this Bread shall live forever, and not die as your fathers did—though they ate bread from heaven" (John 6:58, TLB).

Jesus is our meal offering made of fine flour.

He was "anointed Jesus of Nazareth with the Holy Ghost and with power" (Acts 10:38, KJV). He had the oil of the spirit, the purity and aroma of frankincense. There was no leaven, no evil, in him nor any necessity for added sweetness or honey. His message was not bland, without salt, but clear and pungent. He was the salt of the earth that had not lost its savor.

Although you and I can't physically lay the Lord on the altar as a meal offering, we can serve, feed, and minister to others in his name, knowing that he who offers a cup of cool water to anyone has given it to Jesus.

The peace offering for us. As the burnt offering was only for Jehovah God, the peace offering was to be shared with others. God received his portion (the fat parts of a bullock, a lamb, or a goat which were burnt on the altar), and then the priest received his portion (the breast that was waved and the thigh that was presented) which was to be eaten by his family in a holy place. This offering was a forerunner of the communion Christ shared with his disciples and an example for us today as we partake of the bread and the wine.

Paul says, "Is not the cup of thanksgiving for which we give thanks a participation in the blood of Christ? And is not the bread that we break a participation in the body of Christ?" (1 Cor. 10:16, NIV).

> Whoever eats the bread or drinks the cup of the Lord in an unworthy manner will be guilty of sinning against the body and blood of the Lord. A man ought to examine himself before he eats of the bread and drinks of the cup. For anyone who eats and drinks without recognizing the body of the Lord eats and drinks judgment on himself (1 Cor. 11:27–29, NIV).

As the blood of the lamb cleansed the Hebrew of his sins, the blood of the Lamb, sacrificed for you and for me, has already cleansed us.

Jesus himself said, as he gave his disciples a symbolic cup, "This is my blood of the new testament, which is shed for many for the remission of sins" (Matt. 26:28, KJV).

How important it is for us to understand the Old Testament so we can grasp the meaning of the New. How exciting communion could become for us if we caught the deep concept of why Jesus died "for the remission of sins" and could see that Jesus paid the price once and for all.

"He did not enter by means of the blood of goats and calves; but he entered the Most Holy Place once for all by his own blood, having obtained eternal redemption. . . . Without the shedding of blood there is no forgiveness" (Heb. 9:12, 22, NIV).

We come to God through the blood of Christ not by our money or good works. He is our sacrificial lamb; we have salvation by his substitution.

As we look for God today, we have to leave our worldly conformity in Egypt, keep our faith in the heat of our own personal desert, and seek the Lord with all our hearts, leaning not unto our own understandings. When we have come this far and still don't see the physical figure of Father God before us, we believe Jesus who said, "I am the way, the truth, and the life: no man cometh unto the Father, but by me" (John 14:6, KJV). There is only one way! Christ has paid the price, and we are free!

As we take communion, eating of the Bread of Life and drinking of the Cup of Thanksgiving, we prepare ourselves to move one step closer to the Holy Place and our Father God.

THINK ON THESE THINGS

Read Leviticus 1–7, 17.

1. When did God first show you that you had to leave Egypt? Under what circumstances? What desires of the past has God changed over the last years? In what other ways do you sense God's direction in your life?

2. What kind of a desert are you in today—loneliness? depression? self-pity? Can you figure out why God is allowing you to be there? What lesson might he have to teach you before you become a stream of living water for a thirsty world?

3. Isn't it true of human nature that we cry out for God when we're in need and then forget him in times of plenty? What is the meaning of the saying from World War II, "There are no atheists in foxholes"? Why do you feel God decided to come to earth and live in the tabernacle?

4. Picture yourself as a father who came to live in the town of his married children to bring them gifts and joy and peace. How would you feel if they wouldn't walk down the street to see you but just stayed home grumbling and complaining about what they didn't have that you were waiting to give them? Does that thought give you some idea of how discouraged God must have been when he established his home in the midst of his people and they didn't come rushing to see him?

5. What similarities do you find between Moses and Jesus—in childhood background, in ministry, in miracles, in leadership, in reaction from the people? What does this show you about doing God's work for personal gain or prestige?

6. Now that you've seen the floor plan of the tabernacle, what interpretation do you have of Psalm 100:4, "Enter into his gates with thanksgiving, and into his courts with praise"? Psalm 84:10, "For a day in thy courts is better than a thousand. I had rather be a doorkeeper in the house of my God, than to dwell in the tents of wickedness"? How does this view differ from what you might have thought in the past?

7. What fence did, or does, stand between you and a relationship with God? Why do you think there was no "back door" into the courtyard? What significance is there to you in the verse, "I am the door"?

8. What is the difference in the cost of the Hebrew coming to God and us coming to God? Explain this plan of salvation to someone new this week.

9. How do the trespass offering and sin offering differ? Give an example of each in your own life.

10. What have you done recently just for the joy of pleasing God? When have you last presented a "meal offering" to your pastor or Christian worker? How could you have a communion meal according to the Old Testament?

For Your Notebook

Do a word study on blood, using a concordance and a dictionary, for a deeper understanding of the importance God puts on this fluid so necessary for life and for forgiveness. "For the life of the flesh is in the blood: and I have given it to you upon the altar to make an atonement for your souls: for it is the blood that maketh an atonement for the soul" (Lev. 17:11, KJV).

◇

7. FOLLOW THE LEADER
—AND BE CLEANSED

When God designed the tabernacle and its furnishings, he could have left it unattended, expecting each individual who was seeking him to figure out for himself how to move from the gate into the presence of God. He could have let each person devise his own plan of salvation and create his own unique offering, but he didn't. Instead, he provided a leader—he appointed priests and ordained them to carry out the sacrifices and other duties exactly as he prescribed in order that those seeking would all find the Lord.

For God's People in Bible Times

How did God make his choice for leadership when he had no personnel records or standard job descriptions? If you were God, where would you find qualified men for these spiritual positions out in a desert? There were twelve tribes to choose from, and none were noted for their godliness.

For a résumé on each of Jacob's sons, let's look at Genesis 49 which records the comments given by Jacob on his deathbed when he called his sons together and reviewed their personalities. The following is a summary of what Jacob had to say about each of his sons. As you read, think about which one you would choose as a high priest.

Reuben: You are the oldest but the most unruly. You slept with one of my wives, dishonored me, and were not repentant. Because of that, I'm demoting you, and you will not receive the double portion of the firstborn.

Simeon and Levi: You are two of a kind, men of violence

and injustice, murderers, angry, fierce, and cruel. I will scatter your descendants throughout Israel.

Judah: You were a wild youth, but you have settled down and your brothers shall praise you. You are like a powerful lion and from you will come kings.

Zebulun: You shall live by the sea with your borders extending to Sidon.

Issachar: You are a strong beast of burden and will work hard on the land.

Dan: You are like a serpent in the path that bites the horses' heels and causes the riders to fall off.

Gad: You will be pursued, but you will defend your land.

Asher: You will "produce rich foods fit for kings."

Naphtali: You are "like a deer let loose, producing lovely fawns."

Joseph: You were severely injured by your own brothers who sold you as a slave. Because of your forgiving spirit, you will become as a fruitful tree beside a fountain with branches shading the wall. May God's blessings on you reach to the utmost bounds of the everlasting hills and may your sons be blessed as you receive a double portion through Ephraim and Manasseh.

Benjamin: You are like a wolf on the prowl who devours his enemies each morning.

If you were in God's position, which tribe would you choose to be the family of priests and serve you in your new home on earth? If I were making a spiritual selection, I'd cancel out Reuben, Simeon, Levi, Dan, and Benjamin for their bad records of the past. Zebulun and Gad sound inoffensive but dull. Issachar is a hard worker, certainly a commendable trait for a man of ministry, and Asher and his descendants are good cooks. Perhaps those two tribes could take care of all my needs. Naphtali would make me nervous leaping around like a deer. Judah is the logical choice as his descendants were to produce kings, but sometimes important people don't have a servant's heart. In the final analysis, the tribes stemming from Joseph deserve a break. When I consider the humiliation Joseph suffered at the hands of these brothers, I could make no other choice!

However, God made an unlikely selection. He put the call and the anointing upon the tribe of Levi, a cruel and angry man. Does God make mistakes or does he sometimes choose a person unqualified in the eyes of the world in order to show his transforming power? Even today many of God's most noted servants come out of backgrounds that seemingly do not fit them for Christian leadership. How God loves to take the foolish of the world and make them confound the wise. When Saul was chosen by Samuel to be the first king of the Israelites, his friends were dumbfounded over the selection. They asked among themselves, "What is this that has happened to the son of Kish? Is Saul also among the prophets? . . . How can this fellow save us?" (1 Sam. 10:11, 27, NIV). Only God could have seen commendable qualities in Saul of Tarsus as he was out killing off the Christians, and only God would have taken a chance on transforming him into Paul the great evangelist who convinced others of the power of God to change lives.

Yes, God is all-powerful, and he delights in taking any unlikely person and transforming him before the eyes of a skeptical world. So God chose Aaron as the first High Priest and his brother Levites to serve with him. This Aaron was the same Aaron who served as mouthpiece for his brother Moses in Egypt, the same sanguine who invited the complaining Hebrews to an orgy while melancholy Moses was on the mountain communing with God, the same immature person who made a golden calf out of the women's jewelry and then blamed it all on them—"You know these people. They are bent on mischief! Surely it wasn't my fault."

No wonder God told Moses to take Aaron aside and wash him with water before the dedication. He washed him completely, cleansed him of his old frivolous life, and with God's power caused Aaron to be regenerated, born again. He became a new creature, the High Priest.

From then on, the one-time cleansing of the old life and the daily washing away of new sinful deeds before serving God became a ritual for the priests. To facilitate the frequent cleansing process, God said to Moses:

> Make a bronze basin with a bronze pedestal. Put it between the Tabernacle and the altar, and fill it with water. Aaron and his sons shall wash their hands and feet there, when they go into the Tabernacle to appear before the Lord, or when they approach the altar to burn offerings to the Lord. They must always wash before doing so, or they will die (Exod. 30:17–20, TLB).

> The bronze washbasin and its bronze pedestal were cast from the solid bronze mirrors donated by the women who assembled at the entrance to the Tabernacle (Exod. 38:8, TLB).

Isn't it fascinating that God used the mirror, a symbol of self-examination, to make a basin purposed to wash the sin of self away!

For Us in Today's World

Paul tells us that "We can be mirrors that brightly reflect the glory of the Lord. And as the Spirit of the Lord works within us, we become more and more like him" (2 Cor. 3:18, TLB). And "God is always at work in us to make us willing and able to obey his own purpose" (Phil. 2:13, TEV).

As God assigned Moses to wash the priests before they were to serve him, so Jesus wants to cleanse you and me of sin in our lives. He wants us to come before him and agree with him that we need to be changed. "If we confess our sins, he is faithful and just to forgive us our sins, and cleanse us from all unrighteousness" (1 John 1:9, KJV).

When we bring ourselves as an offering before Christ our High Priest, he forgives us; and as we recognize and confess our sin, he cleanses us. We are saved by the blood of Jesus *once* and cleansed by the water of forgiveness and restoration *daily*. Salvation is a one-time act of faith, but as we make mistakes and don't live according to God's will, we need to seek his forgiveness and cleansing each day.

As Paul wrote to Titus:

> Not by works of righteousness which we have done, but according to his mercy he saved us, by the washing of regeneration, and renewing of the Holy Ghost (Titus 3:5, KJV).

We can be born again and given a new clean life no matter what our past may have been. So:

> Let us draw near with a true heart in full assurance of faith, having our hearts sprinkled from an evil conscience, and our bodies washed with pure water (Heb. 10:22, KJV).

Let us praise Christ as our High Priest—"him that loved us and washed us from our sins in his own blood" (Rev. 1:5, KJV).

Frequently I talk with people who feel God couldn't possibly accept them. Some are innocent victims of childhood abuse who still feel they were to blame. Some have done terrible things they assume God could never forgive. Some have habits which the local church they want to join will not accept.

A God who would choose to transform the Levites into spiritual leaders, and a man like Aaron into a high priest, or Saul into a king and Paul into an evangelist can surely clean anyone of us up if we'll only ask.

"Having therefore these promises, dearly beloved, let us cleanse ourselves from all filthiness of the flesh and spirit, perfecting holiness in the fear of God" (2 Cor. 7:1, KJV).

For God's People in Bible Times

As we have seen, the priests were not chosen because of their training, education, wealth, character, spirituality, or personal holiness. God chose ordinary people and set them apart, sanctified them for his service. So often today as I train people to be Christian leaders, they will say, "God could never use me." They then give lists of their lacks, not understanding that God doesn't need credentials. He confers his own degrees.

When God chose Aaron to represent him he proclaimed:

> Make special clothes for Aaron, to indicate his separation to God—beautiful garments that will lend dignity to his work. Instruct those to whom I have given special skill as tailors to make the garments that will set him apart from others, so that he may minister to me in the priest's office (Exod. 28:2–3, TLB).

I am so glad that God dressed Aaron in spectacular clothes and did not say, "If you are going to be a leader, you must wear only gray and try to blend in with the wallpaper" or "you must be sure your clothes are at least five years out of date and hide all your jewelry!" I'm glad he said Aaron should have beautiful clothes that would add dignity to his work and enhance his leadership.

How beautiful were these clothes to be? The first garment placed on Aaron was a white linen coat, representing the purity and holiness of God. Next came "the curious girdle" or belt tying his undercoat to his body and signifying his willingness to serve. Over this was put a robe of blue, the color of heaven, showing that he had been chosen by God, not by man.

For those of you who thought the layered look was a new idea, picture an ephod draped over the white coat, girdle, and blue robe. The ephod was a special item worn only by the high priest and most nearly imagined by us as a type of cobbler's apron: two pieces of cloth joined at the shoulders. As was the curtain at the gate of the tabernacle, the ephod was woven of fine-twined linen of blue, purple, and scarlet. Added to this were fine wires of gold interlaced into the material and done with "cunning work."

If these were not enough, there were added two stones of onyx to be worn on the shoulders of the high priest. Each of these stones was to be engraved with the names of the twelve tribes; six on each shoulder in order of their birth. These two large stones, estimated to be ninety-five carats apiece, were set in gold and joined to the ephod by gold rope chains. As the high priest moved about, these stones faced up to heaven, constantly carrying the names of the twelve tribes before the Lord as a reminder.

Hung on the front of the priest was a breastplate, not a heavy metal shield as it might sound but a nine-by-eighteen-inch piece of linen fabric of blue, purple, and scarlet interlaced with gold. This cloth was folded in half making a nine-by-nine-inch square with a pocket in the bottom to carry the Urim and Thummim, the divining stones used in making yes and no decisions.

Attached to the front of this linen square were four rows of three stones apiece, each stone representing a tribe. (See diagram, p. 208.)

Can you imagine the beauty and brilliance of this array of gemstones? Picture the largest cut stone you've ever seen and multiply it by twelve. This will give you some idea of how spectacular the breastplate was and of how God wanted his priest to stand out in the crowd.

This jewel-encrusted cloth was attached to the ephod by gold ropes threaded through gold rings. At the bottom, the blue fabric, representing heaven, was tied down with the blue ribbons of obedience. These same blue ribbons were placed on the borders of garments for generations as an earthly sign of obedience to a heavenly God.

"Put upon the fringe of the borders a ribband of blue: And it shall be unto you for a fringe, that ye may look upon it, and remember all the commandments of the Lord, and do them" (Num. 15:38–39, KJV).

Again God was specific when he instructed that the neck opening of the ephod be bound in gold so it would not fray and the bottom edge be embroidered in tri-color pomegranates alternating with gold bells that would tinkle when Aaron came into the presence of God. This breastplate was what we might call a large prayer list keeping the needs of the people out before God.

BREASTPLATE AND ONYX EPHOD SHOULDER PIECES

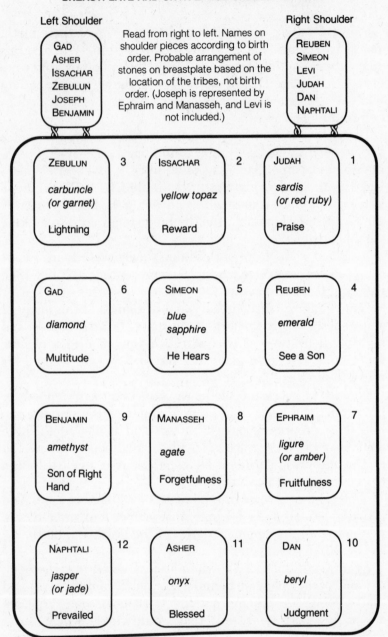

Left Shoulder

GAD
ASHER
ISSACHAR
ZEBULUN
JOSEPH
BENJAMIN

Read from right to left. Names on shoulder pieces according to birth order. Probable arrangement of stones on breastplate based on the location of the tribes, not birth order. (Joseph is represented by Ephraim and Manasseh, and Levi is not included.)

Right Shoulder

REUBEN
SIMEON
LEVI
JUDAH
DAN
NAPHTALI

ZEBULUN 3 *carbuncle* *(or garnet)* Lightning	ISSACHAR 2 *yellow topaz* Reward	JUDAH 1 *sardis* *(or red ruby)* Praise
GAD 6 *diamond* Multitude	SIMEON 5 *blue* *sapphire* He Hears	REUBEN 4 *emerald* See a Son
BENJAMIN 9 *amethyst* Son of Right Hand	MANASSEH 8 *agate* Forgetfulness	EPHRAIM 7 *ligure* *(or amber)* Fruitfulness
NAPHTALI 12 *jasper* *(or jade)* Prevailed	ASHER 11 *onyx* Blessed	DAN 10 *beryl* Judgment

This chart is based on information from *The Tabernacle of Moses* by Kevin J. Conner and *The Tabernacle—The Priesthood and the Offerings* by Henry W. Soltau. (For publication information, see bibliography p. 251.)

"In this way Aaron shall carry the names of the tribes of Israel on the chestpiece over his heart (it is God's oracle) when he goes in to the Holy Place; thus Jehovah will be reminded of them continually" (Exod. 28:29, TLB).

On his head the high priest was to wear a turban made of white linen. His head was to be covered as a sign to God that he was submissive and obedient. This diadem, mitre, or crown was also an indication of royal station, thus combining the idea of kingship and humility. Across the front of the turban, tied on with blue ribbons, was a plate of pure gold engraved with the words: *Consecrated to Jehovah.*

"In this way Aaron will be wearing it upon his forehead, and thus bear the guilt connected with any errors regarding the offerings of the people of Israel. It shall always be worn when he goes into the presence of the Lord, so that the people will be accepted and forgiven" (Exod. 28:37–38, TLB).

After Aaron was correctly clothed, he and his brothers were officially consecrated to the Lord. Aaron put on his white coat, curious girdle, blue robe, ornate woven ephod, bejeweled breastplate, white turban, and engraved gold medallion. These seven items were worn during the seven days of dedication.

Moses, under instructions from God, had the anointing oil made by skilled perfume makers. The mixture contained eighteen pounds each of pure myrrh and cassia, nine pounds of cinnamon and sweet cane, and one and one-half gallons of pure olive oil (see Exod. 30:22–24, TLB). This special oil was to be used for holy dedication only. God said,

> It must never be poured upon an ordinary person, and you shall never make any of it yourselves, for it is holy, and it shall be treated by you as holy. Anyone who compounds any incense like it or puts any of it upon someone who is not a priest shall be excommunicated (Exod. 30:32–33, TLB).

A special offering of the ram of consecration was also made at the dedication of Aaron and his sons as priests. Moses put the blood of the ram on the Levites' right ears, right thumbs, and right big toes. After their dedication the priests were to serve as intercessors, connectors, and go-betweens. As the guilty sinner came to them at the altar with his sacrifice, the priests were to stand in for him, and the high priest with his breastplate of names was to continually bring them all before the Lord. The high priest became the connecting link between sinful man and holy God. He represented the people as a lawyer would stand in for a client; he was the line of communication between the caller and the receiver (see Exod. 29).

For Us in Today's World

How do you and I find God when we don't have Aaron around and our names aren't engraved on precious gemstones? Who is our intercessor? Do we need some holy man in a costume to hold us before God? Where is our leader?

The book of Hebrews gives us an answer. "Jesus was faithful to God who appointed him High Priest, just as Moses also faithfully served in God's house" (Heb. 3:2, TLB). "Christ . . . is our High Priest, and is in heaven at the place of greatest honor next to God himself. He ministers in the temple in heaven, the true place of worship built by the Lord and not by human hands" (Heb. 8:1–2, TLB).

Our Jesus wears the white robe of righteousness and the girdle of a servant. As the high priest, who served in the tabernacle, bore the names of the twelve tribes on his shoulders, so our High Priest carries each one of us before the throne of our Father in heaven.

As Aaron carried the separate tribes before God on his bosom, so our Lord "poured out his life unto death, and was numbered with the transgressors. For he bore the sin of many, and made intercession for the transgressors" (Isa. 53:12, NIV).

Yes, Jesus bears our sins until he can present us as faultless in the very presence of God.

As the high priest interceded for the sinner so is Christ "sitting at the place of highest honor next to God, pleading for us there in heaven" (Rom. 8:34, TLB).

As the priest washed the sins away in the bronze laver, so

Jesus washes his church "to make her holy and clean, washed by baptism and God's Word; so that he could give her to himself as a glorious church without a single spot or wrinkle or any other blemish, being holy and without a single fault" (Eph. 5:26–27, TLB).

As Aaron wore a mitre on his head, so Jesus was "crowned . . . with glory and honor" (Heb. 2:7, TLB). As the gold plate said, "Consecrated to Jehovah," so our Lord was set apart and sanctified for us.

As the priest was chosen from among men, "it was necessary for Jesus to be like us, his brothers, so that he could be our merciful and faithful High Priest before God, a Priest who would be both merciful to us and faithful to God in dealing with the sins of the people" (Heb. 2:17, TLB).

As Moses anointed Aaron with oil made from a secret recipe never to be duplicated, so the Holy Spirit anoints us for Christian service. Peter stated, "And you no doubt know that Jesus of Nazareth was anointed by God with the Holy Spirit and with power, and he went around doing good and healing all who were possessed by demons, for God was with him" (Acts 10:38, TLB).

As Moses put the sacrificial blood of the ram on the priests' right ears, thumbs, and big toes, so we in dedication to our Lord should constantly listen for his voice even in the midst of daily noise and confusion; we should serve and encourage others with our hands; and we should walk in the courtyard of our God following the path in which he leads.

"God was patient with them forty years, though they tried his patience sorely; he kept right on doing his mighty miracles for them to see. 'But,' God says, 'I was very angry with them, for their hearts were always looking somewhere else instead of up to me, and they never found the paths I wanted them to follow'" (Heb. 3:9–10, TLB).

O God, may we be faithful in finding the paths you want us to follow.

"Moses did a fine job working in God's house, but he was only a servant; and his work was mostly to illustrate and suggest those things that would happen later on. But Christ, God's faithful Son, is in complete charge of God's house. And we Christians are God's house—he lives in us if we keep our courage firm to the end, and our joy and our trust in the Lord" (Heb. 3:5–6, TLB).

Now that we see Jesus as our High Priest, making intercession for you and for me with the Father, how can we apply this in our own lives so that we can follow the pattern set by our Lord? We can't go to the Holy Place, but we can bring the needs of others to the Lord in prayer; for as Peter says, we are a royal priesthood. "You have been chosen by God himself—you are priests of the King, you are holy and pure, you are God's very own—all this so that you may show to others how God called you out of the darkness into his wonderful light" (1 Pet. 2:9, TLB).

In review, God chose Aaron as high priest to go between the guilty man in need of cleansing and God himself. As the high priest went before God, he brought the name of the sinner who was then forgiven.

In New Testament times, God chose his son Jesus as our leader, as the intercessor for us. As our High Priest, Jesus brings our needs before the Father. He is our go-between when we wish to enter the Holy Place and stand before God.

By following the steps of our High Priest, we will come into the presence of God. "Yes, the old system of priesthood based on family lines was canceled because it didn't work. It was weak and useless for saving people. It never made anyone really right with God. But now we have a far better hope, for Christ makes us acceptable to God and now we may draw near to him" (Heb. 7:18–19, TLB).

Let us follow our leader and be cleansed.

THINK ON THESE THINGS

Reread Exodus 28–29; then read Leviticus 1–9.

1. How logical it is to think that God only chooses godly people to do his work; yet how obvious it is in the Bible that God chooses unlikely souls. Can you think of any Christian leaders whose backgrounds, education, and training did not fit what we assume to be the norm? What is God's requisite

for leadership? How do you prepare to become a leader? What is the difference between leadership and servanthood?

2. How can we be mirrors that reflect God's glory? According to 2 Corinthians 3:18, what works inside of us to institute changes in our life? What can you do personally to become more like the Lord?

3. What does the word *confess* really mean? How is it used in 1 John 1:9? We've seen how Moses cleansed the priests; how does God cleanse us today?

4. Do you feel God has "put a call" on you? What makes you sense this call? What do you think God is calling you to? Are you willing to let him have his way? Why or why not?

5. What was significant about Aaron's wearing on his shoulders the two stones with twelve names engraved on them? How does this compare with our keeping a prayer list?

6. What is an intercessor? How is this term used to apply to the high priest of the Old Testament? to Jesus? to us? How often do you intercede? What method do you use to remind yourself to pray? Why was the old method of choosing the high priest discontinued? (See Heb. 7:18–19.)

For Your Notebook

Add to your seven list:

Aaron's seven items of clothing
Seven days of dedication
Seven days in our week

Make a comparison chart of Aaron the high priest and Jesus the Great High Priest. The following list will help get you started.

AARON	JESUS
Called of God	Called of God
Atonement by blood of goat	Atonement by his own blood

You might be interested in looking up the history of the twelve birthstones for each month of the year and copying these into your notebook. Do you feel there is any connection?

Bonus Story

◇ ———————————————————————————— ◇

LOOKING FOR GOD IN RELIGION

A few years ago I spoke at a meeting where I was introduced to Beth, a lawyer's wife. The minute I met her, I knew
she was special. We became long distance friends, and each
time I'd come to her city, I'd call her up. She would always be
amazed that I remembered her and flattered that I found her
a fun friend to be with. She heard my testimony many times
and agreed that we all need to find God. Beth was a good
person who went to church faithfully and had even minored
in theology at college. She would frequently remind me of
these facts so I would know she was spiritual, even though I
never pushed her for any commitment. I just interceded;
I just carried her quietly before the Lord.

When we brought CLASS to her city, she attended because
she felt she "owed it" to me. In the small group session on the
first day, she was amazed at how open and honest the people
were. She reported, "They don't seem to care what the others
think of them." Later she told me she couldn't sleep at all
that night. She paced the floor and wrestled with God as
Jacob had, although she didn't realize what was taking place.
On the second day of CLASS, she went home before the
small groups convened. She couldn't face the open vulnera-
bility. She was trying to "keep it all together."

On the third day she was surprised that the groups met
before lunch, and she was trapped into going. She was dumbfounded that "ordinary people" could take a Bible verse and
make it apply to their lives while she who had "minored in
theology" couldn't. "I don't know what's wrong with me,"
she cried as we sat together at lunch. "I'm an intelligent person. I've studied religion, but I don't know what to do with

one simple verse. I just came to CLASS to please you; I didn't know this whole thing was going to get to me like this. What's happening to me? Why are my insides all fluttering and shaky?" As I explained that God was working in her life, she said, "You've had your eye on me right from the first time we met, haven't you?"

At that moment one of our staff members, Patsy Clairmont, got up to give her humor message explaining how humor is a great asset in speaking, but we must always be sure that it leads to a point. At the conclusion Beth said, "I'm just as funny as Patsy. I make people laugh all the time, but I haven't found anything productive to do with my humor."

"Do your stories have a point?" I asked.

"That's the problem right there," she added quickly. "That's the problem with my life. It's full of funny lines, but it doesn't have a point."

By this time everyone had left the lunch room to return to the seminar where I was due to begin teaching, yet I couldn't leave Beth at this critical moment. Suddenly I saw Patsy and called her over. "Beth has a sense of humor just like yours, Patsy; but she needs you to show her how to bring it to a point." Patsy did bring Beth's life to a point. She told her the tremors in her stomach were labor pains preparing her for a new birth and that her minoring in theology did not mean she had been born into the family of God. As I spoke in the sanctuary, Patsy birthed Beth as a babe in Christ without my presence.

I wish I had been the midwife, but instead I was the intercessor, the one used to carry Beth to the presence of the Lord where she was able to present her body a living sacrifice, holy, acceptable to the Lord which is her reasonable service.

◇

8. ENTER THE HOLY PLACE
—AND SEE THE LIGHT

As we follow the footsteps of the Hebrew looking for God, we find that we've gone about as far as we can go on our journey. We've come out of Egypt and through the wilderness. We've looked up to God, dwelt in the desert, and sought the Lord where he may be found. We've entered into his gates with praise, and we've paid the price of sacrifice. We've met the priest at the altar, followed his instructions, and been washed in the water. We know the High Priest substitutes for us, and we are grateful that he intercedes with the Father on our behalf.

We are now ready to enter the Holy Place, and we've heard that inside this tent covered with skins is a lampstand shedding light, a table of showbread, and an altar of incense. As we've followed our leader through the courtyard, we've observed that only the high priest is allowed inside. How can we enter into the presence of God?

"One thing have I desired of the Lord, that will I seek after; that I may dwell in the house of the Lord all the days of my life, to behold the beauty of the Lord, and to inquire in his temple" (Ps. 27:4, KJV).

For God's People in Bible Times

In the days of the tabernacle, anyone could enter into the courtyard as long as he brought a sacrifice, but only the priest could enter the Holy Place. While the outside gate through the linen fence was wide enough for all to enter, the door into the sanctuary was narrow. That is, it was only for the priests, those who had been anointed, cleansed, and made ready to stand in the house of the Lord.

The outside of the tent may have been plain and unappealing so people wouldn't desire God for the wrong reasons, but the minute the priest stepped inside, he was awed by the beauty and majesty of his surroundings. In the courtyard the furnishings were bronze; in the Holy Place they were gold. Inside the light from the golden lampstand cast a shadow over the gold-crowned table of showbread. And the sweet-smelling incense wafted a welcome aroma.

No doubt the priests had whispered about the spectacular sights in the sanctuary so everyone wished they could catch a glimpse of the grandeur. But the ordinary person had no hope of entering the Holy Place, he could only look upon the outside of the tent and imagine what the priests enjoyed in their special privilege of sight, taste, and smell. Once inside, the priest was to keep the incense burning, to trim the wicks on the oil lamps, and to eat the bread put before them.

The first item the priest saw as he entered was the gold lampstand. This was not a candelabra designed for wax candles, such as we are accustomed to today. Instead, it was a stand which held oil and wicks. Beaten out from one piece of pure gold, it had a central shaft and three curved arms on each side.

The lampstand was ornately decorated with almond buds, and the seven cups were almond blossoms. This use of buds and flowers showed that God's light was alive and growing. The almond was chosen because it was the first tree to bloom in the spring and because it represented new life, new growth, resurrection. The meaning of the word *almond* was "wait and watch."

For Us in Today's World

Based on our own good works or righteousness, we cannot enter into the Holy Place any more than the Hebrew could. But we can come to God as we become one with our High Priest Jesus Christ. We get into the Holy Place of God's presence on his recommendation as he declares us to be "a chosen people, a royal priesthood . . . called out of darkness into his wonderful light" (1 Pet. 2:9, NIV).

Although the gate to salvation is wide, the door to God's presence is small, only large enough for those who have already given their lives to Jesus our Lord who proclaimed, "Enter through the narrow gate. For wide is the gate and broad is the road that leads to destruction, and many enter through it. But small is the gate and narrow the road that leads to life, and only a few find it" (Matt. 7:13–14, NIV).

The outside view of the Christian life is frequently not attractive to the nonbeliever. The impression is often one of legalism, piety, and sacrifice. As the tabernacle was covered with skins belying the beauty inside, so the life hid in Christ only becomes apparent after we have chosen to enter into his glorious presence. Only through the reflected light of the believer can the world catch a glimpse of what awaits them inside the narrow gate. Paul instructs the Christians: "Do all things without murmurings and disputings: That ye may be blameless and harmless, the sons of God, without rebuke, in the midst of a crooked and perverse nation, among whom ye shine as lights in the world" (Phil. 2:14–15, KJV).

Are we living in a crooked and perverse nation today? How important it is that we provide illumination, that we shine as lights in the world? You may be the only glimpse of Jesus that your neighbor will ever see.

If we are to be lights in the world, we must be pure and of one mind, just as the gold of the lampstand was of one piece with no alloys or soldering. As believers, we are branches uniting in one vine—Jesus Christ—just as the branches of the lampstand connected to one central shaft.

Jesus himself said clearly, "I am the vine; you are the branches. If a man remains in me and I in him, he will bear much fruit; apart from me you can do nothing" (John 15:5, NIV).

When I think of the beaten gold of the lampstand, I'm reminded of the suffering Jesus was to go through and the trials we as believers have to face. "In this you greatly rejoice, though now for a little while you may have had to suffer grief in all kinds of trials. These have come so that your faith—of greater worth than gold, which perishes even though refined by fire—may be proved genuine and may result in praise, glory and honor when Jesus Christ is revealed" (1 Pet. 1:6–7, NIV).

Only when gold is refined by fire does it become a thing of beauty; only as we are tested and tried are we purified and sanctified unto his service. As the almond was chosen to represent new birth, so we only come into full flower for the Lord as we are born again into new life. "Praise be to the God and Father of our Lord Jesus Christ! In his great mercy he has given us a new birth into a living hope through the resurrection of Jesus Christ from the dead" (1 Pet. 1:3, NIV).

As the golden lampstand was the only light in the Holy Place so is Jesus the only light in a world of darkness. "In him was life, and that life was the light of men" (John 1:4, NIV).

In these dark days, people are looking for God as never before, but they don't want to accept the light. "The light shines in the darkness, but the darkness has not understood it" (John 1:5, NIV).

In the book of Revelation, foretelling the future for the Christian church, John writes, "I turned around to see the voice that was speaking to me. And when I turned I saw seven golden lampstands, and among the lampstands was someone 'like a son of man' dressed in a robe reaching down to his feet and with a golden sash around his chest. . . . His face was like the sun shining in all its brilliance" (Rev. 1:12–13, 16, NIV).

Jesus, our High Priest, will come again and be the light of our dark, evil world. "There will be no more night. They will not need the light of a lamp or the light of the sun, for the Lord God will give them light. And they will reign forever and ever" (Rev. 22:5, NIV).

As the priest of the past stood in the light of the lampstand, Jesus our High Priest provides the light for each believer today and in the future. He'll come again as the Angel of Light, and he will reign forever and ever. To find our God we must first see the light of Jesus.

Bonus Story

◇ ——————————————————————————— ◇

LOOKING FOR GOD IN THE LIGHT

After sitting at a table writing all day, I went out to the jacuzzi at the motel to relax my right arm and back. There I met a pleasant Canadian couple, Carl and Sue, who were on vacation, and we began to talk. When they asked what I was doing, I explained I wrote Christian books and I needed a short break from my work. I told them about *Looking for God in All the Right Places,* and Carl replied, "I'm a Christian, but just recently I met God on a new level." He then told me of a dream he had where he'd been walking down a road at dusk. Lights began to come on and he could see the city straight ahead. As he trudged along, the stars began to shine and the moon came over a mountain.

Suddenly, everything went black, and he was alone in the dark. Flames licked up around his feet for a fleeting moment, and then they died away. There was no light, no stars, no moon, no shadows, no people, no sound. He screamed for help and there was no response; he demanded light but the answer was darkness. Soon he realized he was in Hell.

"Where are the flames?" he called out. "I thought Hell was full of fire." There was no answer, only total darkness, an utter absence of any tiny ray of light.

Then he cried out to God, "Father forgive me, I'll do anything you say if you'll take me out of the darkness into the light. Show me light; give me hope."

As Carl repeated this to me, he said he had awakened crying, and for the first time he realized what God's Word meant when it said, "The Lord is my light and my salvation—whom shall I fear?" (Ps. 27:1, NIV).

When God talked to the Hebrew people about their

disobedience and deception, he explained if they didn't mend their ways they would be punished. "The Lord will afflict you with madness, blindness and confusion of mind. At midday you will grope about like a blind man in the dark. You will be unsuccessful in everything you do; day after day you will be oppressed and robbed, with no one to rescue you" (Deut. 28:28–29, NIV). The absence of light is an affliction of the Lord, a groping in the dark, the way of the wicked.

As we discussed darkness in the hot California sun, Carl concluded, "I've believed in God forever, but I hadn't fully understood the necessity of Jesus' saying, 'I am the light of the world. Whoever follows me will never walk in darkness, but will have the light of life'" (John 8:12, NIV).

Carl groped for God in a dream of darkness and found him in a new light.

◇

9. EAT THE BREAD
—AND GIVE THANKS

As we stand in the light, we see the table of showbread before us. Now that we're here, may we partake of this bread frosted in frankincense? Is it for us? Could we put some in our basket and take a loaf home as a souvenir?

For God's People in Bible Times

Once inside the Holy Place standing in the ever-present light, the high priest could see before him the table of showbread. Built somewhat like a piano bench, the table was acacia wood overlaid with gold. There was a gold crown or edging to keep the bread on the table when it was being moved throughout the desert (see Exod. 25:23). The twelve loaves of bread, made of fine flour, represented the twelve tribes of Israel. No matter how big or small the tribe, they all had the same size loaf showing that numbers are not important to God.

In *The Tabernacle of Moses*, Kevin Conner says that the table had both a godly and a human side: gold for God and wood for humanity. The bread stood for God's provision for his people. "Let them give thanks to the Lord for his unfailing love and his wonderful deeds for men, for he satisfies the thirsty and fills the hungry with good things" (Ps. 107:8–9, NIV).

Bread has always been considered the staff of life, the basic food. When the Hebrews were hungry in the desert, God provided manna, a sticky white bread which appeared mysteriously in abundance each day for forty years. "Give us this day our daily bread" later became part of the Lord's model prayer. Bread was so significant in the sustenance of the Hebrews in the wilderness that a jar of manna was one of the three things put in the Ark of the Covenant, along with Aaron's rod and the tablets of Moses, to give a remembrance of God's perpetual provision for man's needs.

The showbread, literally "bread of presence," was frosted with frankincense, a sweet-smelling white gum signifying purity and placed on the table by the priests as an ever-present display before God. Since each tribe was represented, God could see a symbol of his people in the "presence bread," sometimes called "continual bread," and could feast on the fellowship of his believers forever. Not only was the bread of spiritual significance as a constant memorial and a presence, but it was to be food for the priests. The high priest as part of his ritual was to change the bread once a week. "Every sabbath he shall set it in order before the Lord continually" (Lev. 24:8, KJV).

God was given the fresh new bread, and the twelve loaves that were removed became the bread for the priests that week. They ate the Bread of God; they partook of God's presence; they entered into communion with their God.

For Us in Today's World

As the showbread was a memorial of God's provision and his presence, so our Lord Jesus asks us to take the sacred bread of communion in remembrance of him (see Luke 22:19).

As the presence bread was to be before God at all times, so is Jesus our "bread of life" available to us moment by moment that we might continuously feed our souls with his spiritual nourishment. "I am the bread of life. He who comes to me will never go hungry" (John 6:35, NIV).

"I am the living bread that came down from heaven. If a man eats of this bread, he will live forever. This bread is my flesh, which I will give for the life of the world" (John 6:51, NIV).

"This is the bread that came down from heaven. Our forefathers ate manna and died, but he who feeds on this bread will live forever" (John 6:58, NIV).

Jesus himself told us that we need spiritual food, and he is our bread; he will sustain us. As the priests ate holy bread, so can we receive strength from our own High Priest.

As the priests in the tabernacle ate the showbread in fellowship with God, so Jesus wants his disciples to have communion with him. "Is not the bread we break a participation in the body of Christ?" (1 Cor. 10:16, NIV).

Instead of twelve loaves, Jesus presented himself to God as one loaf. No longer are we to think of ourselves as from different tribes or backgrounds, but as a united body in Christ. "Because there is one loaf, we who are many, are one body, for we all partake of the one loaf" (1 Cor. 10:17, NIV).

When choleric Paul gave instructions for "The Lord's Supper" he told the Corinthians they were first to examine their lives. "For whenever you eat this bread and drink this cup, you proclaim the Lord's death until he comes. Therefore, whoever eats the bread or drinks the cup of the Lord in an unworthy manner will be guilty of sinning against the body and blood of the Lord. A man ought to examine himself before he eats of the bread and drinks of the cup. For anyone who eats and drinks without recognizing the body of the Lord eats and drinks judgment on himself" (1 Cor. 11:26–29).

Then Paul looked out to the group before him and added a personal and pointed explanation. "That is why many among you are weak and sick, and a number of you have fallen asleep!" (v. 30).

For us today Paul's words hold true: we're sick and tired of living because we have not examined ourselves before God, we have not given thanks for what we do have, and we have not eaten of the Bread of Life for our spiritual sustenance.

Jesus is our daily bread, fresh every morning. When we eat of him we will be strengthened, we will have joy, and we will live forever.

How do we eat of Jesus each day? There are two kinds of nourishment: physical and spiritual. There are few of us who do not get enough food each day. Since overeating is considered a chronic American health problem, we don't need to be encouraged to eat more, but our spiritual food is

God's Word. There is no way we can grow spiritually if we are not eating daily of the Word.

Moses explained this to his people. "He humbled you, causing you to hunger and then feeding you with manna, which neither you nor your fathers had known, to teach you that man does not live on bread alone but on every word that comes from the mouth of the Lord" (Deut. 8:3, NIV).

Job declared, "I have treasured the words of his mouth more than my daily bread" (Job 23:12, NIV).

The Psalmist writes: "The Law from your mouth is more precious to me than thousands of pieces of silver and gold. . . . How sweet are your promises to my taste, sweeter than honey to my mouth!" (Ps. 119:72, 103, NIV).

Jeremiah also loved God's Word: "When your words came, I ate them; they were my joy and my heart's delight" (Jer. 15:16, NIV).

When I first hungered after the Lord, I found this Jeremiah verse and devoured God's Word. Bible study became my life and for my two years in Bungalow One, I spent six hours or more each day in study. Had I spent that much time eating, I would have been bulging; instead, I filled up on God's Word. As Peter said, "Like newborn babies, crave pure spiritual milk, so that by it you may grow up in your salvation" (1 Pet. 2:2, NIV).

Often I hear women say, "I wish I knew the Bible better" or "I wish I could use the Scriptures as you do." When this happens, I ask them, "How much time do you spend each week in study?" We all want to be spiritual giants quickly. We would like "instant verses" as easily as "instant potatoes," but to know God well and to grow in the Word, we must spend time studying joyfully for nourishment.

Paul writes, "The word is near you; it is in your mouth and in your heart" (Rom. 10:8, NIV).

"For everything that was written in the past was written to teach us, so that through endurance and the encouragement of the Scriptures we might have hope" (Rom. 15:4, NIV).

As the priests ate of the bread of the Presence, so we will taste of the presence of our Lord Jesus as we eat daily of his Word and give thanks.

◇

10. SMELL THE AROMA
—AND WORSHIP GOD

Can you believe we're almost at the end of our journey? We've been through gardens and deserts, on mountains and in valleys. We've followed our map and collected baskets of memories we'll never forget. We've been allowed to enter the Holy Place, reserved only for the priests. We've seen the light, and we've eaten the bread with thankful hearts. But what is the aroma we smell? Where is it coming from? Let's look.

For God's People in Bible Times

We remember that in the outer court of the tabernacle there was the bronze altar of sacrifice, a place of continual bloodshed. In the Holy Place was built an altar of gold where the sweet aroma of incense was constantly wafting toward heaven. (See diagram p. 172). This altar of incense was made of acacia wood and covered with gold, as was the table for the bread, but it was taller than any other piece of furniture in the Holy Place. Both altars had horns denoting power, but the altar of incense also was bordered with a crown of gold, signifying the glory of God.

The incense, like the oil of consecration, was made from a special recipe of four spices dictated by God himself. Anyone duplicating it for his own pleasure would be excommunicated, kept from fellowship with God. How it must grieve our Father today as he sees so many making their own recipes for worship, taking part of his divine plan, but rejecting his power, sounding saintly but following a false god.

The holy perfume was to be burning constantly. "Aaron must burn fragrant incense on the altar every morning when he tends the lamps. He must burn incense again when he lights the lamps at twilight so incense will burn regularly before the Lord for the generations to come" (Exod. 30:7–8, NIV).

The aroma ascending to God was to be constant, not a thing of the moment. David said, "May my prayer be set before you like incense; may the lifting up of my hands be like the evening sacrifice" (Ps. 141:1–2, NIV).

The altar of incense was the last object passed before entering into the Holy of Holies, the very presence of God. Without the offering of prayers and praise the priest couldn't come to the Lord.

For Us in Today's World

As we learned earlier, the altar of sacrifice represents Christ on the Cross giving up his life for us. Likewise, the altar of incense stands for Christ risen, glorified, and interceding for us with the Father that his prayers might be continually wafting to heaven as a sweet-smelling aroma. How grateful we should be that Christ didn't just say "it is finished" and disappear, leaving us to our own problems. Instead, he is always praying on behalf of his believers, noticing our needs, and pleading our case before the Judge. Jesus is our "golden altar before the throne" (Rev. 8:3, NIV).

As the incense burned on the altar and ascended to God, so our prayers start in the heart and reach up to heaven when we pray in the power of our intercessor, when we pray "in Jesus' name." As the golden altar stood in the way of entrance into God's presence, so we are hindered in our search for him when we do not pray.

Paul tells us, "Be joyful always; pray continually; give thanks in all circumstances, for this is God's will for you in Christ Jesus. Do not put out the Spirit's fire" (1 Thess. 5:16–19, NIV). Don't let the incense of prayer burn out. Tend it in the morning and in the night. "Pray in the Spirit on all occasions with all kinds of prayers and requests. With this in

mind, be alert and always keep on praying for all the saints"
(Eph. 6:18, NIV).

We must be alert and not let the fire within us go out. We
don't want to be lukewarm Christians whose pitiful prayers
never get above our heads. The Jesus of Revelation said, "I
know your deeds, that you are neither cold nor hot. I wish you
were either one or the other! So, because you are lukewarm—neither hot nor cold—I am about to spit you out of
my mouth?" (Rev. 3:15–16, NIV).

How many of us are constantly looking for God but are not
serious enough about our search to make the necessary sacrifices? We're not bad people with cold hearts; we're just not
hot after God's program. We're lukewarm believers, and God
is ready to spit us out.

If we've come this far and we're standing a few steps from
God's presence, what do we need to do to get his attention?
As the incense wafted up to the Lord, and pleased him, so we
must pray without ceasing that he will hear our voice, a voice
that may be crying in the wilderness. "Be imitators of God,
therefore, as dearly loved children and live a life of love, just
as Christ loved us and gave himself up for us as a fragrant
offering and sacrifice to God" (Eph. 5:1–2, NIV). Let's give
up our tepid trust in a nebulous God and become burning
incense whose aroma reaches into the very nostrils of our
heavenly Father.

But how do we keep the fire going? In CLASS we find
Christians who are dedicated to good works but have a lukewarm prayer life. They have had instructions in all kinds of
godly pursuits, but somehow they've missed prayer. Some
have avoided learning about prayer for fear they'd be expected to pray.

After I'd taught Bible studies in our women's club for years,
I decided it was time I taught them to pray. I announced that
the following week we'd divide in small groups, and I'd lead
them in simple sentence prayers. The next week only one-
third of the regular attendance showed up. They liked listening to me and getting their spirituality secondhand, but they

surely didn't want to get into it if they had to take any risks. What if they didn't pray right? What would people think?

The Lord doesn't want pretty little prayers designed to impress others. He wants us to send up fervent prayers, heated prayers—prayers strong enough to reach him. "The effectual fervent prayer of a righteous man availeth much" (James 5:16, KJV).

In CLASS we have been effective in teaching people how to pray when we compare calling on God in prayer to calling up a friend on the phone. Everyone knows how to use a phone. Everyone knows how to let their "fingers do the walking." Everyone knows that in time of trouble you reach out and call someone. For us God's phone number is JER–3303 (Jeremiah 33:3) "Call to me and I will answer you and tell you great and unsearchable things you do not know" (NIV).

We then do a little skit where one staff member, Patsy Clairmont, calls a friend. With every call, she encounters some sort of trouble—busy signal, no one home, interference on the line, unlisted number, need of an operator's assistance. Our prayer chairman, George Ann Dennis, responds from God's perspective and with Scripture. God's never too busy, he's always at home, his number's available, Jesus is our operator, our intercessor, our connection with the Heavenly Mansion.

On our evaluations, we often find this lesson is the favorite. And people who are afraid to pray see that it's easier than picking up the phone. They don't have to compose lofty pleadings; they have only to dial JER–3303. God is a God of clear circuits. As we pray without ceasing, he will hear and answer.

Do you want to find God? Give him a call. He's waiting to give you an answer.

So often our prayers are for ourselves. "Help me God. I'm in trouble again." As Jesus became our example in prayer, he showed us how to pray for others, how to be an intercessor for others as he is for us.

As we intercede in prayer, we literally go between the person in need and our God. We become a willing body, a bridge over troubled waters, bringing our friend and his burdens from wherever he is to the presence of God. In essence, we're saying, "Here he is God. I care enough about this person to bring him from his desert heat into the protective tent of your presence." Likewise, we can ask others to lift us up in prayer.

As Oswald Chambers says, "In intercession you bring the person, or the circumstance that impinges on you before God until you are moved by His attitude toward that person or circumstance."[6]

The reason few of us become intercessors is that there's no credit connected with lifting up a heavy burden daily in the confines of our closet. Platform evangelism is a showcase for God's power through us as seen by an audience and gives us the feeling that God is proud of our humble harvest. We imagine some heavenly wall of granite with the names of our converts carved in stone like the Vietnam Memorial. Although there's no recognition for those who previously prayed, who planted, who watered these prospects up to the point of conversion, God sees those who lift up their friends in faith before his face. What he sees us do in secret he rewards openly.

As the high priest interceded between man and God, so Jesus is our intercessor and so should we constantly uplift our friends. "Admit your faults to one another and pray for each other so that you may be healed. The earnest prayer of a righteous man has great power and wonderful results" (James 5:16, TLB).

Our earnest prayers waft as incense up to the heavenly Father. How he loves to smell the aroma as we worship him in prayer. We can then feel his power and know there will be wonderful results.

THINK ON THESE THINGS

We have arrived! We are at the threshold of God. As we enter into a different country in our travels, an agent reviews our passport and our papers. He looks at our picture to make sure we are not using a false identity. He may even open our bags and check the price we've paid for our souvenirs. We don't cross the line until we've passed the test.

Before we cross the line, let's check our own credentials. Let's make sure we've taken the ten steps leading up to the presence of God.

1. *Leave Egypt—and Follow the Cloud.* Have you packed up your spiritual bags and left the world behind? Have you realized the folly of trying to keep up with the Joneses? Have you made the decision to forsake the pleasures of sin and get serious with God? You could look for God in all kinds of places, but you won't come into the cloud of his presence and see the glory of his countenance until you're willing to leave Egypt, walk through the Red Sea, and let the waters close behind you. Have you left Egypt and followed the cloud?

2. *Listen to God—and Obey His Commandments.* In this day of "do your own thing," no one wants any rules. Yet God gave us a sense of order and a need for discipline even if we rebel against it. Have you listened to God? Have you heard his voice crying out to you in the wilderness? God has given us a simple principle of life: When we obey his commandments he blesses us; when we disobey he punishes. As Christians let's not confuse spiritual freedom with a license to sin. Have you listened to God and obeyed his commands?

3. *Make a Home for God—and Visit Him Often.* As we look for God in churches and in chapels, we often forget that he wants to live right inside of us. He wants our body to be the temple of the Holy Spirit, and yet we still think we have to go somewhere to be spiritual. If only we had a bigger church, colorful stained glass, throbbing notes from the organ, new choir robes, or a powerful preacher—we would be sanctified.

God asked the Israelites to build him a home right in their midst, in the desert, on shifting sand. He didn't care about maximum visibility or freeway accessibility. He wanted them to make a place for him where they were. He wanted to be at the very center of their lives. That's what God wants from us; he wants us to make room for him in our hearts 168 hours a week. Have you made a home for God, and do you visit him often?

4. *Dwell in the Desert—and Be Content.* Although we are to keep our eyes on the Mountain, we often find ourselves living in the desert. Preachers sometimes tell us that God wants us all to be healthy, wealthy, and wise. They even present testimonies that seem to equate the Christian life with "Lifestyles of the Rich and Famous." While it's exciting to think of driving a Rolls-Royce, very few of us will ever have that opportunity. We'd all prefer to have plenty of money and live a less stressful life, but sometimes we're going to be hot in the desert. Does that mean then that we are spiritual failures? No. We should accept the fact that sometimes God sends us to live in a desert to teach us some practical lessons. "I have learned, in whatsoever state I am, therewith to be content" (Phil. 4:11, KJV). Open your mind to hear what God has to teach. I've found out that for me, the faster I accept my situation and become content in it, the sooner God moves me on. As we learn to live in the heat God gives us the cool of the day. Have you dwelt in the desert and become content?

5. *Seek the Lord—and Enter His Gate.* We have learned on our journey of looking for God that there's only one way to open the door to God's presence and that's to go through our Lord Jesus. "No man cometh unto the Father, but by me" (John 14:6, KJV). Any religion that leaves Jesus out or considers him only to be a good role model isn't ordained of God. We can only find God when we go through Jesus. Being good isn't enough. We must abandon a quick-fix quest for God and seek him with all our hearts.

> Turn your eyes upon Jesus,
>   Look full in His wonderful face,
> And the things of earth will grow strangely dim
>   In the light of His glory and grace.[7]

Have you been seeking the Lord and have you entered his gate?

6. *Pay the Price—and Be Set Free.* There's no such thing as a free lunch, yet the fee to see God is not paid in money but in sacrifice, "a broken and a contrite heart." As the Hebrew brought a lamb to sacrifice as an atonement for his sins, Jesus gave himself up as the Lamb without blemish or spot to die once for our sins that we might be saved. He didn't do it in a flashy way to draw attention to his martyrdom; he allowed himself to be nailed to a cross between two thieves in a most demeaning manner. He was willing to go all the way for us.

We don't get to God on our own merits, outstanding though they may be; we approach him, not with lamb in hand, but with the credentials of Christ, "Jesus paid it all." Do you know your price has been paid and you are set free?

7. *Follow the Leader—and Be Cleansed.* As the Hebrew had to come before the priest to have his sins forgiven, we bow before our High Priest, the Lord Jesus. We don't need to follow an earthly leader or find a father confessor, as helpful as this might be. We have only to meet Jesus. "Jesus was faithful to God who appointed him High Priest" (Heb. 3:2, TLB). He is our leader. Can you accept Jesus as your High Priest, as one who pleads your case and is the son of the Judge? What better position could you possibly be in? There's no jury to be chosen and you'll always win the case. Jesus forgives 100 percent, he remembers your iniquities no more, he washes you white as snow. Have you followed the leader, our High Priest? Do you know you are clean and forgiven?

8. *Enter the Holy Place—and See the Light.* What a privilege to enter the Holy Place formerly reserved only for priests. What a revelation to stand in the light and the glory of the Lord. As the lampstand was made of pure beaten gold, so was our Lord purified through his trials until he emerged as fine gold. Jesus is the light of the world, and as we are his reflection, we are to shine "in the midst of a crooked and perverse nation." When we do shine for Jesus, his light will attract those who are seeking illumination. Have you entered the Holy Place and do you see the light?

9. *Eat the Bread—and Give Thanks.* The table of showbread was placed in the Holy Place by Moses as a constant

reminder to God of the twelve tribes of Israel. Each week the priests set fresh bread before God and took the week-old bread to eat for their own physical sustenance. Today as Christians and members of a royal priesthood, we celebrate Holy Communion as we partake of the bread (Christ's body broken for us) and the wine (Christ's blood shed for the remission of our sins). As we participate in the holy celebration and give thanks to our God, we are not to see it as a meaningless ritual of crackers and grape juice, but as a symbol of the body and the blood of our Lord Jesus who died for you and for me that we might be saved from our sins and have everlasting life.

God also asks us to eat of his Word that we might grow and be able to share the Living Bread with others. Have you been eating the Daily Bread and giving thanks?

10. *Smell the Aroma—and Worship God.* The altar of incense, the third piece of furniture in the Holy Place, was closest to the presence of God. From this altar there rose constantly a sweet-smelling aroma to God. Today Jesus is our "golden altar before the throne," and his prayers in our behalf waft up to our heavenly Father. In turn, he desires that we pray for others so that the sweet aroma of our intercession will reach the Father. We should no longer consider prayer as a laborious Christian duty, but we should picture each prayer floating from our mouth to the presence of God and causing him to smile with the sweet smell of our words of intercession. We make God happy when we pray for a friend. Do you smell the aroma as you worship God?

Now that you have checked off the essentials for coming into the presence of God and your credentials have been accepted, you are prepared to meet the Father. As Jacob said, "How awesome is this place! This is none other than the house of God; this is the gate of heaven" (Gen. 28:17, NIV).

Bonus Story

◇ —————————————————————————————— ◇

LOOKING FOR GOD IN PRAYER

Every year our CLASS staff members each choose a verse to represent them on our prayer list. We give our choices to our CLASS principal, George Ann, who compiles them and returns a copy of all the verses to each one of us. With these selections in our hands we can pray for each other using Scripture to personalize our prayers. One year, for example, I chose Philippians 3:10, giving me four clear aims for my Christian life: get to know Christ; feel the power of his resurrection; share in his sufferings; and become like him.

As the staff and I prayed for me, keeping the words of this scripture in mind, I saw changes in the depth of my commitment to the Lord. During this time I also used Philippians 3:10 as the basis for a message to others which I called "Aim and Action of the Christian Life."

Most amazing to me has been the reaction of audiences as I have mentioned this method of prayer support. To many the thought of praying for each other through Scripture is a new idea. Many come up and want to see the list of verses the staff has for each other. As I open my organizer, they peer at the names and verses and say happily, "Why, I could do that?" And of course they can, and you can, too.

One of the reasons people don't pray is they don't think they have anything to say. Even when alone, they're afraid God will think they're stupid if they don't have deep thoughts; yet when I show them how to personalize a verse and insert a friend's name, they often become eloquent.

I've received letters filled with excitement from women who confessed to a lukewarm prayer life that had been reactivated when they found they could talk to God through a verse.

One of these women sent me a copy of how she prayed daily for me on my verse, Philippians 3:10.

> Lord, today I pray for Florence. I don't know where she is, but I pray for her according to your Word. I ask that she get to know you better. To do that she'll have to spend more time with you. Give her the time today to study your Word and learn of you as the perfect example for our lives. Lord, may she feel your power. In the long days she puts in that would tire any of us, would you let her know that you are there: encouraging, strengthening, upholding her. Lord, as you suffered and as she has experienced grief, let her know that she is not alone, let her see the value in the trials of life to refine the character as into fine gold. Give her the joy to spread to others in need as she ministers to and comforts the afflicted. And most important, Lord, help her to keep her eyes on the goal: Jesus, the author and the finisher, designer, completer of her life, that she may one day become like you.
>
> I pray this for Florence in faith, in hope, in love, and in your name, the precious name of Jesus. Amen.

How easily the words flow in prayer when we are basing our requests firmly on God's Word. How grateful this lady was to go from a poor prayer life to an intimate relationship with God. Our God doesn't have an answering machine or a secretary; he takes every call himself.

Standing in God's Presence

◇ ——————————————————————————— ◇

We have come a long way from the Garden of Eden, and we're ready to stand in the presence of our God. What do you think it's going to be like as we enter into the Holy of Holies? When we were children, many of us often imagined what God would look like. Sometimes we were helped by pictures in our Bible storybooks. The God I envisioned was always stern; surely he did not take life lightly and would never smile. I may have confused him with Moses as I remember him in a long white robe holding those big stone tablets.

As I progressed in my Bible stories, I agreed with the Hebrews who asked God for a king they could see. Wouldn't it be easier to follow the leader if we could see him? Wouldn't nonbelievers be more impressed if they saw us bow down before a real king on a golden throne? I began to picture God as King Saul, a head taller than all the rest. How imposing to have a tall and handsome God with a dignified air of authority. Then came David who had such charisma that women swooned in his presence. He killed Goliath and any other giants that got in his way. Besides his bravery, he played the harp and wrote psalms. He was a spiritual giant. Surely God would be like David. But what about Solomon? He was so rich that even the Queen of Sheba was overwhelmed with his possessions. Here was a king with a real palace and a temple of his own. He was so intelligent that he was noted for his wisdom and so spiritual he wrote proverbs for the rest of us to live by.

If I were to create the perfect God, he'd have the depth and authority of Moses; the stature and looks of Saul; the personality, bravery, and talent of David; and the wealth and

wisdom of Solomon. I would place him on a golden throne in
the Holy of Holies, put a jeweled crown on his head and a
Bible in his hand, have musicians playing harps and servants
bowing in obedience.

How about you? What do you think God is like? What do
you think we'll find as we go through the veil to God? You've
come a long way. What will the reward be like?

For God's People in Bible Times

Once each year the high priest was allowed to go into the
Holy of Holies and come into the very presence of God who
said, "There I will meet with thee, and I will commune with
thee" (Exod. 25:22, KJV). On this one Day of Atonement, the
high priest wearing his special garments with the names of all
the tribes on his shoulders, came before God to plead for his
people.

To enter this special room, the priest had to go through the
veil that separated the two chambers. This curtain, embroidered with cherubim, was woven of fine linen in the three
colors used throughout the tabernacle: blue, red, and purple.
The veil, representing separation, presented a barrier to anyone wanting to look into the Holy of Holies. This curtain was
hung by gold hooks onto four gold-covered wooden pillars.
As the high priest came into God's presence through the veil,
he saw shining before him the *ark of the covenant,* a chest
made of acacia wood overlaid with pure gold.

What is an ark? The first ark mentioned in the Bible was
Noah's made of gopher wood, pitched within and without,
and representing the preservation of people and animals and
the salvation of the human race. The second was the ark of
reeds and tar made for the baby Moses to preserve his life and
save him from being killed by the Pharaoh. The ark of the
covenant was the third, and in this golden chest was preserved a jar of manna (God's provision for his people), the
tablets of Law (God's principles of behavior), and Aaron's rod
(God's symbol of power and leadership).

The ark had a crown of gold around the top and a golden ring on each corner to hold the staves used in carrying the ark from place to place as God directed. The ark not only preserved what was inside, but its presence in time of battle saved the Israelites from defeat, its presence at the Jordan parted the river and saved the people, and its presence at Jericho caused the walls to fall and saved the Hebrews from destruction. Later, King Saul went to the ark for help, David made a special tent to house it, and Solomon installed the ark in the temple. Throughout the wanderings of the Israelites, the ark was considered the symbol of God, but Jeremiah predicted that in later years they would forget the ark. "'In those days, when your numbers have increased greatly in the land,' declares the Lord, 'men will no longer say, "the ark of the covenant of the Lord." It will never enter their minds or be remembered; it will not be missed, nor will another one be made'" (Jer. 3:16, NIV).

The lid of the ark was crafted of pure gold with a gold cherubim at each end and was called the mercy seat, the place where God gave out mercy. The wings of the cherubim overshadowed the ark in a symbol of protection and the heads bowed down to look at the mercy seat. As the priest approached God's place of mercy and grace, he brought the blood of a sin offering and sprinkled it seven times on the seat. In God's mercy, he forgave the sins of all the people for one more year.

David once called out to God, "For you have been my refuge, a strong tower against the foe. I long to dwell in your tent forever and take refuge in the shelter of your wings" (Ps. 61:3–4, NIV).

Another time he wrote: "On my bed I remember you; I think of you through the watches of the night. Because you are my help, I sing in the shadow of your wings" (Ps. 63:6–7, NIV). David had seen the ark, and knew God's mercy. He had experienced refuge and shelter in the shadow of his almighty wings.

Once a year the high priest came before the ark of the

covenant and saw the cherubim on the mercy seat, but where
was God? Was he on vacation? Was there no throne? As the
high priest entered the Holy of Holies he was struck not by
furniture and decorations, but by the brilliance of God's presence. "The glory of the Lord filled the Tabernacle" (Exod.
40:35, TLB).

For Us in Today's World

Had we lived in the days of Moses, we would not have been
allowed to enter the Holy of Holies and come into the presence of God. We might have given up right here after this
long trip through the desert. Unless one of us became the
high priest and gave inside information to the rest of us, we'd
have no idea what was inside that ugly tent covered over with
badger skins. We could guess and imagine, but we couldn't
get close enough to know. We would be allowed to come
through the gate into the courtyard, we could see the doorway into the Holy Place, but we couldn't even visualize the
veil with its message of "No Admittance."

What has happened since that time to allow you and me to
come into the presence of God? As we have seen, the tabernacle, with all its furnishings built to God's specifications, was a
prototype of what Christ would become for us.

- The sinful Israelite had to come to the gate—Jesus is
our gate, our door, our way. No one comes to the Father
but through him.
- The Israelite had to bring a sacrificial lamb—Jesus is
our lamb, the Lamb of God, without blemish or spot.
- The Israelite had to meet the priest—Jesus is our high
priest who makes intercession for us.
- The Israelite saw the bronze laver of washing—Jesus
has washed us clean in the water of regeneration.
- The priests cared for the lamps and saw the light—
Jesus is the Light of the World.
- The priests presented and ate the bread—Jesus is the
Bread of Life and his word is as sweet as honey.

• The priests kept the incense burning—Jesus is our sweet-smelling aroma to the Father.

• Only the high priest went through the veil into the Holy of Holies—Jesus is the veil of the New Covenant.

How exciting it is to be touched by the symbolism in the tabernacle, and how dramatic it is to see God's great plan brought to fruition in the life of his Son, our Lord Jesus.

As he is our door, our lamb, our high priest, our light, our bread, our incense, he is also the veil through which you and I can enter into the full presence of God.

"Therefore, brothers, since we have confidence to enter the Most Holy Place by the blood of Jesus, by a new and living way opened for us through the curtain [veil], that is, his body, and since we have a great priest over the house of God, let us draw near to God with a sincere heart in full assurance of faith, having our hearts sprinkled to cleanse us from a guilty conscience and having our bodies washed with pure water" (Heb. 10:19–22, NIV).

Here in these few verses, we see how our Jesus shed his blood for us, became the open way for us, removed the veil that kept us from God, and became our high priest. He did all this so that we could draw near to God if we had a sincere heart. Only Jesus' blood cleanses us, only the living water of Christ can wash out our guilty conscience.

When did Jesus open the way for us? When were we, who were not ordained as priests, first allowed into the presence of God? On the day when Jesus was crucified, when he "gave up the ghost," the veil was ripped in two, the door was opened. Although the tabernacle was no longer set in the desert, Herod's temple in Jerusalem had become God's residence, and it had been built with the same floor plan as God had given Moses. The high priest functioned under the same Law; the veil was still the barrier to the Holy of Holies. At the very moment of Jesus' death, a supernatural power tore the veil.

"And when Jesus had cried out again in a loud voice, he gave up his spirit. At that moment the curtain of the temple was torn in two from top to bottom. The earth shook and the rocks split" (Matt. 27:50–51, NIV).

Not only did the curtain tear, but it was done from top to bottom to show it was a miracle and not a human transaction. At that same time, the Old Testament rituals and sacrifices were replaced by the New Testament.

"For this reason Christ is the mediator of a new covenant, that those who are called may receive the promised eternal inheritance—now that he has died as a ransom to set them free from the sins committed under the first covenant" (Heb. 9:15, NIV).

"We have this hope as an anchor for the soul, firm and secure. It enters the inner sanctuary behind the curtain, where Jesus, who went before us, has entered on our behalf" (Heb. 6:19–20, NIV).

You and I no longer are held in bondage without hope. Jesus has set us free! We no longer have to find a tabernacle or a temple. We no longer need to bring a lamb to the altar. Jesus has paid it all. We're saved by the blood of the Lamb.

"When Christ came as high priest of the good things that are already here, he went through the greater and more perfect tabernacle that is not man-made, that is to say, not a part of this creation. He did not enter by means of the blood of goats and calves; but he entered the Most Holy Place once for all by his own blood, having obtained eternal redemption" (Heb. 9:11–12, NIV).

Because Jesus sacrificed his life for you and me, we are redeemed. We have been bought up and paid off; we have been rescued, ransomed, and relieved of our burdens.

"For Christ did not enter a man-made sanctuary that was only a copy of the true one; he entered heaven itself, now to appear for us in God's presence. Nor did he enter heaven to offer himself again and again, the way the high priest enters the Most Holy Place every year with blood that is not his own. . . . But now he has appeared once for all at the end of the ages to do away with sin by the sacrifice of himself" (vv. 24–26).

Jesus opened up the holy places for you and me to enter

and stand in the presence of God who has raised Jesus from the dead and set him at his own right hand in the heavenly places (see Eph. 1:20 and Mark 16:19).

As the Hebrew high priest brought the sins of the people to the mercy seat for God's forgiveness, we can come before the throne of grace and glory and God will show us mercy.

"If we confess our sins, he is faithful and just to forgive us our sins, and to cleanse us from all unrighteousness" (1 John 1:9, KJV).

"Let us then approach the throne of grace with confidence, so that we may receive mercy and find grace to help us in our time of need" (Heb. 4:16, NIV).

As we come before the throne of grace for preservation and salvation, we can know that as the manna was given in the wilderness, so Jesus is our bread and *provision*. As the Law was proclaimed by Moses, so Jesus sets down our *principles* for living. As Aaron's rod spoke of God's authority, so Jesus through his Spirit gives *power* to our personal ministries.

What an amazing book the Bible is! How perfectly the Word of God constructed the Old Testament and the tabernacle and brought it all together in the New Testament and the Lord Jesus Christ. Could anyone but God have woven these plans and predictions into a whole cloth and then placed the mantle on you and me that we might stand in his presence.

"And we, who with unveiled faces all reflect the Lord's glory, are being transformed into his likeness with ever-increasing glory, which comes from the Lord, who is the Spirit" (2 Cor. 3:18, NIV).

How exciting to know that as we come before our God with unveiled faces, we will reflect his glory. Although we've not been on the mountain with Moses or in the Most Holy Place bowing before the mercy seat, people will know we've seen the Lord because there will be a glow about us. The glory of the Most Holy Place will be our companion. As it was said of Joseph, Moses, and Daniel, those around them could tell that these men had been with God. In Acts 4:13 people could see the difference when the disciples had been close to Christ: "When they saw the courage of Peter and

John and realized that they were unschooled, ordinary men, they were astonished and they took note that these men had been with Jesus" (NIV).

When we find God, others will notice the change. Not only will we look more radiant as we reflect the Lord's glory, but the Holy Spirit, the power and energy of the trinity, will transform us into the likeness of Christ. Bit by bit there will be changes as we commit our lives to Jesus and obey his will for us.

We will begin to manifest the fruit of the Spirit. As we stand in the presence of God we will have more *love* for others than we ever thought was possible. We will be able to exhibit the joy of the Lord even in adverse circumstances. The *peace* that passes all understanding will keep our hearts and minds safe in Christ Jesus. *Patience* that we never had will come over us in a wave of compassion and understanding for those we could barely tolerate before. An attitude of relaxed *kindness* to others will replace our self-seeking natures, and a real *goodness,* a true desire to help without thought of human credit, will become apparent to those we meet. For some of us who have wavered in our dedication to God in the past, the gift of *faithfulness* will be added, and people will see that we've been with Jesus. There will be a new *gentleness,* a softness in our face and in our actions that will attract people to us, and we will gain *self-control* over some of our habits and tempers that have hindered others from seeking the Lord.

When we stand in the presence of God and bow before his Mercy Seat in repentance, he will forgive and transform us into new creatures in the image of his Son. We won't be able to take pictures of God to show our friends we've really been in the Holy of Holies, but we won't need physical proof. For once we've seen Jesus—"the exact likeness of the unseen God" (Col. 1:15, TLB)—we'll never be the same again.

Wouldn't it be great if today you and I could go to a certain place, even in the desert, and know that when we entered the Most Holy Place we would see God in a bodily form, face to face? Even the high priest on the Day of Atonement didn't see

God. He went through the veil and saw the glory of God, the light of his presence. Even as the Hebrews followed God in a cloud by day to shade them and a pillar of fire by night to warm them, they didn't see him in bodily form.

"No one has ever actually seen God, but, of course, his only Son has, for he is the companion of the Father and has told us all about him" (John 1:18, TLB).

Jesus is both God and Man, and he came to earth that people might see him and believe in the Father who sent him. "Before anything else existed, there was Christ, with God. He has always been alive and is himself God" (John 1:1, TLB).

"But although he made the world, the world didn't recognize him when he came. . . . Only a few would welcome and receive him. But to all who received him, he gave the right to become children of God. All they needed to do was trust him to save them. All those who believe this are reborn!—not a physical rebirth resulting from human passion or plan—but from the will of God" (vv. 10–13).

As Noah saved his family, as Joseph saved his father and brothers, as Moses saved the Hebrew race, so Jesus has saved us. All we need to do is trust him, and he will save us and give us the blessing as members of his eternal family. As we believe in Jesus, we pass from the outer courtyard, through the Holy Place, past the light and the bread, inhaling the aroma as we go through the veil into the presence of God. "Some of us have seen his glory—the glory of the only Son of the heavenly Father!" (v. 14).

As each one of us is willing to leave our Egypt and wander in the wilderness seeking God with all our hearts, as we walk through Jesus our door, accept him as our lamb without spot, come before him as our high priest, stand in his light, eat of his Word, and send our prayers up as an aroma, we go through the torn veil and see the glory of the Father. As Jesus sacrificed himself for us, he opened the way for us to approach God.

"It was through what his Son did that God cleared a path for everything to come to him—all things in heaven and on earth—for Christ's death on the cross has made peace by

God for all by his blood. . . . He has done this through the death on the cross of his own human body, and now as a result Christ has brought you into the very presence of God, and you are standing there before him with nothing left against you—nothing left that he could even chide you for; the only condition is that you fully believe the Truth, standing in it steadfast and firm, strong in the Lord, convinced of the Good News that Jesus died for you, and never shifting from trusting him to save you" (Col. 1:20, 22–23, TLB).

Unless we understand the Old Testament practice of the substitutionary lamb, we can never see why the death of Christ on the cross takes away the sins of each one of us who believes in him, why we are saved by the blood of the Lamb, why Jesus is our intercessor pleading our case before a holy God.

"Now God says he will accept and acquit us—declare us 'not guilty'—if we trust Jesus Christ to take away our sins" (Rom. 4:22, TLB).

Yes, Jesus has stood in for us, and we are standing in the presence of God, basking in the warmth and brilliance of his glory.

"For because of our faith, he has brought us into this place of highest privilege where we now stand, and we confidently and joyfully look forward to actually becoming all that God has had in mind for us to be" (Rom. 5:2, TLB).

Can you imagine that Jesus died for us that we might stand in the presence of God? "Even if we were good, we really wouldn't expect anyone to die for us, though of course, that might be barely possible" (Rom. 5:7, TLB).

From my days as an English teacher, I remember the touching conclusion of Dickens' classic novel, *A Tale of Two Cities*. It's set in the time of the French Revolution when the peasants were gaining control and sending all the noblemen to the guillotine. The plot revolves around three people. Luci Manette is the beautiful heroine. She is pursued by two men who look very much alike. Charles Darnay is a refined and cultured nobleman. Sydney Carton is an alcoholic lawyer.

Luci marries Charles while Sydney remains a friend, loving Luci from afar. At the end of the book, Charles is captured by the peasants and is on his way to be put to death. As he stands in the wooden wagon which is taking him to the guillotine, he looks back longingly to Luci who is standing tearfully on the corner. Their eyes meet in a final farewell. At that point, Sydney quietly jumps into the wagon, pushes Charles out, and takes his place.

Sydney loves Luci so much and so selflessly that he is willing to die so that she and her husband might be free.

Sydney stood in for Charles; he was willing to take his place even unto death. He took the punishment assigned to someone else. He loved unconditionally. That's what Jesus has done for us: he stood in for us, he took our place, he accepted our punishment, he loved us unconditionally, he justified our position with God the Father. And now we stand before God cleansed and free.

We may not see the Father face to face until the day he calls us to his eternal home. But we know we are in his presence when we accept the gift he has placed before us—the gift of his Son who died that we might be put right with our Father God. Yes, Jesus gave himself for us that we might stand before God with nothing left against us. And when we accept his gift, we are acquitted; we're not guilty; we are free!

I hope you're not disappointed that God doesn't appear in the Holy of Holies as a king on a throne, but as a light of glory filling any room he enters. I hope you don't mind that Jesus, the son of God, came to earth as the son of a carpenter and never set up a kingdom of palaces and princes. Throughout history there have been many kings who have come and gone, but there's only been one Jesus—our humble leader who loved us so much that he was willing to die that we might live. Other rulers have fought wars and captured countries, but our Jesus is the Prince of Peace. He's the same yesterday, today, and tomorrow; and when we spend time with him in our own holy place, people will see the difference. We won't need posters of the tabernacle, postcards of the golden ark, or pictures of God in his glory. When we return from our trip through the holy lands, we won't need souvenirs. People will know we've been with Jesus.

◇

NOTES

TAKING THE FIRST STEP

1. *U.S. News and World Report*, 4 April 1983.
2. *Ibid.*
3. *Ibid.*
4. *Ibid.*

TEN FALSE STARTS

1. Sharon Mahoney-Schwamb, "Marjorie Holmes: A Long Story Getting Better," *Christian Herald*, July/August 1986, 18–21.
2. Robert Steed, "And the Greedy Shall Inherit the Airwaves," *Atlanta Weekly*, 14 April 1985.
3. *Ibid.*
4. Sundeep Waslekar, "India's Gurus Fall Victim to West's Shrinking Market," *Los Angeles Times* (date unknown), Pacific News Service.
5. George Lurie, "Town's Nightmare Ends," *USA Today*, 4 November 1986.
6. *What About Those Dangerous Religious Groups?* (Grand Rapids, MI: Radio Bible Class Publications, 1986).
7. Nikki Finke, "Bibles, Blond Locks: The New Rastafarians," *Los Angeles Times*, 15 March 1987.
8. *Ibid.*
9. *Ibid.*
10. *Ibid.*
11. "College Follies '86," *California Magazine*, August 1986, 59–63.
12. *Ibid.*

13. *Ibid.*

14. *Houston Post*, 2 January 1987.

15. *Ibid.*

16. Book review of Shirley MacLaine's *Out on a Limb* in *USA Weekend*, 9–11 January 1987.

17. *Ibid.*

18. Annetta Miller, "Corporate Mind Control," *Newsweek*, 4 May 1987, 38–9.

19. *Ibid.*

20. Lynn Smith, "The New, Chic Metaphysical Fad of Channeling," *Los Angeles Times*, 5 December 1986.

TEN STOPS IN OUR SEARCH FOR GOD

1. The four types of temperaments as I define them in *Your Personality Tree* (Waco, TX: Word, 1986) are the *Sanguine* who wants to have fun, the *Choleric* who wants to be in control, the *Melancholy* who wants everything to be perfect, and the *Phlegmatic* who wants peace.

2. Oswald Chambers, *My Utmost for His Highest* (New York: Dodd, Mead & Co., 1935), 286.

3. *Ibid.*, 45.

4. Rabbi Harold M. Schulweis, "Beware the Mere Mortal Who Guarantees Salvation," *Los Angeles Times*, 17 December 1978.

5. Elizabeth Dent, "Lord, Thank You for Being My Guide." Used by permission of the author.

6. Gary Smalley and John Trent, *The Blessing* (Nashville: Thomas Nelson Publishers, 1986), 17.

7. Brother Lawrence, *The Practice of the Presence of God* (Old Tappan, NJ: Fleming H. Revell Co., 1958), 8.

8. *Ibid.*

9. *Ibid.*, 52–3.

10. Carolyn Jensen, "Spiritual Z's" as published in *Christian Herald*, July/August 1986. Used by permission.

11. Oswald Chambers, *My Utmost for His Highest* (New York: Dodd, Mead & Co., 1935).

12. *Ibid.*, 109.

TEN STEPS INTO THE PRESENCE OF GOD

1. Oswald Chambers, *My Utmost for His Highest* (New York: Dodd, Mead & Co., 1935), 345.

2. Charlotte Elliott, "Just As I Am," 1836.

3. Kevin J. Conner, *The Tabernacle of Moses* (Portland: Conner Publications, 1974), 5.

4. D. Bernard Hoenig, "The Return of the Shekel," *Christian Life*, August 1983, 38–9.

5. Oswald Chambers, *My Utmost for His Highest* (New York: Dodd, Mead & Co., 1935), 287, 344.

6. *Ibid.*, 348.

7. Helen H. Lemmel, "Turn Your Eyes Upon Jesus." Copyright © 1922 by Singspiration Music/ASCAP. Renewed 1950. All rights reserved. Used by permission of the Benson Company, Nashville, TN.

◇

BIBLIOGRAPHY

DeHann, M. R., II. *God's House of Symbols*. Grand Rapids, MI: Radio Bible Class.

Conner, Kevin J. *Interpreting the Symbols and Types*. Portland: Conner Publications.

———. *The Tabernacle of Moses*. Portland: Conner Publications.

Ritchie, John. *Tabernacle in the Wilderness*. Grand Rapids, MI: Kregel Publications.

Soltau, Henry W. *The Holy Vessels and Furniture of the Tabernacle*. Grand Rapids, MI: Kregel Publications.

———. *The Tabernacle—The Priesthood and the Offerings*. Grand Rapids, MI: Kregel Publications.

◇

WORDS AND MEANINGS

(Listed in the Order They Appear in Scripture)

GENESIS—beginning
ADAM—taken from red clay
WOMAN—taken from man
EVE—giving life
SERPENT—Satan
CHERUBIM—celestial being used as a guardian
CAIN—wanting possessions
ABEL—empty vanity
ENOCH—dedicated to discipline
TRANSLATED—move to heaven without death
NOAH—relief
ARK—salvation, protection
RAIN—cleansing, refreshing
FLOOD—judgment of God
COVENANT—contract, agreement
RAINBOW—sign of God's covenant and presence
DOVE—peace, Holy Spirit
ALTAR—place of sacrifice
SACRIFICE—atonement for sin or praise to God
TOWER—a high, lofty structure
BABEL—confusion
ABRAM—exalted father
ABRAHAM—father of nations
SARAI OR SARAH—princess
LOT—covered, protection

HAGAR—wandering fugitive
CIRCUMCISION—requirement of God's covenant with Abraham
ISHMAEL—God hears
ISAAC—laughter
REBEKAH—fascinating beauty
ESAU (EDOM)—covered with hair
JACOB (ISRAEL)—grabbing the heel; deceiver
ISRAEL—prince of God
BIRTHRIGHT—special privilege given to firstborn son; denotes succession to father's rank; double-portion inheritance
INHERITANCE—possessions or blessings passed on to heir
BLESSING—irretrievable words of love and acceptance given once to the oldest son
LABAN—shining white
RACHEL—gentle as a lamb
LEAH—weary, languid
REUBEN—see a son (God has noticed my trouble)
SIMEON—one who hears
LEVI—attached
JUDAH—praise
DAN—vindication and justice

NAPHTALI—my struggle, wrestling

GAD—what good fortune

ASHER—happiness

ISSACHAR—reward

ZEBULUN—a gift for my honor

JOSEPH—may God add another

BENJAMIN—son of my right hand

GALEED—witness heap

MIZPAH—watch tower

PENIEL—seeing God face to face

EGYPT—worldliness, sin

POTIPHAR—justice

MANASSEH—made to forget

EPHRAIM—fruitful in slavery

EXODUS—going out; book of redemption

GOSHEN—frontier is near

MIDIAN—strife, contention

MOSES—drawn out of water

BASKET—divine provision for man's need

ZIPPORAH—little bird

GERSHOM—foreigner

CANAAN—inheritance of saints, land of milk and honey

AARON—light on a mountain

PASSOVER—celebration in memory of God's passing over the Hebrew homes and killing firstborn sons of Egyptians

HYSSOP—common weed used in rites of purification; faith

YEAST—contamination of the world, sin

RED SEA CROSSING—separation from the world; salvation

MANNA—God's provision "What is it?" (little white flakes like honey bread)

MT. SINAI (MT. HOREB)—mountain of God

TABERNACLE—tent pavilion

SABBATH—day of rest and honor to God

PILLAR OF FIRE OR CLOUD—sign of God's presence

BRONZE—judgment

SILVER—redemption

GOLD—divine glory

SEVEN—perfection, completeness

TEN—law and government

TWELVE—divine order

FORTY—probation, testing